SAVING SUN BEARS

One man's quest to save a species

DR SARAH PYE

Saving Sun Bears: One man's quest to save a species
February 2021

ISBN: 978-0-9806871-3-2 (paperback)
ISBN: 978-0-9806871-4-9 (hard cover)
ISBN: 978-0-9806871-5-6 (ebook)
ISBN: 978-0-9806871-6-3 (Audio book)

Published by:

ABN: 86 230 144 690
P.O. Box 288
Buddina, QLD, 4575
www.sarahrpye.com

Cover design: Gram Telen
Layout design: Gram Telen
Cover photo: Lin May Chiew, BSBCC
Author photo: Greg Gardner

 A catalogue record for this work is available from the National Library of Australia

Praise for
Saving Sun Bears

"When I first met Wong during filming of BEARTREK, I was so moved by his love for sun bears and their future... it went way beyond science. Now I'm proud to call him a friend and so happy that Sarah has captured his life in the words of this beautiful book. Be prepared to laugh and cry as you read his story, and be prepared to fall for Wong as everyone who crosses his path does."

—Chris Morgan, documentary filmmaker, UPROAR

"I was recently immensely privileged to meet Dr Wong and film the release of three sun bears back into the wild. Wong is an incredibly committed and charismatic man, and I highly recommend this inspirational story about his life and important work."

—Dame Judi Dench, actor and activist

Acknowledgements

Thank you, Wong, for being courageous enough to open your life to my gaze.

Thank you to Wong's family, friends, colleagues, and the staff of the Bornean Sun Bear Conservation Centre for welcoming me into your worlds.

This story was written as part of my Doctor of Creative Arts Degree at the University of the Sunshine Coast. Thank you to my supervisors, particularly my primary supervisor Dr Paul Williams, for sharing your knowledge and expertise so generously. Thank you too, to the Australian Government for supporting its creation with a scholarship.

Lastly, thank you to my family and friends for your undying support, listening ears, and critical eyes.

Table of Contents

Dedication

This book is dedicated to the next generation.
May you leave the world in a better condition
than it was handed to you.

Preface

In the original version of this manuscript, each chapter was headed by a quote from the most famous bear of all, Winnie-the-Pooh. I spent almost a year attempting to track down a myriad of copyright holders for permission to quote A.A. Milne, but to no avail. Who would have thought it was so difficult, and expensive, to reference a writer you admire?

Dejected, I complained to my friend George — my own Wise Owl. "Why don't you use your own quotes?" he said. I have taken his advice. Instead of words from the mouth of Pooh, I have attempted to encapsulate the theme from each chapter by pulling a line from within its pages.

Alan Alexander Milne, I tip my hat to you.

CHAPTER 1

Natalie

*Deep green was the colour of belonging
and she climbed towards it.*

May 16th, 2015 was Wong's birthday and his dreams were about to come true. Yet emotions seldom travel alone, so he also suppressed a sadness as he prepared to say farewell to a close friend. Wong hoped he would never see her again and took a few minutes to say his goodbyes before moving to a safe distance. The translocation cage had been tipped ninety degrees on its side, and he knew once he pulled the rope in his sweaty hand, there was no turning back. He glanced at his watch. 10.40 am. Then tugged. The door slid open and five-year-old Natalie dashed about ten metres. She slowed as her brain unpicked the unfamiliar concoction of odours accosting her nostrils. The unnatural smell of sanitised human skin behind her mixed with the organic, almost pulsating essence of crunchy leaf litter. A strange underlying note tugged at something deep within her subconscious. The scent of mineral-rich mud transported her back to a time walking beside her mother, and she crinkled her nose as she sauntered deeper into the undergrowth, savouring the olfactory brew at the back of her throat. Deep green was the colour of belonging and she climbed towards it. Within minutes, she was free.

As he waited to see if she would double back, the frenetic activity of the last few days settled on Wong's shoulders with the tropical rainforest humidity. His mind wandered back over his relationship with Natalie and the journey that led to this moment. Her courage had made her the most suitable candidate for release, but her impatience had nearly been the project's downfall.

Natalie was three months old when she was surrendered to the Sabah Wildlife Department only a few hours' drive from where he stood. Villagers claimed, as is often the case, they had found the cub abandoned in the forest, but Wong suspected it was more likely that Natalie's mother had been snared by poachers while she watched in horror.

In the sterile safety of my Australian office, I tentatively push play on footage of a snared sun bear, trying to get a sense for Natalie's suffering. I squirm in my swivel chair as the glass-shattering scream pierces my very soul. Who knows how long Natalie's mum suffered while her baby cowered nearby. Alerted by the screeching, poachers would have left their camp, armed with knives. After the kill, they would have severed her mother's oversized paws before slicing open her stomach and extracting her gallbladder. The paws would have fetched a handsome price as a delicacy in bear-paw soup, and the gallbladder was worth as much as US$42 per gram on the black market. Her life? Worth nothing.

If you discount the trauma of her capture, Natalie was a very lucky bear. Other cubs have made it no further than the cooking pot or been sold into the illegal pet trade, their claws and canine teeth removed to avoid injury to their captors, sealing their fate. Instead, dehydrated, weighing five kilos and no bigger than a large teddy bear, with her claws appearing way too big for her body, Natalie was surrendered to authorities on December 23rd, 2010. Wong's 'right-hand-man' at the Bornean Sun Bear Conservation Centre, Wai Pak, was charged with feeding her a bottle five times a day. He struggled to get the milk formula right, but eventually she stabilised and started to put on weight.

In January 2011, Wong returned from his studies in the US and met Natalie for the first time. He introduced a 'walk the bear' program in the open forest to develop Natalie's natural instincts. She put her trust in him, following Wong into the forest, just as she would have followed her mother, and he emulated bear activities, honing his own digging and climbing skills unwittingly.

Natalie was no bigger than a large teddy bear. Courtesy BSBCC

At first, all Natalie wanted to do was jostle with him, and Wong found himself suffering bites regularly. If he wore heavy welding gloves, she would bite harder, so he gave up on protective clothing. He disciplined her with taps on the nose, in the same way you might train your dog.

Natalie learnt quickly, and on Wong's birthday in 2011, after six months of training, he took her to a patch of forest and relaxed on his haunches, watching her amuse herself. In delight, she demolished fallen branches to reveal tasty termites, showering herself with sawdust and wood chips, then tried to lick them up quickly, before they bit her. She turned her attention skyward as the first raindrops filtered through the canopy. Wong watched in awe as Natalie avoided the pending mud by deftly running up the nearest trunk, her paws bent further than the ninety-degree norm for human feet and hands. As the clouds passed, she settled into a crook and took a nap high in the tree. Wong huddled below, wet and reluctantly waiting. When she finally returned to ground level, he pulled himself from his crouch and started running for the bear house. Natalie followed.

It was no surprise that Wong learnt as much from Natalie as she did from him. Natalie was the first bear Wong observed that could move horizontally through the forest. "She was a good climber to a point where she went up to the canopy and crossed from tree to tree like the squirrels," he tells me on our scheduled Skype call. "She could push the branches to their limit, which taught us how little we knew about sun bear behaviour."

I scroll through images of the young Natalie on Wong's blog and a maternal wave washes over me, the urge to reach out and cuddle her. She looks so sweet and harmless: her mouth turned up at the edges, resembling a human smile, with tiny half-moon ears and an inquisitive expression. This cuteness is often the downfall of her species. I can appreciate what compels villagers to keep sun bear cubs as pets. Wong tells me when their pets are confiscated, many are astounded to learn they are actually breaking the law.

Tired from her adventures, Natalie ate well, graduating from milk to two small meals of rice porridge each day. Before long, she put on significant weight until she was too big for Wong to carry. Then came the day Wong dreaded. He and Wai Pak were 'walking' her together. They played in harmony until Natalie began to get tired. Like a human toddler, she became frustrated when it was time to go home. Wong tapped her on her nose to get her attention. Usually she snapped back into submission, but this time she started to growl. Wong immediately knew the relationship had shifted. The hand-worn stick he carried for protection shrank in insignificance. Even as a cub, Natalie had the capacity to cause serious harm. Instantly, Wong launched his body on top of Natalie, pinning her head to the ground and simultaneously barking "Run!" As Wai Pak disappeared through the bar-like trunks, Wong tossed the fifteen-kilo Natalie in the air to buy a few seconds, jumped to his feet, and followed at top speed with Natalie fast on his heels. All three made it to the bear house without incident, but the realisation hit. The risk was now too high. It was time for Natalie to graduate.

Wong integrated Natalie into the equivalent of a child's playgroup with three other cubs of similar age: Julaini, Rungus, and Ah Lun. Just as kindergarten is an important step on a human child's journey towards independence and socialisation, so this new group of friends enabled Natalie to practise play-fighting in earnest. Wong watched as the cubs bared their teeth and emitted guttural barks, rolling around the bear enclosure locked together. He knew the less contact Natalie had with humans, the better her chances of survival in the wild. It was best if Natalie feared his species—she needed to keep a respectful distance if she was going to avoid the same fate as her mother.

In early March 2013, the four cubs had accumulated enough skills for the next step, and the door leading to Pen B in the 1.44-hectare natural forest enclosure, on the edge of Kabili-Sepilok Forest Reserve, was opened. As expected, adventurous Natalie was the first to stick her head out into the sunlight, but she turned around immediately and retreated inside. It took a whole week before any bear was brave enough to go further. Rungus eventually, and cautiously, followed the sweet smell of honey trailing down the ramp and disappeared from Natalie's view. Four hours of nervous pacing passed before she was willing to trade the familiarity of her captivity and follow her friend to a place where the endless sky smelt of danger, and her dense black fur drank in direct sunlight, warming her skin. Although they were secured by ironwood fences and electric wires, this was as close as they could come anywhere in the world to natural bear habitat while remaining in captivity, and it wasn't long before the friends only came back to the bear house at night. Over the next year, Natalie's confidence outpaced her companions until she was climbing higher into the canopy, swinging on vines in the rain. Some afternoons, she commandeered abandoned orangutan nests, or fashioned her own, settling down to rest. Wong watched in wonder. Did sun bears learn this skill from their primate neighbours after jealously watching them rest in safety and comfort high in the treetops? Or did orangutans perhaps learn from sun bears, perfecting the process?

Each nest Natalie built was higher than the last, until one day in July 2014 when she found a position 40m from the ground, gathered the soft new growth from the rainforest canopy, arranged it into a platform in the fork between two stable branches, and stayed away from the bear house for five nights. Wong was beside himself with excitement. Natalie's courage and adventurous spirit was a form of self-selection. She would be the first bear contender for release.

Wong set the fundraising wheels in motion. A local TV channel said they would pay for a military helicopter if they could film but, as the day approached, their support fell through. Then another film crew jumped on board, but filming permission was thwarted by red tape. Time was ticking. On July 23rd, 2014, the planned release came crashing to a halt when Natalie did something no one thought possible.

In the middle of the rainforest fruiting season, short-tailed barbets seemed to beckon as they flew towards fruiting fig trees just out of Natalie's reach. Her pupils dilated as she climbed higher than the other bears towards the sunlight. She passed the vines in the mid-storey, skilfully transferring her weight from one spindly branch to another, and before she knew it, she was in the canopy and outside the compound.

Sepilok Forest Reserve is surrounded by human habitation, and with Sepilok Orangutan Sanctuary sharing the same forest, it is still one of the most internationally visited areas in Malaysia. An encounter between bears and tourists posed too much of a risk to simply wish her well and wave goodbye, so a search-and-recapture operation began.

Natalie fully grown. Courtesy Jocelyn Stokes

Two vets drove all night from Kota Kinabalu. Sipping coffee to keep them awake, they joined the two resident Sepilok vets at 4am, each heading one of four tracking teams that dispersed through the forest. They were tasked with placing and baiting a total of eight barrel traps in forest clearings, and taping eleven motion-tripped cameras across overgrown tracks. Day one, nothing. Day two, nothing. On day three, one team came face-to-face with Natalie. Relieved, they advanced, trying to get close enough to dart her, but Natalie rose to her feet barking aggressive warnings, and they were forced to retreat. Her would-be captors glimpsed her twice more, and Wong and bear-keeper Thye Lim's frustration was palatable when they clicked through the grainy black-and-white images each morning only to find she had been actively sniffing around the traps at night.

A month passed. Natalie was as elusive as the mythical yeti-like Batutut said to inhabit the Bornean rainforest. Then one night, as the fruiting season drew to a close, Natalie's hunger got the better of her. She could smell fruit as she walked down the boardwalk Thye Lim used to conduct perimeter fence checks (having her photo taken for posterity on the way). She climbed back into pen B and sauntered up to the bear house to eat her peers' food scraps. For the next few nights, Thye Lim gently laid a food trail all the way up to her cage. As in the fairy-tale of Goldilocks, Thye Lim tells me the amount needed to be 'just right': If he used too much food, she ate her fill and turned around; if the treats were spaced too widely, she lost interest. He and his partner (and fellow bear-keeper) Lin May decided to pitch their sleeping bags in the bear house and wait, but Natalie could smell them. Every time she came close, the other bears' barks alerted her to human presence. Nights passed until, after thirty-seven days, human ingenuity, and the smell of durian fruit, trumped Natalie's appetite.

Durian was introduced to the West about six centuries ago. It didn't catch on due to its aroma, which food writer Richard Sterling described as a mixture of 'turpentine and onions, garnished with a gym sock'. The smell is so off-putting that durian is banned from many hotels and flights. In 2018, two tonnes in the hold of an Indonesian flight caused passengers to mutiny, the plane grounded, but it's an odour which sun bears love. Knowing her penchant for the fruit, the team modified

Natalie's den so it became one huge cruelty-free mouse trap with durian the penultimate treat. When she stepped inside to taste, the steel guillotine door sliced downward behind her.

A health check showed Natalie had lost five kilos, but physically she was in good shape. She needed to be quarantined for a month while blood results were analysed for transmittable diseases, and at first she was angry with her confinement. Before long, depression replaced aggression, and for days on end, she cocooned herself in the metal basket attached to the wall in her den with her eyes fixed on the forest outside. The taste of freedom still sweet on her tongue, honey was no longer of interest. Wong hoped her mood would improve when she was reintroduced to her social group, but when the time came, she wasn't interested in playfighting Julaini or Rungus. Ah Lun shunned Natalie, chewing her own paw, barking and hitting the bars between them while she paced back and forth with stress. It seemed Natalie had lost her friends in her quest for independence. She had also lost any semblance of freedom. Her adept climbing skills meant she could no longer be trusted to remain in the rainforest enclosure, but neither could she integrate. For Wong, it became essential to fast track Natalie's final release—both for Natalie's mental health, and for the contentment of the other bears.

As I read through the incident and project reports, it is clear that the speed Wong wished for was not possible. Not only did Wong need to raise 50,000 ringgit (about US$12,000) to hire a helicopter and team, but he had to research release sites, decide on appropriate tracking devices, and clamber through political policy hoops before the Sabah Wildlife Department would offer their blessing. He then needed to fatten Natalie up a bit, fit her with a snug GPS collar, monitor her for a month in the forest enclosure, and train his chosen release team in data processing. It took six months before Natalie's cage touched down on the mud flats of Tabin Wildlife Reserve. The miracle is that it didn't take longer.

To track Natalie's whereabouts, Wong settled on the German Vectronic Aerospace GPS collar. Not only did it boast successful projects in fifty countries, tracking eighty species, but a nearby research centre had one available. In the dense tropical rainforests of Borneo, or in hollow logs where Natalie might shelter, consistent satellite connection was impossible, so, to save battery life, Wong programmed the collar to attempt four location readings each day and transmit to the manufacturer only when it had amassed four successful readings. Calculations showed that this could result in plotting data of Natalie's movements for more than a year before the battery gave up. Next, he needed to test it on Natalie, so she was anaesthetised.

Natalie woke with a dry tongue and her head felt heavy. Time had mysteriously perished and her body clock struggled to reset. It took her a few minutes to feel the weight of the perforated collar and chunky transmitter hanging around her throat like a Saint Bernard's barrel. She half-heartedly tried to shake it free, but an anaesthetic headache pounded, so she sunk down on all fours and rested. Unbeknownst to her, Wong monitored data from the little black box remotely. It was her ticket back to the rainforest. Freedom was again within reach.

Just as sand in an hourglass appears to quicken as it nears the end, time rushed over the next two weeks as Wong juggled logistics. Then, as the tropical sun lost its bite on May 15th, 2015, the vet from the Wildlife Rescue Unit, Dr Laura, anesthetised Natalie again and gave her a full physical health examination. As Natalie started to stir, she was gently placed on a bed of leaves in the heavy, metal-barred transportation cage which was loaded onto the back of the pickup truck and latched down. When she woke, she could barely turn around. The length of the cage was shorter than my arm span; the width halved. A claustrophobic primeval response caused her heart to race. Her breath shortened and she barked in anguish.

There were a few rain showers during the two-and-a-half-hour drive to the Sabah Wildlife Department's office in Lahad Datu, which helped keep Natalie cool, and for that, Wong was grateful. From the driver's seat, he could hear her occasional stressed cough, but the journey was remarkably uneventful. As Natalie recuperated for the night in her cage, under medical surveillance, most of the team checked into a hotel. Wong slept fitfully. Sun bears handle extended confinement very differently depending on their past experiences. Some scratch incessantly while others try to bite through the metal cage, potentially causing self-harm. His body was between soft sheets, but his mind was on Natalie.

Natalie sensed the approaching heat as the boom of horny frogs was replaced by the dawn chorus. A myriad of creatures took turns to give thanks for making it through another night, indicating time as clearly as a clock face. When the team reconvened at Natalie's cage at 5am, she seemed remarkably calm.

The release party hit the road before Natalie started to feel uncomfortable, arriving on the edge of Tabin Wildlife Reserve at 6.30am and scanning the sky for the chartered helicopter. Although he was based in Kota Kinabalu, the pilot had spent the night at Sandakan heliport, half an hour's flight away, to ensure an early start. It's an indication of Wong's pragmatic nature when he tells me he suggested that two of his office staff go along for the ride: "Who else has an opportunity to fly in a helicopter without paying 30,000 ringgit?" he laughs as he reminisces. It occurs to me that after all he has experienced, Wong's boyhood enthusiasm is still intact.

Natalie slurped from the offered water bottle as the unfamiliar soft thud of blades sliced through the air, rising to a crescendo of wind so strong the grass seeds stung her eyes. As the hurricane subsided, staff members Gloria and Firo disembarked, beaming, and the logistic shuffle of people and bear began. When media sponsorship hadn't materialised, Wong had hired the most cost-effective helicopter. Natalie's cage would only fit inside once the seats were removed. Wong made a mental note to insist on an underslung harness, with the cage suspended below the aircraft, for future releases. On this occasion, though, he discussed the plan with all participants, made sure the flight crew could unbolt the furniture, then embarked on the first shuttle to evaluate the release site with Thye Lim, Ranger Augustine, and Photographer Gill.

I'm trying to get a feel for Natalie's new home. A few taps on my keyboard and statistics about Tabin Wildlife Reserve emerge. The protected area is apparently 122,539 hectares in size, and this number flies right over my non-mathematical head. More tapping and I have it in context. It is seven times the size of Moreton Island, whose distinctive sand dunes beckon from my Australian Sunshine Coast home, twenty times the size of Manhattan, or twice the size of Singapore. I discover the land in Tabin was selectively logged around the periphery in the 1980s, before being awarded protected status in 1984 to help preserve dwindling numbers of native wildlife including pigmy elephants, rhinos, orangutans, clouded leopards, and a small population of proboscis monkeys. I know Wong estimates there are probably about 120 sun bears too, but there is so little known about their existence that they weren't part of the decision to protect. Tabin is managed jointly between the Sabah Wildlife Department (focusing on fauna) and the Sabah Forestry Department (responsible for the flora).

This was the first time Wong had seen the lowland rainforests of Tabin from the air. As they flew away from human impact, the creepers, tall grass, and bamboo, which had opportunistically filled the gaps caused by selective logging, were replaced by a closed canopy and darker vegetation. When I ask for his impressions, Wong describes it as flying over broccoli. From his usual ground-level perspective, he was used to imagining tall trees as individual high-rises playing host to different species as the altitude changed. But from above, he could also see a living, interconnected community. The occasional ancient dipterocarp tree rose as high as eighty metres above the crowd, acting as a landmark to wildlife and humans and enabling it to efficiently launch its pink-tinged 'two-winged fruit' on the wind.

As they neared the core of the reserve, his heart sang. No matter which direction Wong looked, it was void of telltale palm oil plantation rows. One of the biggest attractions in the reserve was a series of gently oozing natural mud volcanoes. The high mineral content attracted wildlife including elephants and bearded pigs who had left footprints in the mud as they supplemented their diets by licking the salt and calcium deposits. Like a middle-aged man's bald patch, the volcanoes were denuded of vegetation, offering a perfect helicopter landing zone. The pilot hovered then landed softly, tiptoeing on the crust of the mud. Equipment boxes were unloaded and carried to the shady edges, blades accelerating again as the aircraft lifted like a dragonfly from a lily pad. Before long it landed again with its precious cargo, Wong's team waiting like a royal greeting party. Four of the crew squelched Natalie's cage to the undergrowth at the edge of the clearing.

Wong's moment of reflection was interrupted by the sounds of celebration. His team chattered with adrenalin, his smile broadening to match. Wong glanced over at the now-empty cage. It tugged at his heart and he glanced back at the thicket, sending a prayer skyward.

Wong waited for his inbox to fill with data from Natalie. If she was doing well, her location would beam up from the collar to a satellite, back down to the manufacturer in Germany, and on to him. He checked his emails obsessively. After three days, the first data came. Natalie had moved from the release site and a picture slowly emerged.

At first, Natalie kept close as she learnt the peculiarities of her new surroundings. She knew she existed only in relationship to other organisms, and she had to fill in the gaps of her knowledge fast if she was to survive. Where humans saw a tree, she saw a world—a thousand species living and interacting together. She may have been at the top of the rainforest food chain, but she understood her survival depended on the smaller creatures of the forest. She had to find food, enough food, or starve.

I envisage her following the hum of honeybees to the base of a tall mengaris tree, gazing longingly at their comb colonies hanging like earlobes below the branches above. She tries to find purchase in the smooth bark of these rainforest giants, but she's thwarted and rests against the buttress roots in frustration before stripping fallen logs and licking termites instead. Under a crumbling log she discovers a pill millipede, its armour locked in a sphere. This is a familiar treat so she pierces the shell with one of her canines, rolling it around her tongue before pulverising the shell in her molars and chewing the living morsel. Her empty belly is partially placated, and now the rains come. The percussion of heavy drops hits broad, flat leaves, resounding like drum skins and shattering into a spray. It lands on her fur with the softest tickle. As dark descends, she is alert. Sleepless nights are punctuated by wild bears shuffling below her haphazard nest, a civet cat stalking her prey throwing moon shadows like monsters.

Natalie's frenetic movement finally slowed as she chose a home range five kilometres away from the release site. Wong found this comforting. It was likely she had found a good food source without impacting on another bear's territory. After two months, however, there was even less movement. Thye Lim tells me the accuracy of the GPS readings is about twenty metres, and the positions were so close it was likely she wasn't moving at all. Wong didn't know if this meant Natalie was injured, dead, or she had dropped her collar somehow, but he suspected it was the latter.

Unlike trees I am used to, which fruit in a predictable season, the rainforest trees of Borneo, Sumatra, and Peninsular Malaysia have mass fruiting events in a seemingly random pattern. The truth of how and why they do this was a new arm of human discovery. In the wild, sun bears gorge themselves when food is abundant, and substitute what Wong calls 'fall-back' food, which includes things like termites, earthworms, and small insects when rainforest trees aren't producing. This means their weight yo-yos throughout the year, and although Wong had secured her collar tight to allow for slippage, it was possible Natalie had lost enough weight that her head had slipped through the collar. The only way to find out was to send out a search party. Luckily, it was the dry season, so access was possible.

A team of six intrepid explorers set out from Sepilok on September 7th, 2015, meeting up with one more, Chris Tan, from Scuba Zoo filming crew, at Lahad Datu. Communication had been poor: Chris was under the assumption he had signed up for a one-night adventure. After an energy-building breakfast at team member Suhairin's house, they loaded camping gear, food, and tracking equipment into a long wooden boat and headed upstream. The river level was low, and they tentatively crept their way around fallen branches in the direction of Natalie's release location. Mid-morning, a fallen tree blocked the flow. Thye Lim was relieved they had bought a chainsaw. Eventually, with daylight barely on their side, they set camp to the deafening rise and fall of cicadas.

The following day, they continued deeper into the darkening forest, nearing the collar location painfully slowly. When they consulted their ordinance survey map on the morning of day four, they realized the contour lines were getting closer, which meant a steep climb ahead. Thye Lim decided they would leave the camp intact, continuing with day packs instead. At the top of a very steep rock climb, the team stopped for lunch. He took advantage of limited phone service to call Wong, giving him a positive update on progress. Thye Lim spoke too soon—things went downhill from there, literally and figuratively. As dusk descended, they were at least two hours away from the collar, their remaining food was back at the campsite, and as they approached a riverbank, they could hear elephants trumpeting nearby. "Wong always says take a compass, and make group decisions," Thye Lim tells me. "He says always pull out: safety comes first, data comes second." It was good advice but not followed, the decision to continue one they would regret. The team was hungry and tired; multiple egos pulled in different directions.

At 5.30pm, hoping a ping from Natalie's collar might buoy spirits, Thye Lim turned on the radio and scanned. In addition to sending a GPS signal to a satellite, Natalie's collar emitted a Very High Frequency (VHF) signal from 6am to 6pm. Silence. Dejected, they lit a fire with driftwood on the dry creek bed, to keep warm and ward off wildlife, organising watches through the night to ensure the group's safety. Unfamiliar hunger pangs gnawed at their stomachs, prompting the capture of four small fish and five frogs, which were roasted and shared. It was a long night, especially for Thye Lim. Responsibility weighed heavily, and every rustle in the bushes amplified his fear. Chris Tan's family was also worried, after expecting him home two days before. They called the Scuba Zoo office, only to be told no one knew his whereabouts.

With dawn came renewed commitment, moderated by low glucose levels and short tempers. They scraped any remaining flesh from the consumed frog carcasses and started walking. After three hours, the receiver and antenna were turned on and a strong signal showed the collar was only one hundred and twenty-eight metres away. The weight of responsibility on Thye Lim's shoulders lifted slightly. He turned the receiver off to conserve battery, and half an hour later, turned it on again without the antenna. The collar was within ten metres, and before he could organise the team into a transect line five metres apart, Mizuno found the collar lying flat on the leaf litter, undamaged. They were elated. There was no evidence of blood within a twenty-metre radius: no stains, no smell, and thankfully, no carcass. Just like a crime scene, photo records and notes were taken. It looked as if Wong's prediction was correct: Natalie's collar had simply fallen off.

Low on energy and still over fourteen kilometres from Campsite Two, Mizuno, Hasni, and Thye Lim shivered from the cold. They trudged back slowly to avoid accidents, relieved when they arrived at dusk. Jokes released residual fear while cookies and raw instant noodles assuaged their hunger. Thye Lim placed the collar in a clearing to transmit so Wong would know they had found it. Then sleep—a tent can appear palatial after a night without. Refreshed, they found that the last three hours' trek the next morning came easier. By the time they reached civilisation, they had been gone five days and four nights, walking eighty kilometres through dense foliage. They had pushed themselves mentally and physically, gaining a renewed respect for the forest.

And Natalie? As I pen her story, it has been exactly two years since the collar was located: she's not been seen or heard of since. Wong's wish is that she is healthy and happy. That she found a mate and is teaching her own child how to climb trees. But the world where Natalie lives is not perfect. Bears kill other bears. Food is not assured. Injury is common. Worse, poachers still ply their trade while multinational corporations clear land for plantations.

All Wong does is hope.

CHAPTER 2

The Beginning

*"Speak less, do more," his mum said when his
pace slowed and his tongue wagged.*

The cornerstones of ancestry, family, friendship, and culture are linked with character-building moments. In Wong's case, they were punctuated with skinned knees, blushed embarrassments, and pivotal decisions. To understand more, I have left the cocoon of my Australian office and invited myself to his hometown of Bukit Mertajam in the state of Penang, Malaysia where he is attending his 30-year high school reunion.

I'm on the 401 bus from the airport, and from my view in the front seat, the city limits sign announces I am entering the 'Pearl of the Orient'. I have landed on an island about the same size as Singapore, but that's where the comparison ends. Dense rainforest fights for survival against mildew-clad high-rise apartments in close proximity to one another: their render chipped and brickwork sloppy. Washing lines bow like Christmas decorations. Buildings are abandoned rather than maintained, and blindingly white new ones have sprung up everywhere with no perceived organisation.

Food hawker stands vie for space down the median strip, and I catch a glimpse of an old man slowly and deliberately sweeping around his stand with a bamboo switch. His work is futile, the traffic moving around him like a stream babbling around a rock. Moped riders, in singles and pairs, calmly weave in and out of traffic, their jackets turned backwards to ward off the rain and puddle splashes. A compact car cuts us off, prompting the bus driver to put down his mobile phone. "Lady driver, please be patient," screams the bumper sticker in the back window.

A doll's house Taoist temple, no bigger than a public toilet block, clings to hope in the centre of a freshly cleared square of scraped earth. It is surrounded by billboards attesting to a faster-paced existence with block letters 24 JAM, or twenty-four-hour service.

We slow at a bus stop and the door opens, sucking in an odour of garbage mixed with strong aftershave. A man in a crisp suit enters. Behind him a smiling woman wearing a hijab carries an infant on her hip followed by a younger woman in jeans whose T-shirt announces 'Our smiles should touch now' across her chest. The contrast is jarring. As we approach the centre of town, Malay and Chinese business names become interspersed with other cultural imports—Tesco and Home Pro—speaking of colonial invasions and modern cultural infiltration.

Penang has been a trading hub since the 1500s when ocean-going Portuguese merchants replenished their water supplies while travelling on the spice routes from India to the Far East. At the northern entry to the Straits of Malacca, it is a perfect shelter in monsoon months and became a hotbed of pirates (both sanctioned and unsanctioned by their respective governments) who pillaged what they could from each other. In 1786, Englishman Captain Francis Light took formal British possession of the island from the Sultan of Kedah who had strategically traded it for protection from the Siamese and Burmese armies threatening his kingdom. The new colonial status and the subsequent building of Fort Cornwallis made it safer for the British East India Company to use the island as a base, and the newly named George Town became a bustling hive of activity. In many other colonies of the era, the British created exclusive cultural enclaves, but Captain Light declared Penang a free port to try and upstage Dutch traders, and this drew a vibrant swath of immigrants. They were allowed to claim whatever land they could clear and were encouraged to plant spices. Many came from mountainous farming areas in Canton Province on the Chinese mainland, and with the crop focus eventually switching to sugar, then rubber, the town grew prosperous. About fifty percent of Penang's residents today, including Wong's family, are ethnic Chinese.

We turn into a wide palm-lined avenue welcoming us to George Town and head towards the car ferry terminal where boats depart for the Malaysian mainland and the town of Bukit Mertajam where Wong grew up. I disembark and walk towards the old buildings, my back to the water. As the narrow streets suck me in, I am immediately transported back in time. Two-storey whitewashed terraces lean towards each other as if sharing a secret. I imagine the smell of drying fish, hear the cry of tok tok mee hawkers as I dodge the ghosts of hand-pulled rickshaws, their world overwritten by a sanitised present.

As with all of us, the world into which we are born influences our early years. In Wong's case, the Second World War is a good place to start. His parents' experience shaped the household they created for their own family.

The Imperial Japanese Army landed on the other side of the peninsula on December 8th, 1941, an hour before the attack on Pearl Harbor. Three days later, they started bombing Penang. Five days after that, the British abandoned their post, leaving the rice warehouses in Began Serai unguarded. There was a narrow window of opportunity before the Japanese took control, and pragmatic 19-year-old Soon Kew, who would eventually become Wong's father, knew rice might be the difference between life and death. He jumped on his bike, negotiated the 25km journey, skirted the rubble remains of the iron bridge the British scuttled before their departure, and crossed the river by boat. He made it just in time to loot a sack of grain, balancing it precariously on his handlebars for the slower return journey. How disheartened he must have felt when he washed his cache, to find much of the weight was inedible chalk which drained away. He wondered if the British had added chalk as a leaving present for the Japanese, or as a remedy against weevils. Or perhaps he had simply grabbed old grain which had disintegrated over time. Soon Kew's treasure was a meagre insurance policy.

Like ripples in a pond, the Japanese infiltrated the peninsula, arriving at Soon Kew's village of Sungai Bakap in 1942. Amid the constant threat of bombings, the tailor's shop where he worked shut its doors, and he turned to farming the family orchard with his own father and six siblings. They tapped rubber; cultivated green vegetables, sweet potatoes, and yams; harvested fruit trees. With rice scarce, they owed their survival to their crops.

Food production represented survival for the Japanese too—they ordered British colonial rubber tree plantations cleared and planted with edibles. British schools, with lessons in English, were replaced with the Japanese equivalent. Soon Kew's siblings stopped attending, preferring to keep their distance from the invading force. When they were unable to avoid soldiers in the street, they bowed and kept their heads low to ward off beatings. Girls chopped their hair and dressed like boys to reduce the risk of abduction.

To quash insurgents, the Japanese created the 'Ten Families' and 'Hundred Families' hierarchy: Families were grouped into tens with a leader who reported suspect activities directly to the secret police, or Kempeitai. Ten leaders formed a committee, overseeing one hundred families. It was rudimentary but successful. Coupled with a mandatory rice-coupon system, it kept the villagers in line. Any local caught skimming their rice allocation and giving it to the underground movement, the Malayan People's Anti-Japanese Army, was severely punished. The MPAJA consisted mostly of ethnic Chinese, which caused the Japanese to treat Soon Kew and his family more harshly than Malays and Indians.

Rumours circulated about one long-haired general in the nearby town of Butterworth who was killing prisoners with his samurai sword, so even though Soon Kew and his siblings kept their heads down and tended their fields, they lived in constant fear during the three years and eight months of Japanese occupation. Unfortunately, death still infiltrated their world through rampant disease and scarce medical care. Their mother died in childbirth, and their father died from stomach ulcers which could easily have been treated with proper medication. At a young age, Soon Kew and his siblings found themselves orphaned.

In the midst of all the fear and sadness of WWII, there were tender times. Soon Kew clung to the affection of a meek, petite girl in the village called Put Tai. Their romance grew, and in otherwise dark times, the two were married in a simple Chinese ceremony.

In July 1945, paper flyers rained softly down from British planes like snowflakes announcing the Imperial Army had surrendered. By then, Soon Kew and Put Tai were adjusting to life as new parents with a four-month-old baby girl. They were sceptical of the propaganda from the sky. In England, my own parents experienced jubilant, bunting-clad neighbourhood street parties to celebrate 'Victory in Europe', but nothing of the sort happened in Malaya (as it was then known). The British simply returned and started distributing rice. MPAJA members credited themselves with hero status and demanded compensation from families who didn't participate in the resistance. Soon Kew copped a scolding and paid compensation. Since produce from the orchard was seasonal, and the income it produced was insufficient to sustain all the siblings and their growing families, it was time to shed the old life and start anew. He uprooted his young clan and moved to the bustling town of Bukit Mertajam twenty-two kilometres away, returning to garment making.

By May 1969, the US was focused on getting a man to the moon, Malaysia had been independent from Britain for over a decade, and Put Tai was expecting the birth of her last child. A racially charged election campaign was underway with the two predominantly Chinese opposition parties campaigning hard. When the results indicated a hung parliament, tempers flared and riots broke out. The army was called in with a 'shoot to kill' order and conditions deteriorated. A State of Emergency was declared with nighttime curfews imposed by armed soldiers. The reported casualty count ranged from 200 - 1000.

From her previous eight deliveries, Put Tai knew the odds of children arriving at night were high, so she and Soon Kew pragmatically added white surrender flags to her overnight bag in the hope it would guarantee them safe passage during the curfew. Across distance and time, I feel affinity with Wong's mother. My experience pales in comparison, yet my own daughter arrived in the middle of a North Queensland flood with overflowing creeks between us and the hospital. I imagine her sending a prayer skyward in hopes of avoiding a night delivery, then resigning herself to the inevitable as the contractions came. Soon Kew helped his wife into the car, then prominently attached the white surrender flag on a stick, hoping the patrolling soldiers would see it and decline to shoot. This is the dramatic entrance Wong made into the world on May 16th, 1969.

Tentacles of unrest spread across the globe: within weeks race riots broke out in Singapore; by August, Northern Ireland was in turmoil; within six months religious riots ignited in India.

I've arrived at Station Road where Wong spent his early years. It's a long, straight, wide road with electric wires strung like drying spaghetti between poles along its length. Two-storey terraces line each side. Supported by columns, the upper floors hang over the indented lower floor in a smile of uneven teeth with a massive overbite, providing a shaded walkway. Wong remembers a constant stream of people heading to or from the rail station at one end, making it a vibrant childhood neighbourhood well into the night. There were no department stores back then, and most of Bukit Mertajam's residents had their clothes made to order, so Soon Kew's business prospered in spite of the two other tailor shops on the street. It was an anthill of activity into which, as soon as he could walk, Wong became a participating member.

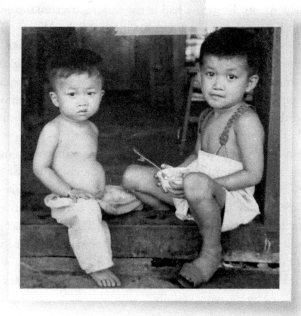

Wong's brothers on the stoop of the shop

Sitting on the raised stoop and counting the minutes before closing time, young Wong could see steam rise from street hawkers' woks across the street. The bell of a tricycle drew closer with sweets on display, and pangs of longing turned in his stomach. The smell of street food permeated his youth, and he developed a craving for it which remains today.

He might not have been old enough for school, but Wong took his task of sweeping scraps of dull-coloured thread from the shop floor before closing time very seriously. Usually, once he was done, he would grab something from the vendors. But Chinese New Year was approaching, so he pulled the blue metal folding door shut a little later than the usual nine o'clock closing time under the authoritative, watchful eye of his father (who he called Apak). Everyone had been working overtime to meet demand before the holiday, and his mother (who Wong called Ah Ji) and his auntie were busy preparing supper. Wong walked back through the workshop, away from the street, through the living and dining area to the kitchen to see what was cooking. Large pots balanced on the top of a big brick stove. His aunt was stoking the three wood fires to keep the temperature even. Smoke curled up through an opening in the ceiling to the sky.

I am invited into Wong's sister's home and shown a similar opening in keeping with traditional Chinese architecture. Sitting in her crowded living room, I ask her and Wong if Apak and Ah Ji mean mum and dad and discover they actually mean aunt and uncle, each family member having a different endearment depending on seniority and position. "I know it is a weird way to call mum and dad, but this is what we do," Wong explains. "I think it has got to do with the belief in the old days that kids were better raised by the whole family."

As soon as Wong was old enough, he took over poking the coals. The fires had subsided while he swept, and keeping the stove at the right temperature was his other important job. "Speak less, do more," his mum said when his pace slowed and his tongue wagged. He liked helping in the kitchen more than the shop. He felt more welcome and useful there, washing vegetables or peeling shrimp while he listened to his mum and aunt Tan Bee Hong's conversation. There was always something to do. Wong absorbed recipes and cooking methods by osmosis.

There were twenty-four years between Wong's eldest sister Siew Mei and himself. By the time Wong was old enough to stoke the fire, many of his eight siblings had already left home.

It was far from a solitary life, however, since Wong's uncle and family also lived in the tailor shop, along with a revolving door of workers. There were usually about twenty mouths to feed. "I learnt early how to be organised and make things work," Wong tells me. "We cleaned up, then after a few hours it was time to start preparing again."

After all his jobs were done in the evening, Wong was allowed to turn on the television. Apak didn't condone idleness, so Wong kept his hands busy trimming threads on the quilt his mum was making from leftover scraps. It didn't take long before his eyes grew heavy and he headed upstairs to rest. He slept on a mattress at the foot of his parents' bed, next to his brother Siew Chong, two years his senior. As he pulled the mosquito net around him, he could hear the muffled conversation of his uncle and aunt saying goodnight to his young cousins in the bedroom next door. His older sisters were still out with his two older cousins. They shared another room with the paid seamstresses. Long after his heavy eyelids had closed, all the young women tiptoed into bed before the current team of male workers strung hammocks where they could. The rainforest timber floor groaned under the weight of people.

As morning light crept through timber shutters, the household occupants awoke, sliding into well-worn routines. Apak (who controlled the money) took his brother to the local wet market to buy produce which they carried back to their wives in the kitchen. Wong, dressed in the pants and shirt his father had made for him, sat at the big round dining table eating the steaming bowl of pork liver broth and noodles Ah Ji handed him with a smile, the smell of frying pork lard still hanging in the air. As the workers started to arrive, taking the remaining seats, he slurped his last sip and went to sweep the workshop floor again as instructed.

When the metal door slid back at 8am, the whir of sewing machines began, workers joining the pattern pieces of the men's pants Apak had measured and cut the day before. Unbeknownst to Wong, in a few years, the grey and brown fabrics would be punctuated with different hues as his sister Siew Yon (known as Vivian) would return from training in Taiwan and start making colourful women's clothes. The fabric colours of his early years were dull, but the atmosphere was far from it. Retired neighbours gathered at the shop. Even though he didn't understand their political discussions, Wong caught glimpses of newspaper headlines over their shoulders and tried to decipher their meaning.

With the kitchen back in order, and vegetables chopped for lunch, Wong ran next door to the billiard shop and begged for scraps of chalk. He situated himself on the concrete floor by his mother practising his letters, wiping away errors and starting again. Ah Ji taught him what she knew, but she was well aware his literacy would surpass her own as soon as he started school the following year. On evenings when she finished sewing buttons early enough, she taught herself to read.

In the afternoon, Ah Ji shooed young Wong out into the garden to play for a while. The other children said she spoilt him, but she had a soft spot for his patient and caring character and seldom found the need to discipline him. While he was gone, she gathered the dirty laundry and alternated between a large washing bucket and a rinsing one, wringing out the clothes with her chapped hands. It seemed her feet were always wet and sore, but a washing machine was a luxury of which she only dreamt. The sun's rays reached the upstairs balcony in the afternoon, so she negotiated around the potted plants and Wong's home-made fish tanks, hoisting bamboo poles to hang the washing in the sun. Her signature flower-patterned sarongs blew in the breeze, balancing the subdued tones.

Meanwhile Wong and his neighbourhood friend revelled in their limited freedom in the square back garden. He drank in the coffee aroma that wafted in his direction from the roaster in the next alley, but there wasn't enough wind to fly their paper-and-bamboo kite. Instead, they picked small hard guavas from their neighbour's tree, drove nails through them, and wrapped a string to create a spinning top. Wong was pleased when his top stayed spinning the longest. Eventually bored, they grabbed a bamboo-poled fish net and bucket, and wandered to the end of the street closest to the station. The small stream beckoned.

As we stare into the puny stream, Wong tells me guppies were introduced to Asia from South America in the early 1900s to control malaria-causing mosquito larvae in urban areas. They escaped captivity and are now one of the most widely distributed freshwater tropical fish in the world. As a youngster, he managed to net half a dozen, taking them back home to his rudimentary plastic-lined bucket fish tanks. He then waved goodbye to his friend, rushed through the house, and added wood to the fire so his aunt could start cooking.

Saturday night was busy on Station Road. The three cinemas in town added an 11pm show to their repertoire, street vendors doing well from the extra late-night traffic. His sisters had promised to let him come with them to the show at the Cathay, and he was excited. There was no cost if he took his own stool along and sat in the front. Maybe they would buy him a plastic bag of sunflower seeds. He liked the salty taste on his lips but had to raise his feet in the air because of the occasional rat scurrying around fallen husks in search of scraps.

The shop wasn't open on Sundays, so the next day, eight family members piled into Apak's pride and joy—his Hillman Minx—and drove back to his hometown. Apak and his siblings still owned their parents' farm. Working it supplemented their income. It was a fertile plot with a stream running through the middle, and their parents' old house was still standing. Seasonal fruit included commercially desirable durian, rambutan, and mangosteen. During fruiting seasons, they leased the rights to the farm, and the lessee would take the fruit to market. The family kept some trees for themselves, and it was these that required constant tending. Even with twenty mouths to feed, the crop was often more than they could consume, so sometimes they gave food away to friends, or the kitchen was turned into a temporary jam factory. "Mum made really good pineapple jam," Wong remembers.

The same tight-knit extended family has called a banquet to welcome me to Penang. Only sibling number three, Siew Min, is missing, Melbourne his home now. As Siew Gaik ushers us through the door, laughter bounces off the restaurant walls, rising and falling in circular waves, disagreements put aside in favour of connection. Wong is called ST here, short for Siew Te. He's the baby, treated with equal weights of pride and indifference, accolades fading into the bamboo-print wallpaper.

Vivian makes her way over to me, asking how I liked her curry puff. The melting layers still linger on my palette from lunch. Eldest sister Siew Mei, who cared for Ah Ji in her final years, takes her place at the round table, kneading her finger joints to keep them limber. I am ushered next to sibling number five, Siew Kok, with the introduction "he's the intelligent one." Quite a compliment when I mentally calculate all the degrees in the room, but he was the first in his high school to get a university scholarship, earning his position. His thoughtful gaze behind narrow-rimmed glasses is more restrained than the effervescent Jimmy, who is toasting with a glass of Chinese tea to my right.

Siew Kok is a devout Christian in a family of Taoists and Buddhists. As he serves me soup from the bubbling concoction in the middle of the table, our conversation is eclectic —jumping from worldviews to books, from vegetarianism to parenting. "When it comes to children, I am the gardener and my wife is the policeman," he says. On the other side of the table, Ben's teenage daughter chimes in, talking about her psychology class, retreating back into the pages of Harry Potter balanced on her knee. The food keeps coming, and the conversation keeps pace.

I am starting to get a feel for the constant busyness of Wong's childhood the next morning as I follow his sister Siew Gaik through the crowded streets of Bukit Mertajam, trying not to get knocked off the narrow path by a tide of bodies. The canvas shopping bag over her crooked arm sways. In her other hand she grasps a plastic bag containing roast chicken she and I have just bought from a nearby vendor. As we negotiate the flow of humanity, the vendor rushes up behind us with extra change, and I get the feeling it's the equivalent of what Australians would call 'Mates Rates'. I am struck with a sense of how respected Siew Gaik and the entire Wong family are in this community. Her father paved the way as chairman of the temple committee for many years, and this is a neighbourhood built on tradition. The loveable, no-nonsense Siew Gaik took over the role of Taoist matriarch after their mother died, and she goes into organisational overdrive as we meet up with Wong and his eldest brother Siew Wah (or Jimmy).

We near the temple to pay our respects to the Hungry Ghost. Long temporary tables have been erected down the length of the covered courtyard to the left of the temple. They point towards a two-storey gold paper effigy with a menacing birdlike face, pom-pom-clad headdress, and knees spread in a defiant pose. A row of plump kneeling cushions lies between the tables and the figure, while various shallow sand-filled boxes support burning red candles on bamboo sticks. Along the edges of the temple grounds, vendors display gold paper pineapples wrapped in cellophane, paper gold ingots, and fake money designed to appease. As we draw closer, the rising hum of human activity mingles with fragrant smoke.

One of the vendors tries to sell Siew Gaik a package of joss sticks but she brushes them off, heading directly to her friend's stall instead. She finds a clear space on the left of the long table, further back from two prostrate whole pigs dripping blood, and starts to unload her bag. Wong arranges whole oranges and bright pink dragonfruit on a small round plastic plate. He unscrews the top from a jar of green tea and pours the liquid into tiny round Chinese tea cups with a capacity of perhaps two sips. Their offering is dwarfed by a tower of steamed buns looking like a French Croquembouche.

White-haired Jimmy hovers, and I get the impression he's here only to placate his sister. Jimmy has moved away from his cultural roots more than some of his siblings, having studied in Japan and married a Japanese woman. On the short drive here, this cultural enigma had disarmingly burst into Cliff Richard and Bee Gees songs without prompting. Jimmy seems almost as out of place as I. His siblings light their incense and work through an ancient ritual. They start at the dragon-like joss pillars that frame the entrance and make their way towards the cushions, falling to their knees in front of the statue with hands glued together, thumbs touching their foreheads in prayer.

Wong and Siew Gaik at the temple

We leave the offering and migrate to the compact temple next door, passing an outdoor stage where three white-faced Chinese opera singers prepare for their next performance. "Mum would have been in the front row on her stool waiting," Wong says in a wave of nostalgia. "She loved the opera." Similar joss-stick rituals take place here, but they are more solemn. I try to fade into the wallpaper and watch in silence, but I am constantly in the way, so I end up sitting on a bench in the corner until Wong and Siew Gaik are finished. The pragmatist in me is pleased when we return to the offering table, pull out the shopping bag, and pack everything away. It seems the ghost has been appeased.

Wong is keen to grab a noodle breakfast from the stalls by the temple, but Jimmy isn't. "It's part of your heritage," I hear Wong say in frustration. In the way of all families, the two are not aligned, so Wong and I leave his siblings and pull up a plastic stool against an occupied table in the only space we can find. Sweet, thick, white coffee; noodles; and donut-like youtiao bread appear.

While we eat, I question the cultural medley I have just experienced. Wong tells me for one month a year, the gates between heaven and hell open, releasing ghosts and spirits of the ancestors into the living world. Chinese children are taught to avoid being out after dark during the Hungry Ghost month because the ghosts are mischievous and like to cause accidents. The offerings seek protection from Tai Su Yah, the ruler of the underworld, and it is his effigy at the temple. At the end of the month-long festival, when safety returns, all the gathered paper offerings and the effigy are piled into the centre of the main intersection and set alight, surrounded by excited crowds.

Taoism was an integral part of Wong's childhood, and he grew up with a belief in the kitchen god, the back-alley god, and the great god who ruled them all. Joss sticks burned in their home each day under a portrait of one of the gods, but the first and 15th day of the lunar calendar were considered auspicious days when the merit of one's deeds was multiplied. These became particularly pious occasions.

Chinese New Year was the biggest celebration each year, and food was an integral part in the same way it was in the English Christmases of my own youth. As young Wong helped his sisters and mother colour and shape dough, he was excited that some of his siblings would soon be arriving from their studies all over the world. He gathered the scraps and took them to the garden for chickens—their last meal. It was slaughter day, dusk fast approaching.

As soon as the fowl were asleep, Apak unsheathed his long knife, or parang, picked them off their perch, slit their throats, and drained the blood into a pan. He would chuck each dying chicken into the bathroom to struggle while he moved to the next, blood soaking into his apron. A large steaming pot on the stove rolled to a boil, and the finally motionless, still-warm chicken would be dunked, making it easier for the women to pluck. In another pot, Wong mixed the blood with salt water, stirring over heat until the blood clotted and hardened. When it was set, Ah Ji would cut the blood into cubes, tossing it into her stir-fry like tofu.

Most Westerners have become so removed from the farming process that I can't imagine an Australian child surviving such an activity without emotional scarring. Although Wong clearly remembers the shock of first opening the bathroom door to blood-splattered walls, he understood that death was part of life, feeling neutral towards the experience. In these years before his schooling began, his growing love for all creatures was somewhat incongruent with the delight of cooking and eating meat. When I probe into the contradiction, he's a little embarrassed. "I'm being bad. I always joke that I am Chinese and eating meat is in my blood—a cultural thing shaped in my childhood," he tells me. "These days I tend to avoid less sustainable foods like sharks and rays… but one day I will become a vegetarian."

CHAPTER 3

Creature Comforts

"If plan A doesn't work, there is always a Plan B;
If Plan B doesn't work, then there's a Plan C..."

When Wong reached the age of five, many of his regular playmates were away at kindergarten during the day. His parents didn't have the money to send him. Instead, Wong learnt from the world around him. That world included the black and white magpie robins his father kept in a cage within the shop. He watched intently as they emitted their shrill conversations, the birds' shoulders shrugging, their tails raised. He unscrewed the jar lid quickly, pinched one of the grasshoppers he had captured in the garden, and pushed it through the bars to the waiting birds. Sometimes his dad caught scorpions to fuel his son's curiosity, and Wong sat fascinated, watching them pounce on their prey at lightning speed with their oversized pincers, then curling their deadly tails to finish the job. There was no Discovery Channel. Wong had the real thing.

His time at the orchard on weekends took on extra importance, feeding Wong's insatiable enquiring mind. There was seldom a weekend he returned to the city empty-handed. No longer content with catch and release, he started bringing jars of guppies home from the orchard. He made a wooden box about a hundred and twenty centimetres long and twenty centimetres deep as a rudimentary aquarium, and lined it with thick plastic sheeting. Without a proper filtration system, algae grew quickly. "I didn't know why this kept happening until I started reading about fish-keeping," Wong tells me. Once he realised, he diligently changed the water every two days, eventually installing a water pump. One day he checked his fish before school only to find a rat had chewed through the pump hose. All his bright orange carp were upside down. Wong was devastated. As he repaired the tank and buried his fish, the tears flowed uncontrollably.

Wong's primary school in Malaysia ran quite differently from the British and Australian systems I have experienced. Typically, children in the first three 'Standards', (or grades), attend school in the afternoon, from 1.30pm to 6.30 or 7pm, while Standards four, five, and six attend in the morning, from 7am to 1.30pm. This cleverly enables the school infrastructure to handle double the numbers, with a swap-over of children and teachers at lunchtime. Even so, class sizes are large, with an average of about fifty per classroom.

In Penang, Chinese families tended to make school decisions based on the quality of school, rather than the religion. Two of Wong's elder siblings attended English-speaking schools while his sister Siew Gaik went to an English-speaking convent school. It wasn't unusual, then, when he was enrolled in Chinese-speaking Jit Sin Primary School, a different school from Siew Chong (Ben), two years his senior. Wong was seven and he had already been exposed to several faiths. It was the first time he had ever been without his mother, though, and he was understandably anxious. He didn't adjust easily to classroom confinement, which cracked the fabric of his utopian world. The first three days dripped like water torture. He couldn't wait for the bell to sound so he could get home where things were familiar. A week later, Wong still hadn't adjusted well to the crowds and unfamiliar surroundings, so in the second week, his parents transferred him to the Catholic school Kim Sen Primary where Ben could keep an eye on him for the first year. Most of the children were of Chinese origin, and all classes, except for English and Malay, were conducted in Mandarin. Friendship groups had tentatively formed in the week before he transferred, but under the tutorage of the Brothers and his female teacher, Yee Pee Yur, Wong slowly started to integrate.

For the first three years, Wong's day began with his chores and caring for his animals. Time flew until mid-morning when he quickly dressed in the crisp white shirt and blue shorts, the standard school uniform for all non-Muslim boys throughout Malaysia, and rushed to meet the blue school bus as it pulled up on Station Road. He knew it wouldn't wait, and he didn't want to drag Apak away from the shop to take him on the old blue Vespa. The wrinkly, wizened conductor stood on the pavement shepherding children onboard, his watchful eye ensuring Wong crossed the street safely. As he jumped onboard, Wong smiled a greeting to the driver, then sat next to his friend Tan Ming Yih who lived next door. The bus pulled away, following the familiar route, gathering more passengers until every seat was full and it groaned under their weight.

The playground behind the one-storey wooden schoolhouse was mayhem when Wong alighted from the bus. Kids kicked a football around the field in the tropical heat and he ran to join them, expending his pent-up energy before the upcoming confinement. When the bell rang, one of his friends picked up the ball and they shuffled to the school hall, washed along by a tsunami of larger children who had finished their lessons. Sweaty from the exertion and squashed like sardines, Wong found it hard to concentrate during the obligatory announcements. He breathed easier when the big kids were dismissed, snapping to attention when his row was instructed to rise and march into the classroom. As the class noisily found their desks, his form teacher shook her head, bracing herself for another day confined with sweaty boy odour, starting to read the roll. There was another child in the class with a remarkably similar name, and Wong tried hard to remember not to answer, "I am here" to the wrong name. Together the two boys had worked out that Ong came before Wong alphabetically, but sometimes he forgot.

Wong dreaded practising his handwriting because sometimes they gave him the cane for not getting the Chinese characters right or not completing his homework, but it was Malay and English vocabulary, with their unfamiliar alphabet, that really taxed his brain. Today, Wong realises that fluency in the Malay language was perhaps the most useful skill he took away from school, but back then, he found it hard to concentrate, preferring to finger the ten sen in his pocket and dream of the plate of noodles it would buy him at recess. Sometimes Ah Ji surprised him and walked the three kilometres with homemade goodies instead, making him feel special. He prized the days when Apak found a large enough gap between customers to pick him up after classes. It saved waiting for the second bus run and got him back to his pets sooner. Ah Ji said Wong was a slave to his animals, feeling sorry that they ate so much of his personal time, but to Wong this was his time.

The top hundred, out of a cohort of three hundred students, were separated in A or B class, and Wong's marks in the early years were never quite high enough to make the cut. The curriculum simply didn't include any of his interests: there were no environmental field trips, no conservation science, and no projects based on wildlife. The two sets of English Encyclopedia Britannica at home, his brothers' pride and joy, were thumbed more often than his textbooks, falling open to pages on dog breeds. As soon as he got home, he rushed to tend to his animals. Luckily, times have changed, and environmental education was added to the curriculum about twenty years ago when educators identified a need. "When everything is beautiful, no one talks about it," Wong philosophises when he tells me things are improving. "Only when things start to go wrong does the voice of balance kick in."

To young Wong, the saving grace at primary school was physical education. He successfully tried out for the basketball team and played for a while but, when the growth-spurt he longed for didn't eventuate, hoops were replaced with track and field. He was a sprinter in primary school until that too was thwarted in Standard 3 by a dislocated ankle that required him to wear a cast for several months. During this confinement, his animals took on even more importance, and it was a fallen urban sparrow fledgling that cemented Wong's life-long love of birds. Cupping it in his hands gently, Wong rushed home to ask Ah Ji what to do. When Wong's mum was a little girl, growing up in the village, she also had an affinity for broken animals, so she put down her armful of laundry and showed her son how to grind rice into flour and mix it with water. She grabbed a toothpick and demonstrated how to feed the tiny bird one morsel at a time. As Ah Ji returned to her chores, Wong nurtured the bird back to health.

Wong was a self-professed night owl, so the transition to morning classes in Standard 4 meant the routine with his growing menagerie was forced to change. He started paying more attention to his studies, climbing the rankings. In no time, he was preparing for the Standard 5 national examination which would determine the high school he attended. Malaysia had government-run and privately run secondary institutions. Students were offered free government school placements based on their ranking, and private schools were considered a fall-back option, used only if a child didn't achieve highly and the parents could afford to pay. Wong would need to settle for whatever school he was offered. He felt the pressure, but he was starting to get the hang of studies, working hard. He squeaked into the top government school in his region. The overwhelming majority of children at state-run Jit Sin High School were of Chinese origin, but all lessons in secondary level were conducted in Malay. To ensure Chinese children transitioned well, they were required to attend an extra school year between primary and high school called Remove. Even knowing their children would be confined in school an extra year, parents like Wong's preferred the quality of education in Chinese-language primary schools. Wong's Malay wasn't that good at this stage, his marks fluctuating in direct correlation to the number of pets he had at the time.

Wong's reputation as a bird and animal lover continued to grow until one day when a neighbour handed Apak a furry, spotted black and grey creature, about the size of a small cat, with instructions to give it to Siew Te. It was a rescued common civet with a tail almost as long as its body. The only time he had seen one before was in the cooking pot when Apak made civet soup. Wong named his new friend Wee Wee and kept her away from his father's knife.

The tailor shop's skeleton was wood, but a concrete block column hugged the edge of the open internal skylight, joining the two floors to the ceramic tiled roof, one part overhanging the other. A water pipe ran the length of the column, and Wong chained Wee Wee around the pipe so she could move freely up and down. She liked to sleep on one roof, in the shade of the overhang. Wong climbed up on a ladder and sat with her. Wee Wee sometimes managed to squeeze her neck out of her collar in Houdini-esque fashion, dashing skyward. Wong clambered after her, calling her name as she deftly leapt from roof to roof along the terrace.

These were the days before the Internet, so Wong couldn't Google the diet of a civet cat. She seemed to like condensed milk, rice, and fruit, so that's what she got but, as she grew, Wee Wee's fur lost its shine and Wong noticed more and more hairs on his clothes. He is pretty sure her unbalanced diet led to malnourishment, and now knows he should have fed her a wide variety of fruits and invertebrates, but hindsight is a glorious thing. A diet of sugary carbohydrates, without adequate fat or raw calcium, led to her premature death.

Wong didn't want to lose another animal, so he climbed to the library on District Office Hill, pausing to catch his breath under the big fig tree, surveying the city sprawling below him. He returned with a magazine called Dog Fancy. It was the first English non-textbook he had ever read, and at the age of about eleven, he devoured its contents. So started a love of knowledge which hasn't waned: Wong discarded his comics in favour of animal, fish, and bird-keeping books, applying all he learnt to his newly acquired house-cat and turtles. All he wanted to do was work with animals, his family dragged along for the ride.

On one of Apak's rare days off, he piled the family into his boxy Hillman and took them to the Penang Botanical Gardens. Wong curiously followed signs to Sun Bears. He'd never seen one before, and as he approached the moat barrier, he could see four stocky black creatures beyond. One stood on its hind legs as children giggled, throwing fruit which exploded on the unforgiving concrete floor. He was saddened by the scene, emotion catching in his throat.

Wong's skills with birds grew gradually until the day when his hobby turned into a small business. By this time, the owners of the tailor shop premises had decided to develop the site. The Wong family packed their memories and moved to a housing estate in suburbia. Apak took the opportunity to semi-retire, but he placated his loyal customers by continuing his work informally. His big cutting table dominated the house, and one worker still lived with them.

As Apak walked home from the market, a flash of colour in the drain caught his eye. It was a small green-breasted African lovebird with its telltale orange forehead and white hooked beak. He suspected it might have hit the side of the house while escaping from a cage somewhere in the neighbourhood. The stunned rainbow fluff-ball barely flinched as he gently scooped it in both palms, taking it home. When his 15-year-old son walked in the door from school, Apak was waiting.

With a grin transforming his face, Wong pushed his glasses up his nose, stretched out his arms, and took the prize up to his bedroom, where he gently placed it in a cage to recover. As soon as the bird was able, it started chirping at the open window, attracting an identical bird that appeared to be its mate. Wong wondered if the pair had escaped together or been released by a reluctant pet owner. Cunning Wong, aided by his brother Ben, lured the visitor into their bedroom using its mate's song as the bait. Once the pair were reunited, Wong's fledgling business as a breeder began. "I had no idea at the time what wildlife conservation was," he tells me, "so all I wanted to do back then was to own a pet shop."

Wong tells me this story as we walk around the edge of a large square grass area towards the main hall at Jit Sin High School. A dozen middle-aged men are kicking a ball around and a corresponding number of women are cheering from the sidelines. Wong's thirty-year high school reunion has begun, the excitement electric as long-lost buddies recognise each other and hug enthusiastically. Wong gravitates to those friendships he still maintains, and laughs nervously around the identities of those people he is frantically dragging from the annals of his memory. I am introduced, then hang around the periphery of both the field and the conversation, observing my surroundings.

The grass is surrounded by manicured hedges, beyond them a walking path, then a two-storey rectangle of classrooms; to the right of me are the government school rooms; to the left, the private school buildings. High school is a territorial place and Wong tells me the socio-economic divide meant the children didn't mix much. Still, Jit Sin High School produced many of the area's leaders, from both sides of the playground. The large hall in front of me is the beating heart of activity, just as it was thirty years ago. Soon it will embrace greying graduates dressed in their finest – assembled to boast, share photos of their kids, and reminisce.

Wong is animated as we enter the wide doors, excited to see how the preparations are coming along. The concrete floor of old has been given a parquet facelift. I can see memories of school plays and award ceremonies clicking across Wong's memory. As we wander around the grounds, he points out where the wooden art shack stood. "My painting taught me about culture, patience, and persistence," Wong tells me, pointing to the upper classrooms. "I painted a mural up there," he says. The locked staircase door thwarts us from investigating whether his legacy remains.

As we walk around the playground, he flinches at the memory of gravel rash before the grass was laid. All the while, like a movie backdrop, the omnipresent mountain watches over us like a benevolent dictator. At the far end of the playground, behind a sturdy metal frame supporting the solid brass bell that has always rung out recess, the Clan Association building competes for power. This group of successful Chinese businessmen, rather like a Rotary Club, owns much of town, including the school, renting individual shops to vendors and paternalistically awarding scholarships. Wong drags me into the inner sanctum to flip through association committee yearbooks, proudly pointing out his father in wooden group portraits.

Just as it is for most teenagers, puberty was a time when Wong's personal values and interests were shaped independently from his parents. The link between Wong's love for animals and his studies came in the form of a comedic, engaging teacher who sowed a love of science, tipping the balance when it came time to choose between a science or humanities stream. The general science of early primary gave way to the three disciplines. Biology was his favourite. Even being asked to drown the sacrificial laboratory rat didn't deter Wong, and when Apak next killed a chicken, Wong found himself helping so he could identify its organs. Biology strengthened his understanding of animals, but he also discovered a creative streak, satiated by the art club. Animals in magazine photos were often his muses, watercolour and pencil his favourite tools.

With oil pastels staining his fingernails, young Wong tightened his shoelaces and headed for the running track where he scaled hurdles until he felt he would drop. There wasn't room for mistakes here. If he lost concentration a falter sent his face careening towards the gravel. Wong enjoyed competing individually, proud when he was asked to represent the state. He made friends with the other state team members, especially a lanky girl named Tze Ling. Her conversation made the long bus rides to athletic meets endurable. Together they stepped off the bus, glancing around at their opponents. The team from the state of Sabah towered above them, their legs rippling with muscle, looking like fully grown adults. Tze Ling giggled nervously under her hand. The birth date of rural children in Sabah was often forgotten, their ability to work in the fields from an early age far more relevant. By the time births were recorded, affecting the year these children started school, they may already be toddlers. Against such competition, Wong learnt to be philosophical, tempering his competitive streak. Luckily, credit was given to athletes to compensate for the time they spent training, boosting Wong's academic standing. Nevertheless, he felt if he failed on the day of competition there was no one else to blame but himself, and that was the way he liked it. When combined with outdoor survival skills learnt at Scouts, the flexibility, the stamina, and the slimmer physique he built training on the track later served him well as a researcher in the field.

Wong wasn't used to sitting on the sidelines of anything, so when his gang decided to create a band, and asked him to join, he rose to the challenge. He became one of five singers, with four additional friends playing guitar. I wonder if his voice is as smooth as his brother Jimmy's, whose dulcet rendition of "Tragedy" by the Bee Gees is replaying in my head. Until the 1980s, Malaysian Chinese sang the songs of Taiwan and Hong Kong in the same way Australians absorbed British pop, so when Wong's band produced original tunes, they were encouraged at local events. "I could have been a pop star," Wong tells me, not completely in jest. Singing improved his credibility with girls too, which was a real benefit for pubescent Wong who was mortified that he stuttered in front of the opposite sex. He longed to confess his growing 'crush' to Tze Ling, but he was worried he wouldn't be able to get the words out. One of his bandmembers came to the rescue, penning a song which could be used to woo her from the stage. Wong practiced well, but on the day of the concert, he was nervous. He strongly encouraged Tze Ling to be there, and when she agreed, he sat her on a seat right under an occasional spotlight. "This song is dedicated from one of our bandmembers to one of his close friends," his bandmember said, close to the microphone. "He wants to tell this girl how important she is." Then Wong began to sing.

Tze Ling remembers the serenade fondly, but at the time, surrounded in a spotlight halo, the introverted young girl felt the blood rush to her face. She was so embarrassed, she longed for an earthquake. Rather than a romance, the shared discomfort sparked a unique and spiritual friendship which has endured the test of time, guiding them both through rough patches. They see each other infrequently, sliding instantly into its comfort like a pair of sheep's-wool slippers.

Eventually, it came time for Wong to sit the Form 5 exams. He crossed his fingers and hoped his marks would get him a place in the Agriculture University of Malaysia animal husbandry diploma program. Even though he was apprehensive about having to leave home and live in the capital of Kuala Lumpur, the diploma was the first rung on a veterinary ladder, and Wong desperately wanted to become a vet. He worked hard and achieved distinctions in every subject except Malay. Without that, he knew he wouldn't be offered a place in the diploma program or, indeed, a place in a government high school to complete Form 6. He was bitterly disappointed. His supportive family banded together and came up with the funds for Wong to enrol in a private school—Han Chiang High School—giving him a chance to retake the exam a year later.

As an ethnic Chinese, Wong needed straight As before he would even be considered for a government-funded university place, and the only university in Malaysia which offered a vet program was government-run Universiti Putra Malaysia. In the wake of the 1969 riots that affected Wong's birth, the prime minister, Tun Abdul Razak Hussin, attempted to address the tinderbox of poverty and economic imbalance with a program called the New Economy Policy. Ethnic Malays (or Bumiputra) owned very little land, were generally less educated, and were lower down the socio-economic scale than other Malaysians, most notably those of Chinese or Indian descent. What resulted was an affirmative action policy, introduced in 1973, which preferenced Bumiputra in education opportunities, business licences, and government jobs. It stipulated that fifty-five percent of university places would go to Bumiputras, and the remaining forty-five percent would be available to Chinese and Indian students. With sixty percent of the citizenship consisting of ethnic Malays, on the surface, the policy seemed a fair way to address the imbalance but, since Chinese had traditionally performed much higher academically, it meant Wong found himself in a very competitive field of his peers. He feels the policy disadvantaged Malaysia on a global playing field because many Chinese subsequently left the country in search of opportunity. World Bank figures reported an estimated one million Malaysians living abroad in 2010, four times the number thirty years before. This brain drain represented two out of ten tertiary-educated Malaysians. Many moved to nearby Singapore where an estimated ninety percent of Malaysians in 2010 were of Chinese origin. The policy was officially abolished in 2002, when the government introduced a program called the Returning Expert Programme to lure them back, but old habits die hard, and Wong says many young Chinese and Indians today still feel discriminated against.

At the end of Form 6, Wong sat his exams. He passed but didn't make straight As, so he wasn't offered a government university position. Wong was running out of options. He re-sat the exam with the same result. His dream to be a vet, the career he longed for, was slipping away.

As he and I sit at his desk and chat over a lunch of leftovers, the chasm between the teenage Wong, facing an uncertain future, and the confident CEO sitting next to me is unfathomable. "If you could time travel, what encouragement would you give to your young self?" I ask.

"I would tell him to stay focused. If plan A doesn't work, there is always a Plan B; If Plan B doesn't work, then there's a Plan C, then D, then E. Of course, you have to try hard – really hard – and never give up," Wong replies.

And that's exactly what young Wong did.

CHAPTER 4

Leaving Home

"Would you rather be eating in a good restaurant, or cooking in one?"

"What shall I do?" teenage Wong asked his favourite sister Siew Gaik, who always seemed to help him find the right path. He wondered if he should give up his dream of working with animals, and fall back on plan B. For the last couple of years of high school, his bird-breeding income had been supplemented by washing dishes in brother Jimmy's Japanese/Chinese restaurant. As he became familiar with the foreign dishes his sister-in-law had chosen for the Japanese half of the menu, he sometimes acted as assistant cook, even stepping into the chef's place when he took a day off. Even in the Malaysian humidity, Wong loved the excitement and challenge of pleasing people with food within a prescribed time frame. Every customer offered an opportunity for success, and every time he passed a plate of food to Jimmy to serve, he felt a sense of accomplishment. Maybe he should be a chef instead?

Many of my interviews are conducted face-to-face in Borneo, and on this occasion, as he recalls the angst of the dilemma, Wong is combining flour and salt water together with his fingertips, his love of cooking intact. The recipe in his head calls for 500g of flour to 250ml of water, but the amount changes depending on the type and age of the flour and the temperature of the water. He adjusts by feel as he rubs. As instructed, I emulsify minced pork with finely chopped onions, garlic, and greens picked from his garden. Unexpectedly, I'm learning so much more than wildlife conservation. Wong thrives on food deadlines, giving himself one hour each night to cook and serve dinner. Today's challenge is Chinese dumplings. He's proud of his dumplings. "I showed my Korean vet friend how to make this," Wong says. "She made it for her mum back home and her mum cried." He rolls the dough into sausages, cutting it into slices. "Do it like this," he says, flattening a dough ball in his palm, topping it with a teaspoon of the mixture, and deftly folding the edges into half-moon parcels. "'Would you rather be eating in a good restaurant, or cooking in one?' Siew Gaik asked me." For him, this one rhetorical question strengthened his resolve. Wong chose to follow his love of animals, but this meant he would have to leave the familiarity of home, the bottomless support of his mother, and of course, his animals. If he were faced with the same chef-versus-animal-research crossroads 'nows-a-days', he tells me, between instructions, it would be harder, but this was twenty-five years before celebrity chefs made it cool to cook.

The door might have closed on the only Malaysian university with a veterinary diploma, but Wong's siblings had set a precedent by seeking scholarships overseas. Sisters Siew Mei and Siew Yon had already completed their studies in Taiwan, Jimmy studied in Japan, Siew Kok went to the States, Siew Min went to Scotland, and Ben had just left for Taiwan. Wong broadened his own vision.

Chinese families adhere to trickle-down economics, and Wong's position as last child came without the blood-tie financial obligations of his siblings. With his brothers and sisters chipping in, and the pressure of kiasu (the fear of failure) mixed with excitement in his stomach, Wong accepted a position studying a combination of veterinary and animal husbandry at Taiwan's National Pingtung University of Science and Technology for the 1989 intake. It was the same year the Formosan Clouded Leopard was declared extinct in Taiwan.

As Wong's departure date approached, Ah Ji was conflicted. He was her baby—her favourite, if you asked his siblings—and this milestone represented the end of an era. Many of her friends told her not to let him go. She deserved to keep him safe at her side, they said, but she was a wise woman and knew she couldn't hold him back. Stoically she helped her baby pack his bag, she checked his ticket, she made sure his brother would be at the airport to greet him, and she took over caring for his remaining menagerie.

Taipei was only five hours from Penang by air, but a world away from the familiar streets of Bukit Mertajam. Wong was grateful to see Ben's familiar face in the arrival hall. Before he knew it, they were catching up on family news on the long-distance bus, passing the central region, where Ben studied, continuing south. As Dawu Mountain rose from the plains, Wong knew he was getting close to his new home. Butterflies collided in his stomach as he set foot onto the largest university campus in Taiwan, incorporating pig, cattle, and chicken farms. Its size was overwhelming.

Ben helped Wong navigate the enrolment process and settle into his dorm room, ensured he could access the funds in his bank account, wished him luck, and headed back to his own studies. Unfamiliarity set in. Wong's Malaysian Hakka accent drew attention, he found people slowing their speech to accommodate him.

Wong lived in a dormitory and ate at the cafeteria, regularly checking his bank account to see how he was faring on funds. The times of asking Apak for pocket money were long gone, and he was struggling. Wong soon discovered he could buy rice and one dish for half the price of a packed lunch, so this became his staple until he commandeered a rice cooker and a small stove, preparing food (against regulations) in his room. "Because I knew how to cook, I could make something out of nothing," he remembers.

Wong noticed some of his classmates worked in the cafeteria at lunchtime. Free food was a perk, so he signed up as a dishwasher during his second semester. There were days he cleaned a thousand plates over a two-hour lunch shift. The repetitive process of pre-spraying, loading trays, rolling them into the stainless dishwasher, locking the door lever down, pushing the start button, and burning his fingers on the clean, hot plates invaded his dreams. He felt relieved when he was given an evening shift, waiting tables in the steakhouse instead.

With such a large campus, Wong bought a push-bike to get from class to class, and sometimes on weekends he ventured into nearby Neipu township to the night markets. The familiar smells from street hawkers made him feel at home and momentarily assuaged homesickness, until a stallholder spat bright red betel-nut saliva at his feet. Wong tried to divert his gaze from the strippers employed to draw crowds. Coming from a Muslim-dominated country, he had been sheltered from such overt displays of sexuality. When there was a sufficient gathering, a salesman weaved through the men to push medicines: some as innocuous as Panadol; others, derivatives of rhino horn or tiger bone.

One day he ventured to a Taoist temple to pray, only to find the holy pig festival in full swing in the courtyard. The familiar incense smoke overpowered the animal odours. Villagers crowded around their festival entries—dead pigs lay prostrate like partly deflated helium balloons with flimsy trotter extensions. Folds of skin cascaded from one black animal's brow, obscuring the eyes. It weighed more than ten normal pigs. The snout was the only indication of its species. Surrounding each obese animal, farmers compared force-feeding techniques. With much fanfare and ribbon wrapping, the winning farmer excitedly took home prize money and street credibility as inflated as his pig. To Wong, the entire process seemed incongruent with Taoist principles. Animals, it appeared, were not revered or respected in the Taiwanese or Chinese cultures of the '80s. As I imagine his shock, I am reminded of a passage from a book by the author of China's One Child Policy, Song Jian, published in 1988, which illustrated the disconnect between man and 'beast'. "We have become the rulers of the entire animal kingdom and conquered all kinds of ferocious beasts that once killed or injured large numbers of our ancestors. Now we have got our revenge on them using their lives to repay the blood debts they owe us from history," Song wrote.

This was the context in which Wong studied animal husbandry. No wonder he found some of his classes an exercise in endurance rather than enjoyment. Pathology class, for instance, was unpleasant but necessary. When a sick chicken was bought in, Wong was instructed to clip one wire to its beak and another to its anus, then plug the wire into a standard household plug. This would kill the bird quickly and efficiently, sending errant feathers slowly to the floor. The chickens then became teaching tools for Wong and his fellow students to study the liver, lungs, heart, and brain, collecting samples and describing abnormalities. Wong learnt well and rose to the top of the class. It was a field trip to the abattoir, however, that caused him to question his chosen career path.

The drum-piercing screams as Wong approached the slaughter pen were excruciating. The smell of death was in the air. Panicked pigs were shocked with an electric prod as workers in white rubber boots herded them through a metal-fenced bottleneck. With hearts pumping, they tried to escape. Climbing over each other. Pushed onto a restrictive conveyor-belt. Pinned and shocked to death. Momentarily, the high-pitched squeals subsided, rising again to a crescendo as the pigs next in line realised their fate. Wong followed one carcass. Still warm, it was dunked in a steaming water vat, then tumbled to remove hairs. Melted pig fat accosted Wong's nostrils with an intensity that made him gag. Further down the process line, the carcass was hung by the feet, which stretched the skin to expose the shape of ribs. The throat artery was severed, squirting a red arch onto the concrete floor. The metallic smell of blood stuck to the back of Wong's throat as a short man in splattered overalls and a hairnet cut the pig cleanly in half with a chainsaw. Internal organs tumbled to the floor. "I don't know how many hundreds of pigs went into the slaughterhouse that day," Wong tells me. "There were live pigs at this end, and they came out as pork at the other end. It was overwhelming."

The abattoir played on Wong's mind when his professor beckoned the class closer for a live pig operation demonstration. On the slab, a tiny pink anesthetised piglet lay on her back and the scalpel slid through her abdomen like butter. The professor mopped up fluids, pointed out various internal organs, then located her intestine, pulling part of it out where they could see. While the students scribbled notes, their teacher cut the intestine in half then picked up a surgical needle and sewed the two ends back together. He shoved the piglet's innards back, lacing the wound together.

Once the demonstration was over, the professor asked for a volunteer to care for the groggy piglet while she recuperated. Wong's was the only hand in the air. The newly named Piggy was taken to the pig farm until the drugs wore off. He wished he could have taken her back to his dorm, but even though the dorm managers turned a blind eye to the smell of curry, he was pretty sure he wouldn't get away with a pet. Instead he relocated three-kilo Piggy to the chicken farm, away from her rambunctious peers.

Every day, Wong rode his bike to feed and walk Piggy in the same way he now walks bear cubs. He knew he couldn't protect her forever. She was a farm animal, after all, but he could make her life comfortable while she was in his care. Piggy put on weight and healed well, and eventually it was time to let go. Just as his dogs and birds had helped Wong cement a love of animals, Piggy made him realise he was more interested in animal welfare than husbandry. Still, he had no idea how you made a living out of caring for animals if they weren't an economic commodity.

Unlike most students, who went home during the long holidays, Wong used the summertime to top up his bank account. Foreign student labourers, as in many countries, were willing to do menial work the locals preferred to overlook. One of these jobs was trimming goat hooves at farms in the rural area surrounding the university. Goats, bred for their meat, were penned on raised wooden platforms which allowed their faeces to drop between the planks. This waste was collected in bags and sold to betel nut farms as fertiliser. Walking on wood, however, meant the growing hooves weren't filed down like they would have been on concrete or gravel. In the worst cases, the carotene curved and twisted so the goats were unable to walk. Wong and a team of six fellow students were paid as trimmers. Most of the goats were manageable females, but they were sexually serviced by bucks the size of fully grown Great Danes with menacing horns. More than their size, it was their smell which made the bucks unpopular.

As Wong approached a large buck, he found the strong musk, which was irresistible to female goats, had the opposite effect on humans. He and his workmates locked eyes with the beast and tried to guess its next movement as they strategically cornered it, slung a rope around its neck, and tied it to the pen wall. Wong manoeuvred into position with a pair of pointed secateurs, grabbed a leg between his knees with his butt touching the animal's flank, and looked down at the foot in his grasp: it forked into two toes, each with a soft flat pad, similar to a dog's. The 'nail' grew around three sides, making it look from a distance like a single entity. Wong worked fast to cut the walls back flush with the soft pad, squaring it off so the goat was using its entire foot to carry weight, not just the nail. His swollen finger joints made it hard to gain purchase as he trimmed incrementally, keeping alert for the telltale pink quick. If he cut it in error, he risked injury as the buck reacted. Musk seeped into his T-shirt, infiltrating his pores. At the end of a back-aching day, he stumbled into the dorm to face complaints from other students as they pinched their noses. Wong jumped into the shower fully dressed and scrubbed himself hard, washing the odour down the drain.

One day in 1992, a friend who worked as a part-time administration assistant in the forestry department, told him some exciting news. Her professor, Kurtis Pei, had been coerced by the government into taking confiscated exotic animals. He was hurriedly setting up a temporary rescue centre using existing buildings within the tree nursery. When Wong rushed over to offer his help, he found ten victims of the illegal wildlife trade in desperate need of care. Wong's passion for wildlife was ignited. In the process, he found his mentor.

On paper, Taiwan's 1989 Wildlife Protection Law was even more comprehensive that the UN's International Convention on International Trade in Endangered Species (CITES). It stated that "Any animal on the conservation list may not be disturbed, abused, hunted, captured, traded, exchanged, illegally owned, killed, or processed, unless under special circumstances recognised in this or related laws." Unfortunately, backhanders to corrupt law enforcers or officials meant the policy had more holes than Swiss cheese. By the time the rescue centre reluctantly accepted animals, for instance, CITES-listed tigers numbered only 5,000 in the wild, yet ground tiger bones could be bought from most Taiwanese chemists for about US$1000 per kilo, to treat cramps, fever, and malaria.

Bornean orangutans and one solitary sun bear starred back at Wong through the bars, making him feel less homesick, and he found himself spending more and more time at the new facility. Wong could only imagine the hardship these beautiful creatures had endured. Ripped from the breast, the young had escaped the fate of their parents, most likely quartered for body parts. Their cuteness was both their saviour and curse. Juvenile orangutans fetched the equivalent of US$6-15,000 on the pet black market.

Astonishingly, there are more orangutans per square kilometre in Taiwan than remain in the native forests of Borneo and Sumatra. When you consider that an estimated one in ten survive the journey, the biodiversity loss is staggering. When the animals grow beyond the size of their cages, becoming unmanageable, or the owner's fortunes change, they are often beaten to keep them obedient, neglected, or simply released onto the streets. In the 1990s, Taiwan had a reputation as the last stop on the road to extinction for such creatures. It's no wonder then, when I ask Kurtis Pei if he was proud of creating the rescue centre, that he answers a strident 'NO!' He is fully aware that the centre was only necessary because of the bad behaviour of his compatriots.

Almost two decades later, the horrific histories of captive wild creatures are front of mind when I report for duty at the Bornean Sun Bear Conservation Centre's (BSBCC) bear house for my own first experience caring for rescued animals. Young keeper Azzry waits while I pick a pair of boots from the shelf. He knows Sepilok with his eyes closed. He's lived here since before he could walk. Azzry's father works at the orangutan centre, and as a young boy, he helped feed infant primates through the night. He's grateful to Wong for giving him a job in which he can forge his own path yet still work with wildlife. As we walk down the path, Azzry rolls off a mental list of rules: dip your boots in disinfectant before you enter; don't touch the cages; walk down the middle of the corridors; be quiet. I feel as anxious as Clarice

Starling entering maximum security in Silence of the Lambs. Then relief: the cages are spacious and light. The smell of urine I had braced for isn't there. Rather than ambient sounds, the industrial percussion from water hoses and stiff-bristle brooms greets me, and the bears in nearby dens wrinkle their noses at my unfamiliar scent instead of the other way round. Azzry introduces me to bear-keeper David Tair as his 'helper-for-the-day' and a fleeting 'not another volunteer' look crosses David's face before he shakes it free then fastidiously shows me the routine. Slowly, over this morning, he warms to my occasional questions.

David Tair was the first full-time employee at the Bornean Sun Bear Conservation Centre other than Wong. His grandfather was a hunter in these forests, and instead of following family tradition, he went into the army. At the time his service drew to a close, David's brother Elis found him this job. Before BSBCC, David hadn't worked with animals, but he says it is similar, in many ways, to the army: "You have to be fit… If there's something you are feeling psychologically, the bears can feel it… You have to choose to die, or live… If you are careless, you die, or your volunteers die. I am very serious. I check and double check. I want to make sure all the cages are safe."

Teamwork, respect, and hard work are David's mantras. When I ask how he finds working with Wong, his emotions are locked behind his eyes. "He's my boss… you must respect the commander… respect is the key." It is questions about the slight, soft-spoken Wai Pak that crack the rusted welds and elicit a smile. After years working together, these two became close and missing his friend is causing David to contemplate retirement.

By lunchtime, I am sweaty and smelly. I mentally catalogue my injuries over a lunch of fried rice and fresh lime juice at the Sepilok kantin. Hot spots on my thumbs sting from chunking watermelon; my biceps feel stretched from stirring rice porridge on the stove; and my admiration for my soft-spoken teacher has jumped a notch. I thank the hardworking kiosk owner who is starting to recognise my face; then, energy levels replenished, walk back down the concrete road. The bear house works like a well-oiled machine, much of the animal husbandry process based on what Wong learnt in Taiwan – both in classes and at the rescue centre. Unlike other centres, however, the animals here have the chance of freedom, and the more I learn about Wong's past, the more I realise why this is so important to him. BSBCC's focus on the welfare of each individual bear adds humanity to every husbandry routine and process.

Back in the stainless-steel kitchen, I divide warm rice porridge into individual feeding trays using the weight charts on the wall, then clip a named clothes-peg on the rim. They cool on the stainless bench while I consult the wall chart. I am struck by the intricate level of physical care as I grind prescribed Centrum tablets and add them to the cooling porridge. After Wong's civet cat died of malnutrition, he learnt the importance of a balanced diet. In the rescue centre, he learnt that mental well-being was equally as important.

Next, I rest a bright red plastic tub of fruit on my hip and follow David around the perimeter fence. As I randomly toss chunks in an arc over the top, he introduces me to his favourite bear, the solitary old-timer Om, chatting to him almost romantically. Another bear stands on its hind legs waiting for me to throw. "That's Damai," David says. My heart flutters.

Damai and I have been on parallel paths for the past five years. She is my own secret crush who arrived at BSBCC six weeks before Wong first offered to take me on a tour of the centre— sweeping me up in his plans. Since then, I have followed her progress from a distance, asking for updates like an overbearing grandparent. I have watched films of her lying on her back balancing a coconut between the soft pinkish pads of all four paws, tearing fibres to expose the core; I've laughed as she gingerly avoided getting muddy when it started to rain; delighted at her climbing speed when the popular and fun-loving bear Fulung chased her skyward. Just as executives proudly display photos of their children next to their computer screen, many of BSBCC's staff displayed pocket-sized likenesses of their favourite bears. It is Damai's portrait on my wall that I gaze at as I write.

With my bucket empty, I see bear-keeper Azzry thumbing through the pages of a thick D-ring binder of illustrated enrichment ideas. It was created by Maria Trenary, senior veterinarian at Oakland Zoo in California, and was growing heavier as humans invented new ways to continually engage bears. Enrichment is synonymous with 'desert' and 'play' in bear lingo. The idea is to hide treats so the bears have to use their skills to find them. Azzry beckons me outside where he and Lester have gathered a mound of ginger foliage. Together, we sit cross-legged on the driveway, each smearing peanut butter on a leaf, rolling it tight, wrapping it with other leaves and stalks, like a bouquet, and binding the fistful with twine. The resulting gifts are piled onto trays until we have forty-four—heaven forbid one bear is left out.

I feel honoured when David asks me to walk down the centre of the corridor tossing the packages high onto the top of the cages. The bears pace, watching my steps, wondering what treat will be forthcoming. At the other end of the building, impatient Mary complains loudly; young Tan Tan scales the bars like an SAS soldier up a rope net before hooking her long black claws and piercing the leaf; blind Gutuk uses his nose to guide him. Within a few minutes the leaves are shredded, twine discarded, paws licked. Some of the bears climb into their steel nests, settling down for the night. I wonder if the sun bears at the Rescue Centre in Taiwan, almost directly north, are doing the same.

Just as BSBCC expanded over time to house more bears, the rescue centre in Taiwan, where Wong learnt his skills, also grew. Social media exacerbated the problem with illegal wildlife deals taking place under the cloak of technology. Subsequently, confiscations escalated. The Rescue Centre now covers four hectares, with a regular population of over a thousand animals and an extensive team—none of whom sugar-coat the tribulations of their inmates. To the contrary, the rescued animals have become a warning to humanity: these tigers were abandoned when a breeder's business failed; this gibbon was thrown out of a high-rise due to noise complaints from neighbours; this tortoise was found at the gate one morning like an illegitimate infant. The soulless eyes of the orangutans break hearts daily and that's how it should be. Some of the same animals Wong once tended have been locked up for 30 years—life without parole.

As the first wildlife biologist and ecologist on staff, Kurtis Pei was not only the Director of the Rescue Centre, but he also accepted the role of advisor to the student bird club of which Wong was a member. This social group was established long before Wong moved to Taiwan. It gained momentum and stature when the government consulted with its members prior to legislating the Wildlife Conservation Act in 1989. The students' input resulted in banning the use of mist nets for bird-harvesting but, as Wong was soon to find out, the practice still continued.

Initially, Wong joined the club primarily for social connection, but after watching a pair of Brahminy Kites make a nest, he was hooked. After a lifelong love of birds, he had no idea simply 'watching' them in the wild was a genuine hobby. He went to the library and found Ben King's field guide, Birds of South-East Asia, with intermittent black and white plates and confusing descriptions. Before long he was on the bird club committee, responsible for organising events.

One Friday about fifteen twitchers met on campus after the last class. He was one of the few who hadn't traded his push bike for something with more grunt, so he jumped on the back of another boy's motorbike (he wouldn't have considered riding pillion behind a girl). On this occasion they headed south towards Kenting National Park on the tip of the island, rolling grassy hills giving way to golden sand and hidden caves. Halfway through the journey, they stopped to photograph coastal vistas and buy snacks from a roadside vendor. When they reached the National Park Service accommodation, they dismounted, parked in angled rows, unpacked their bags, and settled in for an early evening of frivolity. The next morning, they rose at dawn, divided into smaller groups, and dispersed to different vantage areas with clipboards in hand, and binoculars around their necks. They were counting migratory grey-faced buzzards, but this wasn't their only job. Sometimes they acted as bird-guides to tourists, pointing out the constant bobbing of the eastern yellow wagtail or rusty-coloured red knots.

One day, the bird club was asked to count water birds. As Wong followed a black crowned night heron gliding a few metres above the wetlands, he was startled by the sight of a motionless bird in mid-air. He trained his binoculars to discover it was caught in an illegal mist net. Wong was outraged. While his friends looked on with sadness, Wong took off his shoes and waded through the mud in its direction. As he approached, the bird flailed, fine netting tightening around its extended wing. Addressing it calmly, Wong held the small body firmly, untangling its feet, wing, and beak. As the bird flew to safety, Wong noticed the crisp body of an owl, shrouded like a mummy. It hadn't been as fortunate. He and his companions dismantled the net, ripping it to make it unusable, scarpering before the farmer could catch them. Although Wong felt for the farmers' livelihoods, he knew each individual death added up to species devastation, and as a bird-lover, he felt responsible. That incident taught him about entire ecosystems.

It also led him to love.

CHAPTER 5

Love and Commitment

"Tell me how to win your heart, for I haven't got a clue…"

One of the members of the birdwatching group was a Taiwanese student called Chia-Chien. She watched Wong remove his shoes and persevere through deep mud to save the bird. Her heart softened with his every step.

Chia-Chien was a city girl from Taipei studying home economics. Before she started university, her only contact with animals had been at the zoo. She was not an instinctual bird lover, preferring lazy Saturdays sleeping in to dawn twitching. Her friend Wan Fe, a member of the bird club, cajoled her to join. Initially, Chia-Chien agreed for the social connection but it wasn't long before she looked forward to twice-weekly early morning walks around campus and delighted in spotting a new bird.

Wong became the group's event organizer, and as the group swelled, he hired a bus to transport them. On such occasions, Chia-Chien and Wong could converse in more than early morning staccato whispers. As they stared out of the window at the passing paddy fields, Wong told Chia-Chien about Piggy. His love of animals pulled at her heart strings. She asked if she could join him on his next trip to the chicken farm. As Wong recounts those early days, he clasps a dog-eared photo in his palm. Chia-Chien leans towards him with Piggy between them, Wong's youthful face holding expectation and hope for the future. "When I got this photo developed, I realised I had feelings for her."

Wong in the bird watching club. Courtesy Wong Siew Te.

Wong started finding ways to be close to Chia-Chien when possible, sitting next to her on the bus, making sure he was in her survey team. Every now and again, in the security of the group, the couple would hold hands. With the embarrassment of his past stuttering on his mind, Wong finally gathered the courage to confess his growing feelings towards the thoughtful and considerate Chia-Chien. His heart pounded in his chest, as he tried to articulate his feelings, bracing himself for rejection. He sighed with relief the moment she smiled. "There was no struggle period where she had to think about it. She just accepted it, which was really nice," Wong tells me.

The rest of Wong's last semester flew by in the rose-tint of romance. When exams loomed, he would lock himself in his dorm room, memorising positions of cow internal organs, while Chia-Chien went to her night classes. On date nights, they dreamed and ate on Wong's meagre student budget. Chia-Chien met him outside his building, handing over the keys to her motorbike, wrapping her arms around his waist. They headed off to the night markets about fifteen minutes away, bought two plates of noodles, and settled into plastic chairs to talk. Wong's feelings were intensified by the looming expiry date of his student visa. Not wanting it to end, he told her he was going to apply for permission to work in Taiwan.

Meanwhile, Kurtis Pei had noticed his commitment and enthusiasm at the rescue centre. He offered Wong full-time work as a research assistant. It was Wong's first paid position with wildlife. When his last exam finished, he packed his bags, waved goodbye to the dorm and the cafeteria, and rented a room in the same building as Chia-Chien.

Much of the next two years was spent working in the field, learning a new set of skills. Wong started by surveying vertebrates in the nearby forest reserve. Most of Taiwan's lowlands had been cleared. The reserve only escaped development because it was steep. It was too late for the recently extinct Formosan Clouded Leopard, but the goal was to find out what species were distributed across different elevation gradients in the hope of protecting the area from encroaching development.

Reaching the research site at dawn, Wong sat motionless listening to the cacophony of waking birds, recording sightings on his clipboard. As the sun's intensity grew, and the birds settled into their daily routines, he walked narrow trails checking and resetting small mammal traps. He was rewarded with a dead field mouse in one, a shrew in another. He placed them in plastic bags, labelled them, and slid them into his backpack. The third trap had been triggered without a capture so he reset it, noted the number, consulted his map, and moved on. His stomach rumbled, prompting Wong to rest under an ancient oak tree and unwrap the leftovers from dinner the night before. As he stared between his feet, a hidden world slowly revealed itself. A honey ant scurried away with his crumbs; a tiger leech balanced on its fat tail to smell the air before making a beeline for his ankles. As he brushed it away, the stick next to him moved, the insect's camouflage breached. Over time he became alert to the ecosystem around him, treading more carefully on the earth like his soft-pawed predecessor. He became more comfortable in the forest, stamina growing from constant movement, the excess weight of sedentary student life falling away.

Together, Wong and Kurtis trialled the latest field technique: camera trapping. The concept was so new, Kurtis made his own contraption with a set-focus Olympus camera, metal ammo box, and a microwave-triggered sensor. When an animal tripped the sensor, the shutter clicked, recording the animal's passing without sacrificing its life. It was early days for such technology. The spare batteries weighed ten kilos, and Wong struggled uphill with four in his backpack, checking each trap every two weeks.

Wong located one of the traps at a high-traffic crossroads between two animal trails. Focusing his attention, he levered open the watertight box then checked the tiny number on the camera. All thirty-six frames had been taken. Sometimes this was because the microwave trigger battery had caused it to misfire. He wouldn't know until prints came back from the photo lab. Wong was nervous as he took the next step. If he didn't wind the film all the way before opening the cover, valuable negative images would overexpose and be gone forever. As he moved the lever, resistance grew, then eased. He opened the back, placing the roll in an empty plastic film canister. He then shielded the camera from direct light with his body, feeding the tongue of a fresh roll through the sights, clicking the shutter a couple of times. He checked the connections between the camera and sensor, then packed everything back in the ammunition box.

Unlike most jobs, this one didn't end at dusk; shifts simply changed between trapping diurnal and nocturnal animals. The forest grew very cold after dark, and Wong zipped up his jacket, rubbing his hands together to keep the blood flowing. Booming frogs beckoned him from moist hollows, the white pinpricks of their eyes reflecting his head torch. Meandering patterns on the surface of otherwise still creeks alerted him to snakes. Wong struck fast with his long-handled tongs in the same way a sun bear catches termites with its 25cm tongue. It was a fruitful night, his sample sack filling quickly. Its contents would help identify what species lived at different elevations. His eyes were growing heavy, his steps laboured. Wong made his way home, showered off pond scum, and slept soundly.

Wong surveying vertebrates at night. Courtesy Wong Siew Te

In the morning, Wong headed to the lab to identify and process his samples. He pushed thoughts of Chia-Chien and romance aside, and started by skinning his catch. He soaked the skins for two hours in a solution of water and boric acid to neutralise the lime and preserve them. While they were soaking, Wong removed the skulls, put them on a baking tray, and dried them in a low oven. Once cooled, he placed them in a glass aquarium overflowing with carrion beetles who feasted on any remaining muscle tissue, completely cleaning and exposing the bones so they could be compared and catalogued. The rest of the body was placed in a jar of pickling solution and organised on the shelf. Wong didn't know what future research might benefit from his attention to detail, so nothing was wasted.

While Wong found his feet in his first fieldwork position, the co-chair of the International Union for Conservation (IUCN) Bear Specialist group, American Dr Chris Servheen, was in Malaysia meeting with Sabah Wildlife Department. Chris asked permission to conduct a study of sun bears in Borneo. With the department's tick of approval, all he needed was a Malaysian research assistant. Wong didn't know it then, but their paths were destined to converge.

Kurtis obtained funding for the first Taiwanese study of larger mammals using radio tracking, which took place from September 1992 to December 1993. The project was a collaboration with the University of California, Berkeley. It focused on trying to establish the home range, number of animals, and activities of the Reeves' Muntjac, commonly known as the 'barking deer'. Similar awareness was growing around the world: for example, in the United States, President Bill Clinton formed a group of 1,600 scientists to identify species and habitats at risk in the US.

Technically speaking, a muntjac is an even-toed ungulate. So are cattle, pigs, camels, and hippopotamuses. Visually, though, a muntjac is the russet colour of a red kangaroo with similar narrow face and perky ears that appear translucent with the sun behind them. The Taiwanese subspecies stands about half a metre tall, weighing between eight and twelve kilos. The species' name hints at a colonial past. John Reeves worked for the British East India Company in the 19th century. He thought the sprightly animal made great sport, so he took samples back to Britain where they adapted well. A year-round hunting season in southern and eastern England now attempts to keep the involuntary invaders from impacting native species. Most studies on the species had been conducted on the feral animals in the UK. Kurtis wanted to test some of the UK findings on animals in their native forests. He chose the Central Mountain Range which lay directly east from the university, straddling the border between Pingtung County and neighbouring Taitung County. It was near enough that Wong could come back for supplies, yet remote enough that the access road wasn't paved.

Wong finally had a motorbike, so he packed as much equipment as he could carry in his panniers, threw his heavy backpack over his shoulders, and rode carefully along the dirt road, skirting around the occasional rockslide. At 2,000m elevation it was cold. Wong was grateful for the relative warmth of the abandoned huts in the old marble quarry where the camp was based. He unloaded his gear, started up the generator, and wiped the dust from his face. Then he walked along the two-kilometre forest trail to catch his first glimpse of the 4.2km-square study site. He was relieved to find himself in a basin. To the east and west, the slopes marking the edge of his research site looked unstable and steep. Impenetrable peaks extended to the north and south. He unfolded his topographic map to get his bearings, turning the paper around to point in the right direction.

This was Rukai country, steeped in legend. The indigenous Rukai people believed their ancestors migrated from across the sea. When they settled in the Central Mountain Range, their community made a pact with the neighbouring Hundred-Pacer Snake, or Paiwan Tribe to live in peace. To show they were sincere, the Rukai carved a symbol of the snake into the ancestral pole outside their doors. In exchange for this reverence, the Hundred-Pacer Snake tribe granted the Rukai access to the life-giving water of Great Ghost Lake (Taluomalin) and Little Ghost Lake (Payoutsu), together known as the 'Sacred Lake'. They believed the ghosts of their ancestors resided there, so they wouldn't enter the lake's boundaries without a very good reason. Wong hoped the ancestors would tolerate his presence.

Muntjac are notoriously skittish and secretive, so Wong planned to use camera trapping to estimate population, and radio-telemetry to determine their range. For the latter, individual animals needed to be fitted with collars that emitted radio signals. Kurtis hired three local indigenous hunters to help Wong capture the animals. They agreed to refrain from hunting until the study was complete. They also modified the snares so the animals wouldn't be hurt.

Wong watched as the men deftly pulled a small sapling in an arc across the path to create a spring with enough pivotal force to trap the animal, but not cut into its leg. Instead of the traditional wire, a loop of weaved nylon rope was anchored to the earth with a trigger device made of twigs. It would spring into action when an animal's leg touched it. Wong knew the rope might stretch as the animal struggled, giving it back its freedom, but this was preferable to leg injuries. He marked the location on his map. As he walked away to set the next one, he glanced back. He couldn't even see where the trap had been laid.

Five days later, Wong and the hunters walked in single file down hoofed paths, hoping the trap had been successful. As they approached, he could hear the telltale barking of a scared muntjac and hoped the snare had been gentle. Within moments he locked wide eyes with a buck about the size of the goats at the farm.

Luckily it looked like a recent catch. The deer was still feisty. Two symmetrical antlers curved towards each other like an unfinished heart shape. The muzzle was darker brown than the body. Black lines originating between its eyes, outlined a lighter triangle on its forehead. Its ears were fully extended, listening for every nuance of the humans' approach.

Wong needed to move quickly to reduce the animal's stress. He pulled a radio collar from his backpack and turned the battery on. With any luck, it would last twenty months. Like hungry wolves, Wong and the hunters tightened the circle, avoiding the muntjac's hind area. A powerful kick could do damage. While they held the animal pinned between them, Wong wrapped the hundred-gram collar around its neck, locking it into place. Within minutes, the snare was released, the buck bounding away without a backward glance. Adrenalin pumped through the men's veins as they laughed in relief.

As soon as there was a sufficient number of collared animals, it was time to gather data. These days, Wong uses Global Positioning System (GPS) collars. In 1992, however, such devices were in early development. The US Department of Defense had reluctantly released GPS technology to civilians in the 1980s but selectively degraded the signal to maintain an upper hand. This meant, in order to use the technology, it was necessary to compare readings with those of known positions and make regular adjustments to unscramble the data.

When Professor Dale McCullough from the University of California, Berkeley came to join in the muntjac study, he brought the latest GPS with him. It was the first of its kind used for research in Asia. Wong and Kurtis gathered around in excitement to learn how to use it. Then Wong and Dale lugged the new technology through the forest. They started by taking readings of trail intersections, rocky outcrops, and shelters. When they graduated to moving animals, the adjustment process proved far too time-consuming. Kurtis wasn't impressed, so the expensive Magellan GPS had to be discarded. Wong and Dale went back to the radio direction device.

I'm standing with Wong outside the bear house at the edge of BSBCC's forest enclosure and he's showing me how to use a radio direction finder. In one hand, he holds a Very High Frequency (VHF) receiver and, in the other, an H-shaped directional antenna. A cable joins the two like an umbilical cord. "The technology hasn't changed much," he tells me. "This radio is very similar to the ones we had in the early 1990s." Beyond us, sun bear Debbie wanders around the undergrowth with a transmitting collar, the VHF tuned to the correct channel to pick up her frequency. I follow Wong down the hardwood boardwalk, sweeping a horizontal arc with the antennas until he hears a continual pinging sound. Wong stops, identifying the direction where the pinging stops, pointing straight toward the radio wave. Wong moves forward along the fence-line, continuing to sweep as he goes. "When it's really loud, you know you are about half a kilometre away."

When Wong and Dale were at a similar distance from a loudly beeping muntjac, they separated, approaching the animal from two different directions. Wong took his small orienteering compass from his pocket, squinting as he lined it up on two peaks around him to chart his location on the topographic map. Without moving, he then turned the aerial, determined the direction of the animal, and jotted down the compass reading. As he drew a bearing line on his map from his known position, Wong knew the muntjac was somewhere on that line. He reached for the two-way radio on his belt and called Dale. Using a process called triangulation to pinpoint the exact location, he used Dale's readings to plot a second line. The muntjac stood where they crossed. When Wong worked alone, it wasn't so easy. He mapped the first bearing line, then struggled through the undergrowth, ignoring scratches from branches to try to get ninety degrees from his first spot as quickly as possible, chart another location, and take another bearing before the animal sensed his presence and bolted.

Wong and Dale moved around the lake to the east. After a natural fire decimated the forest, quick-growing, impenetrable grass opportunistically invaded. The muntjacs had created elaborate tunnels under the thatch. To follow them, Wong and Dale got down on their knees and crawled. As they advanced on the deer, Wong glanced around the forest floor looking for faeces. Finding some, he pulled a plastic bag from his backpack, picked up the poo, and took it back to the lab. There, he would test nitrogen levels to determine the quality of the animal's diet. This would then be compared to the result from faeces taken from captive animals. Weather and seasonal climate patterns were overlaid to build a more detailed understanding of the animal's behaviours.

Wong learning to use an aerial. Courtesy Wong Siew Te

To record movement, the study used two stationary radio signal receivers, run on solar panels, placed at high points on opposite sides of the research area. These systems automatically recorded signals on one animal for five minutes before moving onto the next one, gathering data on how much they travelled. When data and theory were kneaded together, the habits of wild muntjac emerged: they had a much larger home range than expected, with males and females apparently roaming equally. The females appeared to be more social, often grazing together; males, instead, had distinct territories which they marked with musk. They were susceptible to cold, but the tunnels they created through the grasslands shielded them from frost. Where the forest thinned, and light crept in, food plants grew quickly, and the animals gorged. By late summer, when the monsoon retreated, they struggled as their abundant pantry literally dried up.

As they walked back to camp, the rolled map of data in hand, Wong shared his dreams, including a longing to enrol in an undergraduate program, with Dale. He expressed anxiety that his time as a research assistant was ending. Many of the publications to which he had been exposed in his classes came from either the US or the UK, and he delighted in National Geographic and the Discovery Channel, both which originated in the US. Wong surmised there was much more happening in wildlife conservation in the US, and asked Dale if there was any possibility of studying there. Dale encouraged his ambition, promising to send him information on the most suitable programs when he returned to California.

With Dale back in Berkeley, Wong voiced his dreams to Kurtis, who had graduated from the University of Montana. Soon after, Kurtis's own American mentor, Professor Richard (Dick) Taber visited. Kurtis needed someone to show him around. Wong's English language skills were much better than the majority of Taiwanese students, making him the perfect choice. The painful hours Wong had spent learning the subject in school had finally paid off. Dick had studied under Aldo Leopold, considered by many to be the father of wildlife ecology and a legend in Wong's eyes. As he showed Dick through the rescue centre, Wong shared his dreams with Dick too, gaining another ally.

Eventually, Dale's list came back with the University of Montana near the top. In the library, Wong found a section of catalogues from overseas academic institutions. He flicked through, glancing back at Dick's list as he went. The striking front cover of one jumped out at him. It was an image of the University of Montana taken from Mount Sentinel. A green-spired, brownstone clock tower stood tall over lush lawns and orange-tinged maples. His heart fluttered. Call it a premonition or a hope, but, at that moment, Wong felt drawn to Montana. He retreated to a chair and flicked through the pages: the college football team was called the Grizzlies; Dick, Kurtis, and Dale had all suggested Montana. Most importantly, he discovered it was the least expensive of the ten options on his list.

As Wong's work visa drew to a close, he started planning his return to Malaysia. He could apply for universities from there, earning money while he waited. He hated the idea of leaving Chia-Chien behind. He was very much in love, but he had no choice. Wong was a realist and a fatalist. He knew the time they spent apart would either strengthen their relationship or break it apart. The two were committed to each other, and part of him wanted to lock her into a promise, but he knew that wouldn't be fair. On one of their last weekends together, they rode to Kenting National Park. Avoiding talk of the future, they swapped memories about their early days, the bird surveys, their friends. The couple wandered through the markets, hand-in-hand, the ache of impending separation tangible. A shirt swung in the breeze at a market stall, catching Wong's eye. Surprisingly, the sentiments were from Lionel Richie in English: "Tell me how to win your heart, for I haven't got a clue, but let me start by saying I LOVE YOU." In a wave of romance, they bought matching shirts, pulling them on to discover the layered pink hearts sat right over their own. Wong laughs nervously as he tells me the story. I'm not sure if he's embarrassed by the soppy sentiment, or the exposure of his raw emotion. "I was young once," he says.

Wong didn't want to go back to work in his brother's restaurant, so he wrote to one of the only two wildlife non-government organisations (NGOs) in Malaysia, the Malaysian Nature Society, based in Kuala Lumpur. They had a vacancy as trainee scientific officer. If he wasn't accepted into university in the US, this would be the perfect fall-back. Wong flew home to Penang via Kuala Lumpur to attend an interview with his potential boss. They connected well, the field experience in Taiwan weighing heavily in his favour. He felt confident, but he had been honest about his US goals. As Wong recounted the discussion with his parents, sitting on the couch in Penang with his dog Jojo on his lap, he regretfully asked them if they thought his honesty might affect his chances of securing the job.

The discussion shifted to his US dreams. Just as they had a few years before, the family brainstormed how they could help him realise this next step. Between them, his older siblings agreed to finance his bachelor's degree. Feeling immensely grateful, he started the application process, ensuring he included a copy of a glowing reference letter Dale had been kind enough to supply. Every submission came with a processing fee and he didn't want to waste his brothers' money by applying to all ten. Wong hedged his bets. His hand shook as he licked the last one-ringgit stamp, the auspicious face of an orangutan starring back at him. With excitement replacing fleeting fear, he pushed two envelopes into the mailbox slot: one to the University of Montana and the other to the University of Idaho.

Wong waited. To pass the time, he bought a stack of cassette tapes. Every evening he pushed the play and record buttons down in tandem, speaking into the tiny microphone, following on from the previous day's ramblings of happenings and emotions. When the wheels stopped turning, he flipped the tape, continuing his candid journaling on the B side. Each week, when the cassette was full, he wrote a message on the paper insert, slid it into its case, and posted it to Chia-Chien. When she sent a similar tape back, he rewound and replayed often. This process kept both their parents' phone bills to a manageable level.

It's 2017. 9pm. Wong and I have spent the evening sitting at his home-desk poring over old photos and jogging his memories. I say good night and head for the guest bedroom. He opens his laptop and logs into Skype. As I turn to close my door, I glimpse the face of Chia-Chien appearing on the screen, her hair pulled back severely in a ponytail. There are a few more wrinkles around her eyes but, just as she was in early 1994, she is in Taiwan and Wong in Malaysia. The two old hands are conducting a long-distance relationship yet again. "Are Winnie and Evie there?" Wong asks after his teenage daughters as my door closes.

Wong's interview at the Malaysian Nature Society was successful, and he moved to Kuala Lumpur to start an inventory of flora and fauna in one of the oldest rainforests in the world—the Royal Belum State Park in the northwest corner of Peninsular Malaysia. The Malaysian Nature Society wanted to gather enough data to convince the government to change its status to a protected national park. This was an area rich in threatened species including the majestic Malayan tiger, the extremely rare Sumatran rhino, the evasive sun bear, the hook-nosed tapir, and the fast-moving white-handed gibbon. For half of Wong's work, he was based at headquarters coordinating visitors and researchers. The other half, he drove five hours to the field camp, close to the Thai border, helping scientists trap birds and small mammals. This was his first time working in low elevations and tropical conditions. It was a completely new world of alien creatures.

Wong's traineeship was measured by learning, not longevity. In May, the University of Idaho contacted him for more financial information. As he prepared to gather documents and jump through the hoops, another letter arrived. It had been posted in the cold dry climate of Missoula, 13,000km away. As he tore open the envelope, he could almost smell pine forests. "Congratulations…" it began.

CHAPTER 6

Far Horizons

"The sun bear chose me, I didn't choose the sun bear!"

As he walked through the airport gate in an unfamiliar country, accents he had only heard on television enveloped him. Wong was greeted by another student, Pit Kee, who had been hired by the foreign-student support office to help him navigate the unfamiliar habitat. Wong felt grateful to have a guide. It was so dark outside, and he had no sense of direction. Pit Kee took him to Grandma Frost's boarding house, where he also stayed.

Wong left his shoes at the door out of habit. He lugged his suitcase down the stairs to a single room in the basement, his toes disappearing into the plush pile carpet. In front of him stood a much taller bed than he was used to. The thickest mattress he had ever seen beckoned. The exhaustion of travel rose through his body, clouding his peripheral vision. He mumbled his thanks, took a shower, then sank into the down comforter.

Wong barely moved during the night. He cracked his eyes open to bright light streaming through the small ground-level window. He pulled back the covers and stuck his face against the glass. The lawn outside was vibrant green, edged with a rainbow of summer flowers. In the neighbouring garden, a middle-aged man waved a hose over his grass. The sky above was an uncluttered baby blue. Wong took another shower. The smell of bacon wafted down the stairs. He followed it to the smiling face of his landlady, the tight-permed, silver-haired Grandma Frost. She patted the dining chair cushion, indicating where to sit. His gaze wandered to the endless knick-knacks and soft furnishings, in stark contrast to those of the sparse home of his childhood.

Energised, Wong was ready for a tour of the campus. As he and Pit Kee waited for a bus, a light breeze blew a fragrant garden bouquet in their direction, so different from home. The bus pulled up on time, and the driver greeted them as they boarded. The streets of Missoula looked as manicured and clean as a film set. Sun-pinked people walked their dogs on sidewalks along each road. Weeds dared not grow in the cracks. "Have a good day," the bus driver said as they stepped down onto the kerb.

With two weeks remaining before Wong's classes began, Pit Kee's tutelage was invaluable. On that first day, he helped Wong open a bank account to deposit his wad of cash; showed Wong where people advertised permanent rooms; and helped him get a student card, buy textbooks, and register for classes. When they ran short on energy, they stopped for lunch at a steakhouse. Bright flashing lights and fairground sounds came from gambling machines in the corner, something Wong had never seen.

About thirty of Wong's required 126 class hours were waived in lieu of his diploma, which propelled him directly into his sophomore year, reducing costs. It also meant he was allowed to live off campus. One of the share rooms advertised in the university newsletter was only two blocks away, and he went to look. Pit Kee forewarned him many of the houses in Missoula were compact to avoid high heating bills in the winter. This one was no different. It had four levels, if you included the obligatory basement. At ground level was a room and bathroom, the first floor incorporated the kitchen and living room, and there were two bedrooms in the rarefied air at the top. Wong signed an agreement with the local woman who would be his share-mate, settling in before his classes began.

Wong pored over class timetables well in advance, identifying the classes he wanted to add and learnt tips to ensure he was competitive when the games began. On the first day, he lined up outside the lecture hall early, enrolment papers in hand, in hopes other students had dropped out. When entry was permitted, he leant on a wall at the back of the class while the professor took attendance and laboured through his expectations, then rushed to queue at the front. There were five vacant places. He just made it. Wong triumphantly took the valuable slip to the registrar to confirm his position then queued at the bookshop to buy the required text.

As soon as he wrapped his hands around Sand County Almanac, Wong wanted to absorb Aldo Leopold's groundbreaking theories on wildlife management. Reading was slow because his English vocabulary was poor, but by the time his professor assigned chapters, he was already way ahead of his peers. After a couple of classes, Wong started recording all his lectures with his overused tape recorder, making sure he remembered to take Chia-Chien's tape out first. After every hour-long lecture, he spent at least two hours re-listening, adjusting his notes, and adding to his lengthy word list. He flipped through tissue-thin dictionary pages searching for the correct spelling of a word before he could learn its meaning; he waded through textbooks, repetitively mumbling Latin species names until he memorised them. "I bet you didn't know a rainbow trout is called an Oncorhynchus mykiss," Wong tells me, smiling. His workload was double that of his American counterparts, but Wong didn't begrudge the extra hours. "If you study what you love," he tells me, "you don't mind spending more time and effort learning about it. On Friday nights, when the American students were out partying, I would usually have dinner with other Malaysian students, then go back to studying." Wong was grateful on the weekends when Dick Taber and his wife Pat dragged him from his books. They wandered through conifer forests of the Rocky Mountain foothills pointing out species and sharing wilderness stories. Sharp mountain air pricked his cheeks, replaced later by an enveloping warmth as they sat around the dining table before a fragrant roast dinner.

Before long, Mount Sentinel had wrapped a cloak of white around its shoulders, the grass crunched underfoot, and sparrows huddled together on telephone wires. Wong willed himself onto his bike to go grocery shopping. He bought a CD of rainforest sounds to slice through the frozen silence, helping him sleep. Layering his clothes was an alien concept, and he turned the heater on a little too often. Shivering, he coaxed himself into the shower to keep up the level of cleanliness Ah Ji would expect. Over time, his skin began to itch uncontrollably and he found it hard to sleep. Wong was scared he had contracted a weird winter disease, so he took himself to the doctor. After prodding the rash for parasites, the doctor asked, "How often are you showering?" When Wong told him three times a day, the doctor grinned. Instead of medication, he suggested Wong change to one daily wash and start using body lotion. Wong wished he could talk to Ah Ji about such cultural differences, but she'd had a stroke the previous year and found it hard to concentrate on the phone. At times like this, he missed home. Instead, he and Chia-Chien laughed about the doctor's visit on their long Sunday night call.

By the time the American autumn rolled around for the second time in Missoula, Wong felt far more adapted. As he locked his bike to the rack outside his wildlife management class and rubbed the circulation back into his fingers, he had no idea the next couple of hours would change his future direction. In front of his class stood an unfamiliar, moustached professor who launched into a lecture about bears. Chris Servheen was co-chair of the International Union for Conservation of Nature (IUCN)

Bear Specialist Group. He supervised students researching non-American bears in China, Taiwan, Greece, Japan, Spain, and Romania. Chris told of his struggle to find someone willing to study the 'unknown bear species' in Malaysian Borneo. Wong felt the rest of the class fade away. It was as if Chris was talking directly to him. He couldn't wait for the lecture to end so he could bounce from his seat and be first in line to introduce himself.

Wong's background in veterinary studies plus large mammal research made him a good candidate, but it was his country of origin that made him perfect. Chris Servheen hadn't supervised a Malaysian student before. "The optimum situation is to get a student from that country," Chris tells me. "Someone who lives in the country, was born there, and can contribute a tremendous amount to conservation, as opposed to an American who is only there for a short time, then comes back." Wong's enthusiasm matched Chris's, so much so that Chris was willing to wait two years for him to finish his degree and apply for the graduate program. As Wong puts it, "The sun bear chose me, I didn't choose the sun bear!"

In the yin and yang of life, the next two years were times of personal growth and tremendous sadness. Wong and Chia-Chien's feelings hadn't waned, and she was keen to join Wong in Montana. Her parents had liked Wong when they met, but they were worried about her moving to a foreign country where she spoke very little of the language. Chia-Chien assuaged their fears by applying to study English in Missoula. In 1996, heart in her throat, she flew halfway around the world to be close to Wong. Instantly, his world was less lonely. Like two snow monkeys locked in a hot-spring embrace, Wong and Chia-Chien warmed each other against the sometimes-harsh world, strengthening their individual resilience as they navigated the unfamiliar culture. They pooled their funds together and bought a cheap used car, adjusted to driving on the right, and widened their horizons. It was a wonderful time, which Wong remembers fondly; unfortunately, it wasn't to last.

Pulled from the depths of sleep by the phone's insistent ring at 1am, Wong rubbed sleep from his eyes. Heart pounding, he realised the crackly voice on the other end was his brother Ben, calling from Taiwan. It could only mean bad news. Wong listened in dazed silence as Ben recounted the details. Just like any other day, Ah Ji and Apak had eaten lunch together. Ah Ji coughed and gulped as she ate, a side-effect of the stroke. Something stuck in her throat and she went to the toilet to clear it, instinctively locking the door behind her. Apak could hear her trying to catch breath, but by the time his elderly bones managed to push the door down, his wife was gone. More than twenty years later, Wong is visibly distressed as he recounts this conversation. The woman who had taught him how to care for rescued animals, had instilled his love of cooking, had selflessly let him travel at her own expense was gone, leaving a painful heart-shaped hole in his chest.

In a disconnected fog, Wong alerted his professors and booked a flight home. Through LA and Japan, he pictured the coffin sitting in the middle of his parents' living room, and willed himself to get there before the cover closed. Her body was not embalmed, so he knew only too well he was racing against nature. By the time his jet-lagged legs stepped into his parents' home, the mirrors and statues were already covered, ceremonial incense permeating the walls. The wooden lid was down.

Wong tearfully said his goodbyes on the fifth day, as the coffin was taken away. On the seventh day, the family stayed at home, knowing Ah Ji's spirit would follow the red plaque on the door, returning to say goodbye. Siew Yon (Vivian) saw her mother moving through the house, and her recounted experience put Wong's mind at ease. Ah Ji returned again for one last goodbye on day forty-nine, before her soul was reincarnated, but by then, Wong was back on the other side of the world.

Duty and love draw Wong to Penang each year for the traditional tomb-sweeping ceremony, or qingming. Seniority is sacrosanct in Chinese tradition, so he and his siblings start by visiting Apak's parents at the cemetery, placing food offerings on a carpet of newspaper, lighting joss sticks and candles at the headstone, covering the mound with a rainbow of paper flags and paper money. They move on to the crematorium to honour their parents, jostling through the crowds leaving offerings on temporary rows of tables in the covered courtyard. Through the industrial-looking doors, rough concrete pigeonholes frame yellowed urns with red lettering. Black and white photos of their parents lead the way, more recognisable than the etched numbers on Perspex. As the youngest, Wong is last to bow low in deference. As they return home, the sombre mood lifts. Offerings are scooped up and added to a joyful feast, strengthening the ribbon of family bonds.

It was the love of his family that helped Wong come to terms with the loss of Ah Ji, but just when a semblance of normality was returning, Chia-Chien's father became ill. He anxiously drove her to the airport, not knowing they wouldn't see each other again for more than a year. The phone and tape recorder once more became touchstones as Wong retreated into his books. Finally, the day in 1997 came when he put down his pen and glanced over the answers on his last exam paper. He was sure he had done well, and as I flip through his university transcripts, his confidence is reflected in an almost-perfect grade point average. With only one more exam between him and the graduate program, he could soon change focus and learn how to handle bears.

There were two healthy populations of grizzly bears in the United States. About five hundred animals were known to live in Yellowstone National Park, split over the Wyoming border into the southern part of Montana. Another population inhabited the northwest corner of the state, in Glacier National Park and the surrounding Northern Continental Divide Ecosystem. Chris had a full-time crew, capturing and tracking black bears and grizzly bears in the northwest as part of an ongoing recovery plan study.

Wong found himself learning from seasoned researchers in the Yaak Wilderness Area. It was a bountiful environment where bubbling rapids buffeted river rocks and rainbow trout pointed upstream like airport weather socks. Unlike the organised chaos of the rainforest, uniform spruce trees stood like trained soldiers, their fallen needles carpeting animal trails and campsites, releasing essential oils when crunched underfoot. The forest knew nothing about political borders, and neither did the species inhabiting it. Grizzlies wandered to Banff and Jasper National Parks in Canada with regularity, unperturbed by their changing classification—no longer considered endangered when they entered Canada. The researchers migrated back and forth too, trapping bears, cognisant of the political tenderness of jurisdiction.

As they drove down a remote road on the US side of the border, Wong and his mentors chanced upon a young roadkill deer. They stopped to scrape it from the bitumen, pleased to be recycling the resource as bear bait and keeping scavenging bears off the road. Unfortunately, they couldn't carry the carcass internationally, so they used it to set the American traps, stopping at Safeway in Canada to beg for expired meat. Wong laughs when he remembers coming back to check the trap only to find the rump steak gone, totally devoured, and the hot dogs untouched. "Since that day, I've never eaten a hot dog!"

Over time, Wong became adept at trapping and collaring black bears, getting close enough to jab them with a dart pole. The ketamine wore off quickly, so he and fellow researchers had to spring into action: removing the snare, taking samples, measuring. Sometimes they would even treat the bear's wounds. As soon as the bear's ear tweaked, or nose twitched, they knew they had about two minutes to gather their gear and scarper.

One day Wong's vision was limited through the trees, but he could hear a frightened bear complaining. This time it was a snared grizzly. All jovial conversation ceased. He used a cigarette lighter to check the direction of breeze, gingerly advancing from downwind. Seriousness washed over their faces as Wong's companions stopped, slid their shotguns from their shoulders and removed the safety, buying themselves a split second which could mean the difference between life and death. There was no room for mistakes.

As they progressed, one of them brushed against a pine, cracking a branch. The frightened male grizzly sensed their presence and charged at full speed, growling. It was anchored to a tree by a tenuous cable around its front leg. Wong worried it could pull free at any moment. He froze, his skin instantly clammy as fear enveloped him. "I nearly peed my pants," he says. As he shut his eyes, the animal exhaled, bravado and breath knocked from its lungs as it reached the end of its tether. As if in slow motion, three hundred kilos of fur and teeth lifted from the ground with such force it landed upside down with a thud about thirty metres away. Wong felt the quake through his boots. As the startled animal picked itself up, Wong's companion lifted the gunpowder-charged dart gun and squeezed the trigger.

Wong's heart was still pounding as he tentatively approached the sleeping giant. A musky smell, like wet dog mixed with pine resin, filled the space between them. He ran his fingers through coarse hairs down to the softer layer below. The front paws were double the size of his own hands, with sharp claws. Staring into the bear's glassy eyes, so menacing a few minutes before, Wong lifted its head in both his hands to feel its weight. The animal's nostrils pulsed as its laboured breath fogged his glasses. The team moved quickly, gently removing the snare, taking blood samples, and fitting a radio collar. It was more important than ever that they were gone when the bear woke up.

Trapping grizzly bears in Montana. Courtesy Wong Siew Te

As his confidence grew, Wong was trusted out alone. Startled, I raise my eyebrows when he tells me this. Out? Alone? In bear country? He was young, naïve, and bulletproof, riding his bike fast down logging roads, the wind in his hair, dodging black bears on the road as he rounded the bend. He searched for radio collars which had released at their used-by date, or found berry patches, like bear candy shops, and mapped their whereabouts. He sang as he searched the undergrowth to alert bears to his presence.

Realisation of the risk hit when a lone hiker was mauled in his research area. The field supervisor, Wayne Kasworm, called him in and handed him a two-way radio and a can of pepper spray to add to his first aid kit.

Over time, Wong identified what types of data he would need to gather if he wanted to unlock the secrets of sun bears—their home range, food habits, potential seasonal movements. By osmosis, he also identified traits he needed in his own research team. While the world's media buzzed with the Kyoto Protocol's call for a sharp cut in greenhouse emissions, he was ready to start his master's. But first he needed to make two very special stops in Taipei and Penang. It was time to make his love for Chia-Chien official.

Ordinary people don't get married three times to the same person, but Wong is no ordinary person. He and Chia-Chien decided it was important to have one celebration for her family, followed by one for his. The third wedding was culturally unique. The local council in Taipei organises regular mass nuptials, and one was planned a week before Wong's real wedding. They shuffled inside the lilac and pink town hall with ninety-nine other couples, taking up their places facing the stage. As they waited for Mayor Chen Shui-bian to officiate, Wong fidgeted with the lapel of his grey suit, and Chia-Chien adjusted her white lace veil. Wong laughs as he tells me Chen Shui-bian is now in jail. After climbing his way to the presidency, he left office four days after Wong's birthday in 2008. Hours later, without the magic cloak of immunity, he was arrested for corruption.

The second wedding was in Taiwan, on January 18th, 1998. Chia-Chien was nervous as she zipped up her Western white wedding gown again, waiting for Wong to pick her up from her parents' home. She lit an incense stick, cupped her palms together, and prayed to her dad, wishing he could be there. Then she knelt before her mum in thanks, emotion welling for them both.

At the door to the hotel banquet hall, Chia-Chien's girlfriends welcomed guests, bowing as they accepted the ang pow—small red envelopes of money given instead of presents. Wong and Chia-Chien took their places at the end of a large round table and glanced around the room. Ten other tables lay before them, cloaked in deep red for luck. Ten places were set at each, a symbol of perfection. Chia-Chien turned in her chair, her squeaky dress bunching at her waist, looking at the stage behind her. It was just as she had planned: an altar-like table, also draped in red, was adorned with flowers and a microphone. Behind it, on the wall, a huge heart-shaped balloon bouquet framed Chinese characters lined in gold, signifying prosperity.

Chia-Chien's uncle spoke thoughtfully in her father's place. Jimmy, as the representative of the Wong family, made everyone laugh, assuring them, regardless of his white hair, he was not Wong's father. Then Wong's professor Kurtis Pei added his blessing. A dozen dishes appeared in staggered progression. The most important, fish, signified abundance; the chicken in red sauce added more luck to their future. "We didn't have to say any vows," Chia-Chien explains. "Just married." Wong was glad when he could shift from his seat, take his new wife by his hand, and move around the tables toasting the future. Then Chia-Chien disappeared with her girlfriends into the changing room where two other outfits hung waiting. She carefully removed her veil so she wouldn't disrupt her manicured hair, and slid into a ball gown, the pink chiffon skirt swishing as she moved. She accepted red laced gloves from her bridesmaid and slipped them on. When she returned to the ballroom, the merriment had begun. The guests were mingling, and their laughter brought a smile to her face. There was one last costume change ahead: the kingfisher blue of her 'see the guests out' dress. All too soon, the night she had planned for so long was over. Together, she and Wong retreated to a room at the Hilton.

Apak's health had deteriorated since Ah Ji's death, but Wong wanted to honour him and his siblings, so the process was repeated in Malaysia during the summer. Suited up for the third time, Ah Ji stole Wong's thoughts as he and Chia-Chien lit an incense stick for their ancestors. He wished she could have been here to see him so happy. Siew Mei stood next to her father's chair, the tray in her hands holding her mother's white china tea set. Wong and Chia-Chien bowed as they presented a cup to Apak. The process was repeated for each of Wong's siblings, red envelopes of luck extended in return. It seemed strange they were giving him more money, for Wong knew that without his siblings' financial support, he wouldn't be standing next to the woman of his dreams or embarking on the research that would shape his future.

CHAPTER 7

How to Catch a Bear

*"The rainforest was more fragile than
most people thought."*

I t was the summer of 1998. As the bus driver turned on the windscreen wipers, pushing dust to the corners, Wong could see a heavily laden logging truck approach. Another slow-going half hour through the selectively logged forests of Ulu Segama Forest Reserve and they left the logging trucks behind as they entered the eastern edge of the Danum Valley Conservation Area. The close proximity of logging offered an unparalleled opportunity for him to study sun bears in their natural environment and assess human impacts.

The sounds of industry were replaced by a more soothing melody. Wong's attention was momentarily stolen as a kite flew overhead. Then the encroaching undergrowth parted to reveal an expansive green lawn and a series of buildings. A huge wooden welcome sign announced Danum Valley Field Centre (DVFC). He felt his heart skip a beat. The buildings before him were equipped with all the essentials for scientific discovery and collaboration. Danum was the coalface of conservation. Wong knew researchers from all over the world would give a limb to be where he was. He hoped he was worthy.

Wong peeled his sweaty thighs from the plastic seat and thanked the driver. The senior scientist, Andrew Davis, gave him an orientation tour, pointing out the laboratories and specimen-drying room, walking him through the drool-worthy library, and showing him to his assigned office. He was handed a basic map. He rotated it to align with directions to the permanent research plots, the suspension bridge over the Segama River, and the observation platforms and towers. Wong learnt the Centre was manned year-round by about fifty local staff and their families. A tropical plant nursery was located at the centre of the study area. Forest workers were housed in a third settlement, Takala logging camp, at the northwestern corner of the study area. The total population rose and fell with a tide of itinerant scientists.

The conversation migrated to what Wong hoped to accomplish. He wasn't sure where to start. There were only two other sun bear researchers in the world. So little was known about the Malayan sun bear that it couldn't be included in the IUCN Red List of Threatened Species. Basic things like how many there were, what they ate, how far they roamed, and how they raised their young were still a mystery. Sightings were extremely rare. He planned to use camera traps and radio collars, just as he had for muntjacs, but he knew finding sun bears would be much more difficult. The rainforest was hostile; sun bears were elusive.

Wong woke early in the unfamiliar surroundings of the outlying annexe building. He would only be here three months this time, so he needed get his bearings quickly. He reached the top of the vertical ladder and stepped out onto the canopy tower platform just as an orange sun pushed through the blanket of morning mist. In the distance, a gibbon hooted as it wooed a potential mate, the sound rising and falling like an air-raid warning. The unspoilt Borneo of his dreams sprawled to the horizon. It was a pocket of Eden boasting more species than Yosemite, at a tenth the size. Some said there were more species here than in Europe. It was home to the largest flower in the world, the largest orchid, the largest moth, the largest carnivorous plant. An iridescent green Rajah Brooke's birdwing flitted past. Wong turned full circle to follow, his arms outstretched, lungs expanding with fresh air.

I am trying to track down the same butterfly, but this time I'm a long way from the pulsating jungle. I'm in London for a writing conference and I've taken a few hours off to visit the British National History Museum. Beneath cathedral ceilings, I face a palatial staircase. On the first landing, a white marble effigy of Charles Darwin surveys the exhibits with surety. Without the man I am searching for, however, Darwin's greatest work might have never seen the light of day. I find my champion in bronze, tipping his hat as he squints skyward through wire-rimmed specs, a butterfly net in his hand and a binocular box strap across his chest. This is explorer, mapmaker, and often forgotten co-originator of the theory of evolution, Alfred Russel Wallace.

During a severe bout of malaria in the Malay Archipelago (during which he named the birdwing butterfly which later circled Wong), Wallace's feverish mind chanced on an idea. The beetles he collected laid thousands of eggs at a time. Perhaps the larvae that made it to adulthood were those best suited to their environment. After he recovered, he scribbled and honed this idea into a theory but had no idea how he could get it published. Wallace sent his paper to someone who could help: an English gentleman with clout, Charles Darwin. When the package arrived, by ship, Darwin's similar theory—penned sixteen years earlier—was gathering dust, halted by his fear of religious objections. Wallace's letter was the impetus Darwin needed. He published, acknowledging his colleague with a public reading of their two theories. Wallace might not have historic star billing today, but he accomplished his goal. He and Darwin corresponded in mutual admiration for years. Meanwhile, Wallace changed his focus to another theory, one which directly impacted Wong's sun bear study.

Evolutionary biogeography studies the distribution of animals and plants across the world. It's a strain of science that owes its existence to Wallace's travels through the Malay Archipelago in 1874. The distance between the islands of Bali and Lombok was only 50km, but Wallace noticed the species of birds and mammals on one island were completely different to those on the other. He drew an invisible line on his map, now called the Wallace Line, which extended north to the edge of Borneo. On the Asian side were tigers, elephants, and hornbills; on the Australasian side, marsupials, platypus, and parrots. He continued around the world mapping species distribution and carving up continents.

I leave Wallace and wander through an automatic glass door labelled Treasures. This room promises twenty-two tantalising exhibits. My heart quickens at a penguin egg collected on Scott's Antarctic expedition, at pages from Joseph Bank's notebooks with pressed cuttings from Australia. Then I stop breathing. Darwin's pigeons lie in state, hand-scrawled labels binding their legs. In the next cabinet, elevated to the status they belong, the extended wings of Wallace's butterflies tell an equally compelling story. I take a photo and message it to Wong, still in the land where the butterflies fly free. "Wow!" comes the immediate response.

For three months in the northern hemisphere summer of 1998, Wong got his bearings. He made his own series of maps, using them to set camera traps close to animal trails, water sources, and mud wallows. Within their angle of view, he laid different types of bait, to find what worked best, settling on chicken entrails. Time flew by, and before long he was once again sitting in a classroom in Montana, planning the next step of his fieldwork. In early 1999, Wong was back at Danum. He bought a car and picked up where he left off. This time, although she had to leave the country every six months to renew her visa, Chia-Chien joined him. The young couple settled into a two-bedroom wooden bungalow called Tiong 1 on the periphery of the Centre, which they shared with one other researcher. After Montana, the humidity took some adjustment, but a shady tree protected the white-railed deck, and louvered slats above the door kept the tropical air from getting stale. Life at Danum settled into a pleasant rhythm.

Wong and Chia-Chien woke to the distant generator starting up at 7am. Chia-Chien gathered Wong's clipboard and they headed to the computer lab where she planned to enter his endless numbers into spreadsheets. As he helped decipher his handwriting, the power cut. In frustration, he headed to reception for answers. Power restored, Wong was able to access the Internet on the computer next to his wife. It was the least exciting part of research but essential. Time disintegrated, and as the light faded, researchers appeared from all directions like zombies, showered, and headed to the canteen. Back in their bungalow, Chia-Chien peeled garlic while Wong beat eggs and heated the wok for his famous noodles. They saved the food scraps for the Centre's pet pigs, George and Michael, just as they had for Piggy. At 11pm the generator coughed and slept.

Chia-Chien found work at a kindergarten in the nearest town of Lahad Datu, teaching the children how to use an abacus, and they often travelled in together on a Friday, appreciative of a night on the town. While Chia-Chien taught, Wong went shopping. He was ready to build four bear traps based on the design of those used in the US to capture wolverines. Two he planned to put in the logged forest. For these he could fell trees on site, but cutting trees was prohibited in the conservation area. When Chia-Chien waved goodbye to her students at the end of the day, Wong was waiting at the gate, the back of the car heavy with lumber, wire, screws, and hinges.

Canadian Bruce McLellan, co-chair of the International Union for Conservation of Nature Bear Specialist Group and an expert trapper, flew from the US to help Wong make the wooden traps. Together they lugged the supplies along narrow trails to sites Wong had chosen, sweat pouring from their brows by the time they bolted the last logs together. To test their handiwork, Wong climbed over the walls, moving towards where the bait would be. As he stepped on the hinged board, a wire tightened, releasing a wooden lever, dropping the lid, and sliding a locking device into place. Wong was trapped in a pine box, but not for long. Together, the two men set the trap again. They attached a string to the lid. A small magnet on the other end interrupted transmission on a radio collar—the same one they hoped to attach to the trapped bear. When the door dropped, the magnet would release, and the collar would start transmitting. "It was really simple," Wong tells me.

Wong checked for a signal several times each day. On the first beep, he and his research assistant Guy rushed to the trap. What they found, however, was not what they expected. One of the two-by-four lid planks had been completely shredded. Through a jagged hole the size of a sun bear, Wong could see a bed of splinters. He lifted the shattered lid. Rounded wall logs had been stripped as efficiently as a planking saw. Wong's shoulders slumped as he realised the exhausting construction work had been futile. Trying to keep positive, he was grateful he still had four metal traps scattered through his research area. Would they be able to hold a bear?

Wong's timber trap was shredded. Courtesy Wong Siew Te

The first was an aluminium alloy barrel trap, custom-made by Teton Welding in Montana. At a finished cost of US$3000, and an additional US$1000 for shipping, this one piece of equipment had devoured most of Wong's research budget. The design cleverly came in nine pieces. Each one was light enough, and small enough, to be strapped to a backpack and reassembled in place. The aluminium didn't rust, so Wong expected it would easily last his entire project. He was right: it is still catching bears today. On top of the barrel, a grate provided ventilation, a solid guillotine door slicing down to close the entrance once a bear took the bait. Wong modelled three additional traps using some of the same features, but he made them in Malaysia out of 55-gallon oil drums. They rusted over time and only dismantled into two, making them harder to transport, but they were a fraction of the cost.

On June 22nd, 1999, Wong swept the air for a signal. The barrel trap close to the east trail beeped back. This wasn't the first time. He was catching so many Malay civets that he joked to Guy that he should change his research species. This time was different. Wong and Guy drove close to the end of the trail. As they slowly approached on foot for the last few metres, they were startled by a deafening bear bark, magnified by the barrel. Through the grill door, angry eyes stared back. He estimated the animal was a muscular forty kilos, its fur matted with dirt and faeces, the chicken-guts bait still hanging. Wong had been so sure it was another civet, he hadn't brought his field kit. He drove back to the centre making mental lists in his head. Dart pole. Zoletil. Chia-Chien. Camera.

When the bear was out cold, Guy and Wong pulled it from the cage. They took measurements and attached the collar. Chia-Chien, as the unofficial photographer, moved around them, Wong's SLR camera to her eye. "It was an interesting life for me," she tells me. When the frenetic activity ended, 'bear 125' was left in the open to recover. The team found a safe vantage point and settled down to wait, keeping themselves amused by choosing a name. They settled on Daley, a shortened version of Danum Valley. Eventually, Daley raised his head, struggled to his feet, shook the unfamiliar weight around his neck, and wandered out of sight.

Wong and Chia-Chien with a captured sun bear. Courtesy Wong Siew Te

Over the next couple of months two other male bears were successfully trapped. Lucky, so named because he had a gunshot wound they successfully treated, was captured twice: once on July 10th, again on August 3rd. Between those two dates, he lost two kilos. Wong worried the collars might be having an adverse effect. Four days later, a fully grown older male, Teton (named after the trap manufacturer), was caught. Even before the collar was attached, he was skinny with protruding hipbones.

Wong introduced monitoring all collared animals for a 24-hour period each week. The best vantage point was the top of the Bukit Ator fire tower. With only one car, this took a bit of shuffling. Guy covered the daylight hours, Wong driving him out early. As the afternoon shadows stretched across the lawn, he again drove out, this time with Chia-Chien, camping equipment, and food. She maintained the monitoring and set up their picnic while he took Guy back.

One day, as Wong's car climbed the steep slope to the fire tower on the return journey, the tyre tread slipped in thick mud. He slowed, inching forward. With only about two hundred and fifty metres to go, the wheels spun. He tried to reverse, splattering his wing mirrors. Wong waited a moment then tried again but the car sunk deeper. He unpacked the equipment, and with his arms full, he walked the last stretch. Wong lit the hurricane lantern and hung it over an array of plastic containers, illuminating their food. Sitting cross-legged, Wong smiled at his wife with contentment. They were working together to a common goal, the loneliness of the past at bay.

Soon after he and Chia-Chien put down their chopsticks, a herd of elephants crashed through the jungle below. They sensed humans above and weren't happy with company, trumpeting their protest loudly. They might have been pygmy elephants, but they were actually far from small. Wong reassured Chia-Chien the tower and platform were solid and they were in no danger, but apprehension descended with the darkness. The sound of scraping, twigs breaking, and angry pachyderms punctuated their shift. At dawn, the visitors were long gone. Wong and Chia-Chien packed their things and made their way to the car, nervously double-checking over their shoulders. The sight that greeted them was shocking. The car was several metres from where Wong left it and looked like it had been in a road accident. The windshield was pushed in, the right fender dented, the bull-bar hanging like a wobbly milk tooth. They brushed shards of glass from the front seats and Wong held his breath as he turned the key. It started, and they inched their way back to camp.

One month after Teton was captured, he was found dead in a hollow log. A month later, Daley's signal was almost stationary. Wong feared the worst. Holding the aerial like a shield, he and Guy advanced cautiously as the signal strengthened. Like Teton before him, Daley was cocooned in a tree cavity. He moved his head occasionally, disinterested even when Wong shone a torch in his eyes. His condition was shocking. He had lost a third of his body weight, and his loose skin showed clear signs of malnutrition. White spots peppered his fur. Wong wondered if he too had been the victim of a poacher's aim. He decided to sedate Daley and investigate.

With no cage for protection, Wong gathered his courage, getting close enough to deliver a dose of Zoletil. When the dart hit home, Daley didn't even flinch. Pulled out in the open, spread on an orange tarp, Wong could see the white dots were not buckshot wounds, but engorged female ticks feeding on Daley's blood. They removed as many as they could and left the poor creature to recover. When Wong came back early the next morning, Daley was dead. A necropsy identified a mouth infection and a haemorrhage on his hip from a severe impact, possibly from an altercation with a pig. Even though he thinks Daley was doomed, Wong still worries he might have killed the bear. "It's hard to know if I had a part in his death," he tells me sadly. "Perhaps the medication or the stress from being handled sped up the dying process."

I've become accustomed to Wong's world and mine being woven together. In fact, some of our independent past experiences also travelled parallel, so I'm shocked when I realise how different our lives were at the turn of the century. As I wrapped myself in domesticity, reading parenting books to adjust to the sleepless nights of a new infant, he tried to unlock the secrets of the rainforest, with no text for support. All three of his collared bears died. All showed signs of severe starvation.

Then, in May 2000, Wong successfully trapped another bear, an underweight sub-adult male he named Lai Xiung ('Come Bear'). Wong and Guy tracked him through the forest for the next seven months, during which they managed to catch glimpses twenty-one times. On one occasion, Lai Xiung was about fifty metres above the ground, lying with his belly flat against the branch, legs hanging down. While he rested, Wong took stock of his surroundings. Bulbous pitcher plants hung down at eye level. A mountain tree shrew, disturbed from licking its sugary deposits, scurried from sight. The ficus tree was in full fruit and the bear wasn't alone. To its left, two helmeted hornbills gorged themselves, and between the branches he caught glimpses of a furry-faced binturong (or bearcat), along with its young. Wong marvelled at the interconnectedness of the scene before him. The pitcher plant's sugar strategically attracted the shrew whose 'thank you' droppings provided essential nitrates for the pitcher plant. If the shrew became extinct, so would the pitcher. In the same vein, if global warming were to impact the fig fruiting cycle, the forest impact would be far-reaching.

Wong walked quietly around the base of the tree looking for bear scats. He could learn a lot from poo. If Lai Xiung had eaten the figs, his excrement would be the consistency of a cow pat with lots of seeds. If, instead, he had feasted on termites or earthworms, the faeces would be more solid and earth-coloured with termite skeletons visible to the naked eye. Wong found a soft sample, bagging as much as he could to put in the freezer for later analysis.

After forty minutes resting in his veritable supermarket, Lai Xiung climbed down to a smaller branch, used his right paw to reach for figs, and stuffed them into his mouth whole. It was the first time Wong had actually witnessed a bear eating figs. He watched so intently, he didn't see the orangutan clutching her infant until she started throwing twigs at him. Wong resisted a five-minute onslaught, before he finally gave up and left.

Unfortunately, by August, the photo trap pictures of Lai Xiung showed his condition had markedly deteriorated. He became so hungry, he learnt to exploit the traps, giving up his freedom a total of seven times for tasty chicken, sitting quietly inside the trap waiting for release. Two more severely underweight bears followed. On September 24th, 2000, when they approached the only trapped female, Lai Mei, she was very aggressive. She had been gorging on figs and the trap smelt ripe from her droppings. After measuring and collaring her, and after she had recuperated, Wong weighed the soft faeces she left behind. He was astounded to find it was equal to ten percent of her total body weight.

Chia-Chien felt nauseous as she took the required photos of Lai Mei. It was to be expected. A few weeks earlier, she had found out she was pregnant. The smell, heat, and humidity set off morning sickness. Wong sped up his measurements, then helped her into the car and gingerly drove the two hours home, stopping often so she could double over beside the car and throw up. This was a new experience for both of them, and as she lay on their bed in pain, Wong was worried she was miscarrying. They were so far away from a hospital, the event scared them both. With four months of research left, Chia-Chien packed her bags and flew to the warm embrace of her mother in Taipei, close to medical care. And the bear? Only eighteen hours from releasing her, Lai Mei destroyed the collar and disappeared.

Wong named his last bear Lai Fu. This bought the entire research tally for his master's research to six collared bears in twenty-six months. Over the study, the images the camera traps produced showed increasingly emaciated animals—bears and pigs. In desperation and emboldened by starvation, wild animals ventured into the Field Centre to find food. One night, a staff member watched George and Michael defend their territory from a marauding wild pig. In ten years at the Field Centre, he had never seen such a skinny animal still alive. The poor creature lumbered back to the forest like a ghost. Lai Xiung also cleverly discovered the Field Centre garbage dump and started to put on weight.

Perhaps, Wong thought, the answer to their hunger was in the wild animal's diet. When time permitted, he retrieved his frozen samples from the freezer. First, he defrosted the scat, put it in a sieve, and washed away the dirt. The large particles were oven-dried for twenty-four hours, soaked again, and dried again before they were ready for inspection. Just like magnified sand, a world of colours, shapes, and textures emerged under a microscope.

Wong's scat findings confirmed, without a doubt, that sun bears were opportunistic omnivores. Although he found evidence of beetles, wasps, stingless bees, turtles, bird eggs, and even small mammals, by far the most prevalent items were ficus seeds and termite skeletons. It seemed figs were an essential part of a sun bear's diet. While lowland tropical rainforest trees in Borneo produced fruit year-round, he learnt they sometimes underwent synchronised mass flowering and mass fruiting. Over a few weeks, nearly all the dipterocarps, ficus, and up to eighty-eight percent of all canopy species flowered in unison, producing huge crops a few months later. These reproductive waves were linked to periods of low rainfall, happening irregularly at intervals between two and ten years. In Segama Forest Reserve, where Danum Valley lies, mass fruitings, called masting events, were recorded in 1986, 1990, and 1996, always after pronounced dry seasons.

Collaborative research between Wong and Norhayati Ahmad provided the missing piece of the puzzle. Yati, as she was known, monitored flowering and fruiting activities in primary forest and logged forest plots from August 1997 to May 1999, then linked them to weather events to form a pattern. Wong helped with the research, and when Yati's study was over, he continued monitoring the same patches for a further nineteen months. Their combined results showed there had been no mass fruiting since 1996. In 1998, El Niño, the warm phase of the El Niño Southern Oscillation (ENSO) was replaced by a period of La Niña, the cool phase. With it came sixteen-year record high rainfall in 1999 and 2000.

Wong had been office bound for four days of heavy rain. He put on his boots and squelched as close as he could to the burst banks of the Segama River. The wooden tread of the suspension bridge, normally two metres above the flow, was invisible beneath a torrent of muddy water. The wooden sign on the closest side was inundated up to its bottom edge. As he watched, illegally felled logs race downstream across his view. His anger rose with the water as a new idea struck him. ENSO fluctuations triggered forest fires throughout Borneo in 1997 and 1998, leaving a deadly hazy in their wake which he suspected wiped out fig wasps. Without the fig wasps to pollinate them, trees aborted their blossoms, halting the development of fruit essential to sun bear survival. The survival of sun bears was dependant on bees in a delicate balance where even the smallest of creatures and plants played their part. Although the green, lush undergrowth gave the impression of constant abundance, he realised he was standing in the middle of a famine.

Wong wondered if famine was a natural way to balance animal numbers in an area where natural predators were few. Or perhaps there were few predators because larger animals couldn't survive in the natural feast-and-famine cycle. Global warming appeared to be affecting weather patterns, but forest fragmentation, deforestation, and logging probably also had their parts to play. Rather than unlocking the secrets of sun bears, his research had uncovered a much greater issue on which the survival of the entire ecosystem relied. The fruit of the ficus underpinned the survival of forest fauna. "The rainforest was more fragile than most people thought," Wong explains to me. "This research elevated ficus to a super-keystone species in the rainforest ecosystem."

CHAPTER 8

Little Things

*Wong made a vow to Little One that
she would never be forgotten.*

In 1994, while Wong was still trapping muntjacs in Taiwan, a young Dutch woman, Gabriella Fredriksson, was completing her master's field work on orangutans in Kalimantan, the Indonesian part of Borneo. She stepped over a thorny rattan vine and pushed aside foliage, stopping to focus her binoculars and scan above. Gabriella could hear something falling from the canopy and bouncing off the branches below. She approached quietly, moving around to get a clear view through the foliage, expecting to see the red flash of an orangutan as it fashioned a day nest. To her astonishment, two black shapes were high above her, hanging off the tree. She rolled her index finger over the dial between her eyes. A pair of bears came into focus, chewing off bark chunks and tossing them aside as they tried to break into a stingless bee nest. "I had never read anything about bears being present in Borneo," she tells me. "No one ever mentioned bears."

Back in Holland, recuperating from a broken knee, Gabriella's bear encounter kept interrupting as she tried to write up her research. She searched for bear experts to find out what was known about the species, eventually contacting Dave Garshelis in the United States. Apart from a failed field research attempt in Thailand, he told her, nothing had been done on wild sun bear research, but he would be willing to supervise her, if she was keen. Just as Chris Servheen mentored Wong, Dave mentored

Gabriella. She joined a bear research team in Sweden to learn more about bear research, and in August 1997 she was back in Indonesia with a different animal in her sights.

Gabriella was sponsored by the same organisation with which she had been affiliated during the orangutan study. Besides orangutans, they cared for ten rescued bears. The Wildlife Department planned on releasing five in her research area. Gabriella was given permission to track them. She didn't think radio collars would stay on the sun bear's broad necks, so she used Dutch-made low-frequency implant transmitters, installed by a local Indonesian vet. "There was a lot of trial and error because no one had done radio tracking in a tropical rainforest," Gabriella tells me. "The implant transmitters were specially designed by a research institute for this project with a low-frequency signal— the theory that in a rainforest, you have a lot of water held in the trees and that low-frequency signals would travel better."

After the release, the bears quickly spread out over a large area. As all Gabriella's research was done on foot in the forest using one receiver and antenna, she struggled over the next three weeks to find the bears. She was despondent, wondering what to do next, when word reached her of a bear sighting in farmland on the edge of the forest. Gabriella and her assistant arrived in time to recapture it, releasing the bear soon after. A few weeks later, the same bear ended up back on the periphery. Perhaps, she wondered, it had been chased out of the forest by its wild territorial counterpart. Gabriella started searching for her other implanted bears on the forest edge, and sure enough, one after the other she found them near human settlements. Three of her study bears were eventually found dead, killed by villagers. Her final report condemned the release of rescued bears.

Gabriella started setting traps for wild bears, but her reputation with confiscated bears had been cemented. Within a few months, the government approached her again. This time they had commandeered a tiny cub, but the orangutan rescue centre was unable to cope with its around-the-clock needs. Gabriella knew the local international school had cared for a range of wildlife. When she approached them, they were keen to add the cub to their gibbon cage, assuring her sun bears and gibbons were compatible. Two weeks later, just as Gabriella was preparing to go back out into the field, the school principal called, distraught. The young bear had killed some of its cellmates.

Gabriella loaded a cage into her truck and took the cub with her, deep into the primary forest. She balanced her research with caring for the infant, cradling it in her arms and giving it a bottle every few hours, taking it for walks in the forest, watching in delight as it padded along behind her heels. Perhaps, she thought, this type of 'soft release' had a chance of success. More bears needed a home, and a year later, Gabriella was living in the forest with three bears, each about six months apart in age.

The bears thrived on both personal attention and the opportunity for independence, testing their boundaries like siblings as they grew. Gabriella fitted them with collars, which didn't fall off after all, but could be adjusted as the bears grew. The oldest two, Ucil and Ganja, were out of sight, but she could hear them play-fighting. Gabby tracked their signals to the base of a huge old tree, strangled by interwoven ficus vines. Arboreal behaviour was so seldom observed. She marvelled at their agility. When she called them, the two females leapfrogged down the trunk, using the splaying lattice vines as steps. They played with her for twenty minutes before they impatiently took off again. She jotted notes, picked up her instrument, and followed.

When Wong started his own bear project, he contacted Gabriella in Kalimantan. He also knew of one other researcher studying sun bears, Japanese doctorate student Fuyuki Nomura (from Hokkaido University), based in nearby Tabin National Park. A comradery grew between the trio, and in 1998, during the first three months of Wong's field research at Danum Valley, they met for the first time at Nomura's research site in Tabin.

Nomura was the first to trap a bear. Over a bowl of steaming noodles, the other two enviously probed for his secrets, keen to emulate his success. In the process, they compared their study sites. Gabriella worked in a remaining patch of primary forest surrounded by plantations and development. In some ways, it was a time-capsule island, but the bears roamed back and forth through the wider landscape. Wong's area at Danum was pristine forest bleeding into logged forest, the impact of industry on sun bears measurable by comparison. Nomura studied bears adapted to a logged forest adjacent to a forest plantation. His was the Ghost of Christmas Future, the results offering a warning if industry continued to ravage the rainforest. Malaysian hardwood exports were twenty-five times larger than they had been in the 1940s, which wasn't sustainable. The area logged each year in the Indonesian side of Borneo alone was the size of Hong Kong. An estimated half of suitable wildlife habitats in Borneo totally disappeared between 1960 and 1990. Researchers knew a return to past habitats, uninterrupted by human encroachment, would be impossible. They agreed that they were fighting a battle against time. Educating and adjusting to the present status to reduce further loss, rather than grieving an idyllic past, were the only way forward.

In October 2000, Wong tidied up the ends of his field research, looking forward to being reunited with Chia-Chien and preparing for the arrival of their baby. He had just enough time to squeeze in a reciprocal visit to Gabriella's research site. By then, Gabriella had managed to trap and collar three wild bears. She tracked them on foot, and also tried to observe them, but they would disappear as soon as they smelt humans. The three semi-habituated bears were a different story. Gabriella and her assistant had been observing them for several years, a rich story emerging. "We could see what the wild bears were eating, what the released bears were eating, and determine if it was the same," she tells me. "We learnt heaps from those bears."

By the time Wong visited, the two females Ucil and Ganja weren't coming back to base anymore, but they still had collars on and were happy to be observed from a distance. The male, Schizo, was still attached to his human family. His need for interaction and proximity, compounded by his great size, was starting to become problematic.

Not long before Wong's visit, Gabriella had accepted her fourth cub. Si Kecil came upon her name by default because no one could come up with a better one. 'Si' is used in front of a proper name in Indonesia to indicate closeness. 'Kecil' means 'little.' Gabriella wanted 'Little One' to spend as much time in the forest as possible, so the cub came with her as she worked. The plan was to move Little One to another site as soon as possible so she could rehabilitate in an area free of other released bears. In the meantime, Gabriella taught a new staff member how to walk the new cub in the forest, how to call her back, and how to feed her in her forest cage, reminding them to keep away from the larger, less predictable Schizo.

Wong was smitten with Little One, just as Jane Goodall had connected with chimpanzee David Greybeard, and Dian Fossey loved gorilla Digit. He had been tracking and trapping bears remotely for so long, he missed the personal connection of his pets at home. Little One filled a void, his first sun bear cub. Wong giggled as he sat the eight-month-old on the lap of his cargo pants, the tips of her hairs tickling his bare chest, his fingers disappearing into back fur as dense as a faux-fur rug. An inkling of her gold ventral patch peeked out from under her chin. Brown button eyes looked up into his, the tan pads on the bottom of her paws waving in the air as he tipped her back and tickled her tummy. "It was wonderful," he tells me. "It really changed me a lot." When Gabriella took Little One for a walk, he tagged along with his camera, third in a duck line. Little One climbed a small branch about eye-height and cuddled it like a child on a fireman's pole. He had never seen a sun bear so close in its natural habitat.

He was struck by the beauty of the natural composition, clicking away like paparazzi.

Wong meeting Little One. Courtesy Wong Siew Te

On Christmas Eve, two months later, Gabriella and one staff member were the skeleton crew left in camp. Gabriella opened Little One's cage and they took off down a narrow path, stopping when the cub found tasty termites, and again when she came across a crunchy pill millipede. Several barbets sounded far away: "took, took, tarook." Gabriella knew this probably indicated a fruiting fig. She wondered if Ucil and Ganja were gorging themselves.

Before she noticed he was there, the fifty-kilo Schizo emerged from the undergrowth, crossing Little One's path. He stopped, wanting to play but, just like a full-grown pit bull terrier, he didn't know his own strength. Little One retreated, scampering up the nearest tree. Schizo followed, bullying her in jest or jealously. Gabriella's heart raced with fear. She had been at the receiving end of Schizo's strength. She shouted out to him in guttural Dutch, anxiously running her hands through her own no-nonsense hair, but he ignored her. Gabriella ran back to camp, dodging trees. Perhaps with help she could lure him away.

When she and her assistant returned, gulping air from exertion, Little One was on the ground, also straining for breath. Gabriella crouched beside her, visually assessing the damage. She found several puncture wounds. As her hands gently squeezed Little One's limbs searching for breaks, she looked up—a detective searching for clues, surmising Little One had fallen from the tree above. Gabriella clutched the cub to her chest, rushing her back to camp.

Little One died that night from internal injuries. Wong was devastated when he read Gabriella's email. Even now he finds it hard not to demonise Schizo. He tells me it's likely the older bear wanted to play, and his rough, rambunctious enthusiasm caused Little One to fall out of the tree. In his grief, Wong made a vow to Little One that she would never be forgotten. It took a while to keep his promise.

Wong and Chia-Chien landed in the middle of a Missoula winter. The distance from her mother hit Chia-Chien as hard as the icy wind. Her five-month-old foetus turned to adjust as she cradled her stomach. There was a vast difference between studying in a foreign country and starting a new family in one. The couple feathered their nest with a support network: experienced American elders, church group peers, other Taiwanese and Malaysian students with young families, and an obstetrician.

The growing bump became a topic of conversation. Instead of tipping acknowledgement to a family member or choosing a name with a religious meaning, Chia-Chien and Wong batted around bear names, settling on Winifred, or 'Winnie,' after Winnie-the-Pooh. In hindsight, it was more fitting than they knew. The bear A.A. Milne based his story upon (Winnipeg, or Winnie for short) most likely lost her mother to Canadian hunters, and in 1914, she was sold into the pet trade. Cavalry soldier Harry Colebourne couldn't resist her oversized Mickey Mouse ears and quizzical expression. He bought her at a train stop and she became the company mascot, accompanying him to London. At the end of WWI, when Winnie reached an unruly size, Colebourne 'gifted' her to the London Zoo. It was there that the real Christopher Robin met her, and the Winnie-the-Pooh tales were conceived. "What if it's a boy?" Chia-Chien posed. That was easy. Keeping to the bear theme, they both agreed on 'Ted.' Teddy bears had been named after President Teddy Roosevelt, and that seemed fitting for the new generation, American-born Wong.

As their unborn child grew, stretching Chia-Chien's skin tight, winter slowly warmed to spring. Chia-Chien's body temperature followed suit, making her uncomfortable. She walked slower around the supermarket, Wong by her side. "I told myself, in an emergency, I could deliver a human being," he tells me. Chia-Chien tossed and turned all night. She couldn't get comfortable. As daylight crept through the curtain cracks on May 9th, 2001, she realised the cramps in her stomach were early labour pains. The time had come. Wong helped her into the passenger seat and drove to the Missoula hospital, worriedly glancing across as the next contraction wave hit. It was a slow day at the hospital, and with time on their hands, the nursing staff hovered like hummingbirds, getting Chia-Chien anything she needed. Early evening, sufficiently dilated, Dr Visscher offered her an epidural. She gladly accepted. Traditionally, Chinese women were not supposed to call out in labour, and the relief from pain helped put Chia-Chien's mind at rest. She grasped Wong's hand tight and, as instructed, bore down.

Dr Visscher beckoned to Wong. He left his wife's side and moved down the bed, swallowing his apprehension at the overwhelming mess of amniotic fluid and blood. Dr Visscher calmed him, drawing his attention to the shine of sticky dark hair starting to crown. As he recounts the first view of his daughter, mental images flick across his memory. "It was both an amazing, and educational experience," he tells me. Two more pushes and a wrinkly human emerged, smothered in waxy white vernix, so much bigger than the other mammals he had delivered. With a grin cracking his face, Wong accepted a pair of surgical scissors. He separated his wife from their daughter, his love instantly doubled.

Woken by the guttural cries of his new daughter, Wong found himself thrown into the topsy-turvy world of any new parent. He squinted at the bedside clock, mentally calculating whether the time between feeds was getting any longer. Beside him, Chia-Chien rose in a sleep-deprived stupor and he slid out of bed in support. It wouldn't be long before Chia-Chien would start pumping, and he could feed Winnie while she slept. He stared down at Winnie against Chia-Chien's breast. Her skin had a yellow tinge and she would need to go back to hospital to check for jaundice. As he looked down on his tiny daughter the next day, wrapped in a light blanket, which looked like a giant blood-pressure cuff, his thesis could not have been further from his mind.

As soon as the school year finished in Taiwan, Chia-Chien's mother waved goodbye to her class of children and flew to Montana to meet her granddaughter for the first time. With the responsibility shared for a while, Wong could intermittently focus on classes and writing, but his mind was never far from Winnie. He rushed back to the married-student housing as often as he could. Over time, family routines were established. Wong and Chia-Chien grew into their community through Winnie, her cheeky grin and milestones celebrated by their neighbours.

Winnie was growing so fast, Chai-Chien moved breakables up another shelf. Outside, the last crisp white hillside of winter beckoned. She stuffed her daughter's chubby arms into the sleeves of her navy-blue parka, zipping the bottom third. Red mittens on an elastic string poked out of the ends. With one hand, Chia-Chien perched Winnie on her hip. With the other, she deftly pulled the red beanie over Winnie's head, two tassels sticking up like her ponytails beneath.

They followed footprints, Winnie bounding ahead. Before long, Chia-Chien was swapping mothering advice with a neighbour, while their two toddlers giggled, fashioning the ice with their tiny hands. Winnie's button nose turned red and she came running, cold fingers outstretched. Chia-Chien rubbed them between her own. It was time to head home to rest. Morning sickness was beginning again.

As the semester ended, Chia-Chien pulled her maternity pants back out of the closet and Wong headed back to Malaysia with a grant from Woodland Park Zoo in Seattle, Washington to complete a study of captive bears throughout Malaysia. The zoo's support for such a study wasn't completely altruistic. Woodland Park Zoo keeper Cheryl Frederick was the sun bear stud keeper for the entire country, keeping records of bear movements to avoid interbreeding. Ten bears had been sent from Sepilok to populate zoos in the US in 1996, another ten in 2000. Part of the agreement was that the US would help with bear conservation in Sabah. Since Nomura had finished his study, Wong was the only remaining person studying bears in the state of Sabah, making him the obvious beneficiary.

Wong touched down in Miri Airport, Sarawak, grabbed his bag, and hailed a taxi. His first stop was the low-hanging fruit, Miri Crocodile Farm, where he knew there were sun bears. As they drove, he probed the driver for insider information on other captives. There was talk about one in a nearby palm plantation. He added it to his list, thanked the driver, and paid the entrance fee.

As he approached the sun bear cages, he could smell a concoction of bear excrement and rotting fruit. A closer look revealed urine seeping through the concrete cracks. An adult bear stood, stunned, in the corner shaking his head repeatedly. He looked as if he was trying to wake himself from a nightmare, but Wong knew the shaking was a sign of psychological trauma. Beyond the cage, a laughing crowd gathered. Wong moved on to investigate. Two sub-adult bears with heavy chains around their necks were tied to posts as a photo opportunity. A teenage boy was trying to teach one of them to high-five, his sisters laughing as their father pointed his camera. Wong felt sick.

As he turned away, out of the corner of his eye, he saw three small birdcages away from the regular visitor traffic, tattered rice sacks stretched to provide shade. The closest two seemed to house puppies, but there was something in the third that made him look twice—the undernourished 'puppy' was circling repeatedly. As he got closer, Wong was devastated. It was a tiny bear cub in obvious distress, repeatedly turning in the 2x1ft birdcage, its dull brown fur indicating extremely poor health. Wong longed to rip the bars apart and rescue the bear, but instead, he tried to calm the cub with words, took pictures, and dragged himself away. There were so many more places to survey. He hoped his stomach would survive.

It was a month of opportunistic conversations leading to intense travel. The more sites Wong investigated, the more bears he found. Regardless of whether the zoos were government-run or private, all the main ones had sun bears. In addition, there were schools with cages in the playground and private collections hidden away from the public. Apart from the odd compassionate enclosure, the majority of bears were kept in appalling situations— mentally, and sometimes physically, abused.

The last state on Wong's bear tour was Sabah. On the northern tip, in the Victory Zoo in Kadat, Wong followed signs around the lake to the 'Panda' enclosure, only to find two adult sun bears staring through bars at the water, just out of reach. How was it possible, he thought, that the zookeepers didn't even know the name of the species they had incarcerated? He was exhausted and disheartened when he arrived at Sandakan, but he still had sites to review. Wong checked his list as his skin stuck to the hot vinyl in the back seat of another cab. There was one bear confined to a small cage at Jalil Alip Recreation Area, close to Paganakan Di, where I stayed in volunteer accommodation years later; his friend had told him of another kept at his uncle's home; a blind bear was reported at the Sandakan Crocodile Farm; and Sepilok Orangutan Rehabilitation Centre, the last stop on his survey, had several.

The taxi slowed under the Sepilok welcome sign. Wong looked out of the window; a photo of a red-headed orangutan infant above his head stared back. He was no stranger to Sepilok. During his master's degree he had visited the vet office behind the guarded gate to collect medication for his anaesthetic jab stick. Another time, he helped carry ten sedated bears into translocation cages for their journey halfway around the world.

Wong was met at the gazebo by Dr Sen Nathan. He's now the Assistant Director of Sabah Wildlife Department, but back in 2004, Dr Nathan was Sabah Wildlife's resident vet. Rather than heading to the orangutan reception, they turned left, crossing a rickety bridge and following the path to a row of seven dank cages.

Bears were sharing cells, like an oversubscribed prison. The concrete underfoot could only be properly scrubbed if the bears were sedated; a powerful hose was the next best option. They had no drinking trough and were only given water three times a day by hose. They had no sleeping baskets, so their feet were always damp. One of the bears constantly licked his feet, leading Wong to suspect a foot infection. Their food was limited to what would fit between the bars and subsequently wash down the drain (rice porridge), fruit only given in small peeled chunks. International visitors who watched iconic orangutans less than a hundred metres away were oblivious. If he had asked, they wouldn't have even known what a sun bear was.

On the other side of the quadrangle, a solitary middle-aged Western woman was preparing rice porridge. She tucked her unruly blonde hair behind her ears as Dr Nathan introduced her. Anne Birtwell, a volunteer from the UK, was the only person caring for the bears. Wong extended his business card and Anne accepted. 'Co-chair of the Sun Bear Expert Team, IUCN Bear Specialist Group', it read. It was a position which sounded grander than it was. There were only two remaining sun bear experts, after all: Wong and Gabriella. But Anne didn't know that, and she wasn't going to let this opportunity slide. With emotion welling, she grabbed his arm tight, imploring him to help the bears.

Rescued cub Nano. Courtesy BSBCC

Wong wants to introduce me to his newest charges, so I'm standing outside those old bear cages, now used only to temporarily quarantine new arrivals at the Bornean Sun Bear Conservation Centre, their past long forgotten. There are two young cubs inside, Noah and Nano, under the maternal care of Lin May. They have just been integrated with each other and they seem to be getting on well. As Wong and I approach timidly, Lin May crouches against the bars at Noah's level, feeding him drops of honey. Black shirt and long pants hang off her slight frame, and her jet-black hair is pulled back. My eyes struggle to adjust because the darkness is stark compared to the newer well-lit and ventilated bear house. Nano and Noah will be introduced to the older bears slowly. Ostensibly, they need to be cleared for diseases, but Wong is also cautious to avoid the fate of Little One. I have been instructed to wear black in preparation for meeting the youngsters. Wong and Lin May indicate I can move closer, but the moment Nano senses me coming, the stress is tangible. He may have adjusted to Lin May, but he's not willing to extend his inner circle. Nano climbs quickly, barking loudly to ward me off. I back away, my ego bruised. I had so wanted to meet the bear, but I am well aware this fear of humans could save his life.

In 2004, Wong used his short time at Sepilok to help Anne care for the bears. They chatted while they worked. He learnt her career was in television, often editing sports broadcasts, networking with stars. He laughed at her audacity as she recounted an incident earlier that year when she had tried to convince a plantation owner to surrender his pet infant orangutan. Thinking she needed a bargaining chip, Anne contacted English footballer David Beckham asking for his help. Beckham sent a signed photo which Anne successfully traded for the infant's life, freeing it from the tiny palm plantation cage. It seemed to Wong there was always a way. It just required thinking outside the square. "What bought you here?" Wong asked, and learnt Anne was working with CNN in Malaysia when a chance meeting with wildlife documentary maker David Attenborough changed her direction. Sir David casually mentioned orangutan numbers were dangerously low, only six thousand left in the wild. A feeling of devastation and responsibility led Anne to commit six months a year to volunteer at Sepilok.

Wong and Anne may have been from different cultures, but their hearts were united in the dream of a better world for wildlife. Before he left, Wong made her a promise: he would do his best to help the bears. It's a pivotal moment he still remembers clearly, the first kernel of BSBCC germinating.

CHAPTER 9

It's a Jungle Out There

Wong was no longer a lone voice smothered by the foliage.

In Missoula, Wong's PhD application was accepted. He was assigned a committee of five, per university policy: Chris Servheen, once again his primary supervisor; the others bringing to the table various expertise including data analysis and biology. Remembering Wong's difficulty capturing elusive bears for his master's, the committee suggested he should play it safe and limit his research to bearded pigs. I struggle to understand this reasoning. Were sun bears essentially too endangered to study? Did they consider it a foregone conclusion that sun bears would become extinct, like the Pyrenean ibex had two years before? Was this advice offered to protect Wong from failure, or make it easier for his committee? Wong felt cornered. He knew no one on the ground would offer financial support for studying pigs, so with his committee's approval, he decided to collect data on both species, submitting only the pig research for his thesis. Essentially, he committed to double the work.

While he prepared to go back into the field, Wong was contacted by biologist Chris Morgan, who wanted to make a documentary about bears and wanted his help. English by birth, Chris was a year older than Wong. He had been working as a counsellor at a New Hampshire summer camp at the age of 18, when a fortuitous meeting changed his career direction. A local bear biologist came to regale the kids with anecdotes about his study. More than the kids, it was Chris who became hooked, pestering for the chance to be involved.

As dark descended, young Chris stood awaiting pickup, torch in hand. He had butterflies in his stomach as he imagined treading softly over fallen pine needles down winding forest paths, using stealth to approach the research subjects. Headlights slowed before him, and Chris jumped into the passenger side, pulling the door closed behind him. They drove to the fork in the road, turning right towards town. Chris was confused: he thought the bears were in the hills. Instead, as they neared the city dump, the insipid odour of rotting garbage stuck to his tongue, announcing its proximity. There, Chris counted fourteen black bears silhouetted in the moonlight. All night he helped tranquillise, measure, and take samples. As the blush of dawn crept across the sky, he chased off the last sleepy bear, smelling worse than he could remember, but grinning uncontrollably. Just as Wong had done after a day at the goat farm, Chris headed straight for the shower.

For the following decade, Chris had worked with scientists in far-flung countries like Spain, Pakistan, and Ecuador. He learnt bears lived in Europe, Asia, South America, and the Arctic, in some of the most diverse ecosystems on earth, yet six of the eight bear species were endangered. All the researchers he met struggled for funds. "I wanted to do something with my life that made sure that changed," Chris tells me. He knew if conservationists managed to preserve bear habitats, the flow-on effect to other species would be astronomical. "Save the eight bear species, and you are basically saving a third of the world's land surface, so bears are a rare conservation tool," Chris says. In 2005, he decided to draw attention to bears through film, pairing with filmmaker Joe Pontecorvo to create an ambitious full-length feature documentary they called BEARTREK. They chose to focus on spectacled bears in Peru; brown bears in Katmai

Park, Alaska; polar bears in Churchill, Manitoba; and sun bears in Borneo. I wonder if Chris would have been as committed if he had known the film wouldn't make its public debut until 2018.

As soon as Wong heard the concept, he wanted to help but he was a little worried—sun bears were more elusive than grizzlies during the salmon run, or black bears on a dump. They decided, in the worst-case scenario, Chris could film him looking for bears and they could visit captives at Sepilok. And so began the journey to secure appropriate permits. Even when Chris employed a Malaysian 'fixer', a professional photographer called Cede Prudente, it was a frustrating two years before his five-person production team could buy plane tickets. The process hasn't improved much over time. Each state in Malaysia has different fee schedules and approval checklists which require a unique set of completed documents including things like a script, storyboard, profile of the production company, company crew list (including birthdates, nationalities, and passport numbers), a production equipment list (including serial numbers), and a filming schedule with exact dates and locations.

While Wong waited for news, life rolled on, punctuated by discussions with Chia-Chien about more children's names. They liked 'Ursula', meaning 'Little Bear', but when Winnie pronounced the name it sounded more like the term for 'starved to death' in Mandarin. They laughed and settled on Evelyn, or Evie. Their second child was born in the same hospital as Winnie in November of 2004, just as their world was threatening to turn white for another winter, and shortly after Britain made it illegal to hunt wild mammals with dogs. When Evie was two months old, the family was on the move again, the first stop Taiwan. The cold seeped into Wong's heart as his family, only just formed, was fractured—three stayed in Taiwan, one went back to Malaysia. At least, he thought, Chia-Chien would have her mother for support while they were apart. Wong snuggled his daughters one last time, burying his nose in their hair, committing their sweetness to memory.

When Wong first told me he had spent years studying bears in the field, I pictured him as an unwashed recluse, emerging from the jungle for the sustenance he couldn't harvest from the trees. It was a surprise to learn Danum Valley Research Centre was a bustling hive of activity and intelligence. Researchers rotated as if through a revolving door. A different batch gathered to share their research and spawn collaborations every Monday night over dinner. Many PhD students narrowed their vision to avoid distraction and to keep to schedule. Reluctantly unencumbered by family, Wong instead filled his time and widened his gaze by helping his peers gather data, expanding his network like ripples in a pond.

When interpretation officer Sylvia Yorath walked into Wong's office, Darwin instantly sprung to mind. In pride of place was the petite-featured, pink-nosed white-fronted langur Wong had found abandoned in the freezer at Danum and lovingly stuffed. Its black Zorro-like eye mask and comical halo of Einstein-like hair made her smile. Her gaze then bounced across the specimen jars until it landed on Wong, cocooned in their midst. Sylvia, originally from Yorkshire, was updating the research displays. She had come to ask for help. Wong often offered copies of his sun bear photos unsolicited. She knew the focus of his lens was a broad as his interest and was sure he would have images of other species she could use. She also knew he was a good ambassador for Danum, so she started promoting him as a possible presenter to the wider public.

At the time, Robert Ong was chairman of the Sandakan branch of the Sabah Society. He agreed to invite Wong to give a talk to members of the non-government organisation who were interested in the geography, culture and history (natural and otherwise) of the state. Wong greeted a rainbow of suits, shawls, and loudly patterned shirts as they shuffled in and took their seats. He cleared his throat, launching into a passionate picture of his research, the dangers to bears, and his hopes and dreams. When he finally paused, Robert wasn't the only person captivated. With chairs pushed aside and handshakes exhausted, Robert arranged a meeting between Wong and his sister.

Cynthia Ong runs a non-profit organisation in the US called LEAP Inc (Land, Empowerment, Animals, People). She had a growing philanthropic network and was developing a locally based non-profit, also called LEAP. Wong arrived prepared with a shorter presentation about his study, ending with the shortfall of funding. It was his knowledge and sincerity that Cynthia remembers. She emailed Wong's proposal and his photo to American philanthropist Nancy Abraham who already supported orangutan conservation and was concerned about the plight of sun bears. Nancy was drawn in by his round face and open expression. Just like I did when we first met, she thought he looked a little like a sun bear himself. Nancy gladly handed over a US$10,000 cheque.

Instantly, Wong's peripheral vision expanded with possibilities. As he crunched through the undergrowth in search of pigs and bears, he rattled off Latin tree names to keep his wits sharp, but his thoughts regularly drifted back to the bears at Sepilok. What if he could create a rescue centre where bears could be taught the skills which would allow their eventual rehabilitation back to the wild? What if such a centre could educate local children and tourists about sun bears, promoting their inherent value to a wider ecological story, rather than as a source of food and medicine? What if such a centre welcomed researchers from around the world, adding to human learning about the species and the rainforest habitat?

Questions bounced around Wong's mind as the universe aligned around him in the form of two men from different sides of the globe. As he arrived at the field office in the middle of another power outage, a fresh new Chinese Malaysian forestry graduate called Wai Pak was checking in. They enthusiastically chatted in Mandarin, the beginning of a pivotal friendship and mentorship.

Soon after, a lanky, pale Scotsman called Ian Hall arrived at Danum Valley Field Centre. He had been working as an expedition leader for Sustainable Development Charity, Raleigh International, but the raw magnetism of the rainforest held him in its grasp. He decided to stay, volunteering his architectural services over three different conservation areas. Although neither man can be sure, they probably met at one of the regular Monday gatherings. Wong loved a chat and Ian offered a receptive ear, soaking up as much as he could learn about the local ecology. "You know when you get a feeling people are interacting with you because they want something?" Ian rhetorically asks me between his Northern Hemisphere winter sniffles and an occasional video delay, "I got a feeling like that from Wong early on, but also knew whatever it was he wanted, I would be interested."

One day as Wong and Ian sat on the wide veranda, and Ian polished his glasses on the bottom of his T-shirt, Wong tested the waters: "I have this idea..." he started. As Wong's dreams tumbled from his lips onto scraps of paper, Ian was pulled along with his enthusiasm. Ian didn't have a design business, Wong didn't have any money, but such details were irrelevant. Youth and ideology were on their side. Their combined respect for, and sensitivity to, the natural world would eventually spawn both the Bornean Sun Bear Conservation Centre and a sustainable design company, Arkitrek.

Wong was no longer a lone voice smothered by the foliage.

Wong's promise to Anne was never far from his thoughts. Wong came to admire the feisty woman who wouldn't take no for an answer. In 2006, they jointly raised enough money to rebuild the dreary, unhygienic confinements. Anne contributed her own funds, Wong used some of his research money, and Nancy pitched in. Wong and Anne's combined experience and sensitivity allowed them to design a basic, but much improved bear facility which pared the dream back to match the budget. The size of the three smaller cages was almost doubled, a gap created between the roof and bars, fans installed, and drainage improved. Then an exercise area was added to each row, accessible by cable-operated sliding doors. The bears would be able to take turns exploring the two concrete baths while their cages were cleaned. Ironwood branches, sleeping baskets, and concrete water troughs transformed the sterile cubes.

As the sound of construction petered out and the workmen gathered their gear, Wong and Anne surveyed the new structure with pride. Just as a skeleton provides the scaffold for the body, it acted as the frame from which homes could materialise. Like interior decorators placing vases and fluffing pillows, they tossed leaf and twig litter over the floor, tipped rocks into one of the exercise area baths, and filled the other with water using the remotely accessible tap. It was September 1st, 2006, and, like a home renovation show, it was time for 'the reveal'. The first three bears were introduced to their new adjacent dens: a solitary male, Om, and the only bear couple, Keningau and Bentik.

Om had been separated from his mother since he was about five months old. People had become his family, and despite the dank cage he had grown up in, Om was always ready to play. When he was introduced to his upgraded den, it had been extended, giving him more room to explore. Om was confused. The sensory experience completely overwhelmed him, and he paced back and forth trying desperately to avoid the crunchy leaves which slid across the floor as he walked. He cowered in one familiar corner, turning away from offered enrichments, retreating internally.

With his back to the wall, Om stared alarmingly at Bentik and Keningau being introduced to the next cage.

Om's anxiety eased slightly on the second day and he approached the bars, sniffing intently, reaching through to tentatively touch Bentik. Wong and Anne were relieved as they watched the ensuing playful interaction, but it didn't last. On the third day, Bentik was over the attention, perhaps concerned Om might be trying to steal his mate. He rose on his hind legs, making himself look as large as possible, and nipped at Om through the bars. Socially inept Om didn't get the message. It was his first chance at a relationship with another bear and he wasn't going to let go. The next day Bentik lost his patience. He wanted to be left alone with Keningau, far from the perceived constant threat of Om's prying eyes. Om came out the loser with scratches on his body and a cut on his foot. He retreated into a corner to suck his paws, growling if Bentik approached the bars, his comfort zone compromised.

Om in his new wall basket. Courtesy BSBCC

When the contractors returned on the seventh day, Wong asked them to put an old tyre in Om's enclosure, similar to the one he had had in the pre-renovated cage. They also installed a second wall basket, as far away from Bentik as possible. It was just what Om needed. The basket became his safe place where he retreated after bear disagreements. Before long, he was throwing toys around his cage, delighting in the noise they made and taking them back to his tyre to chew. Neighbourly confrontations were a thing of the past.

In contrast, Bentik and Keningau integrated to their new environment quickly. Perhaps having each other made the transition easier. Wong and Anne were excited to introduce them to the exercise enclosure. Anne hid dried dog food pellets under the leaves and rocks then, and when she was back in a safe place to observe, Wong wound the sliding door open. Keningau, who seemed to be the more intelligent and adventurous of the pair, rushed in first, balancing along the branches. She could smell the treats, and soon abandoned her exploration in search of the hidden morsels, delicately grasping individual biscuits through the twigs. Bentik followed suit but he wasn't quite as patient. He pushed leaves aside with his snout, noisily snorting up the prize. Wong moved closer to the cage and Bentik looked over expectantly. His mate might be happy with foraging, but he was frustrated, preferring a handout.

On the fifth day, when the bear couple entered the exercise area, a strange-shaped thing awaited them. As Keningau rolled it along the floor with her nose, she could hear liquid sloshing inside. She concentrated on solving the riddle, sitting upright and balancing the heavy ball in her back paws before digging the tips of her long black claws through the hard exterior. Slowly, and meticulously, she worked at the fibres, peeling them back and tearing chunks with her teeth. Eventually, a brown shell was exposed. She turned it over, looking for a weak point. Keningau tapped the three black eyes on one end, finding one soft enough to pierce. She lifted the ball to her lips. The drips were invitingly sweet. Bentik, who had been disinterested up to this point, could smell juice as it ran down his mate's muzzle. As she cracked the ball on the concrete and started scooping out the jelly-like white interior, he made his move, trying to steal her prize. Wong watched as his power overcame her skill but, once he succeeded, Bentik didn't quite know what to do with his quarry. Keningau angrily barked and grabbed the coconut back, carrying it away to a corner. She remained alert to further attack and Wong made a mental note to give them two coconuts next time.

The next day, as Wong returned from lunch, his heart melted to see Bentik and Keningau curled up in their baskets asleep, content. He called Anne over to watch as they rose from their naps, jostling together in silence. He knew they were playing, he tells me, as bears are always vocal when they are angry. Bentik grabbed Keningau by the scruff of her neck with his teeth and they rolled around the ground. For a few moments, it was hard to see where one bear started and the other ended. Bentik got dizzy and sat down to rest, losing interest. Keningau climbed the branch above his head and dangled above him provocatively, swiping at him with her paws until he resumed playing. Wong had never seen sun bears exhibiting sexual behaviour, and he wondered if this was what was going on. Sure enough, the flirting escalated and a couple of days later, one of the team noticed Bentik licking at Keningau's urine before positioning her, as if to mate.

On September 18th, Wong and bear-keeper Rosli got to work at about 8am. They did a quick visual check on the other five bears. Tokob barked, startled by their presence; tiny Mamatai was squashed in her water basin splashing; Wonad balanced halfway up the bars; Ah Chong was curled on his self-made nest of leaves; Om was still inside his wall basket. They ended their roll-call at Bentik and Keningau's cage, planning to let the couple out into the exercise area. Rosli couldn't believe what met his eyes—the two were mating. Rosli had been looking after the bears at Sepilok for ten years and he'd never seen sexual activity before. Wong was over the moon as he later recounted the news to Anne. In less than three weeks, the changes they had made to the enclosures, and the enrichments they had both developed, had succeeded in creating an environment where Keningau had been secure and stimulated enough to come into heat. The added space had made it possible for the couple to practise sexual behaviours, leading to this exciting development. Anne and Wong voiced their inner dreams—perhaps a sun bear breeding program might be possible in the future.

In his buoyed state, Wong had no idea that the following year would deliver two crippling blows.

Just as Gabriella had been approached by the Indonesian government to take care of Little One, Sabah Wildlife entrusted Wong with the release of a young cub called Batik. He took her to the forest to his field site camp where she alternated between her cage and the forest. Wong's joy matched Batik's as she explored her new home, climbing trees, digging for termites. Before long, he felt it was time to release her into the forest to fend for herself. Wong opened the cage for the last time, dismantling the camp so she couldn't return.

As her usual dinner time passed, and night fell, Batik was confused and scared. The sounds of the forest seemed amplified in the dark. When Wong appeared the next day, she approached him with relief, wolfing the dog biscuits he offered. Her frustration grew when they ran out. Whether in anger or punishment, she lashed out, biting him. Wong didn't allow her close again, monitoring from a greater distance over the next few weeks and growing concerned as the shape of her ribs became pronounced, like gills along her flank. He had expected her to lose weight as she learnt to spend more time foraging, but he had no idea how much was reasonable. Would she learn how to survive quickly enough? A few days later, Wong's assistant Chai saw Batik crawl into a hollow. He trained his binoculars on the entrance, but she didn't emerge. Wong was summoned, but by the time he got there, it was too late. Emotion sticking in his throat, he sat with Batik as she took her last breath.

Wong tells me he now knows he released her too early. Her skills were not honed. Together he and Chai lifted her body into a sling and recorded the devastating statistics. Batik had lost thirty percent of her body weight as she unsuccessfully searched for sufficient sustenance. In his grief, Wong questioned the very notion of freedom. Perhaps Batik would have preferred a cushy life in captivity with regular meals, to freedom coupled with the risk of starvation.

Then, on a clear January day in 2007, Wong drove his three research assistants to the end of the Rafflesia Reserve logging road. They were going to look for signs of bears to the north and complete three transects, or predetermined research paths. As they slipped into their backpack straps, Wong checked to make sure the two-way radios were working, and reiterated the plan to meet back at the same spot two days later. "Be careful, stay safe," he said in parting.

Malaysians Chai and Ade, and Canadian Gillian set off to the north. They pitched camp as rain began, zipped up their rain jackets, and continued for another hour in the same direction. Heavy mud stuck to their boot treads; slick wet leaves were as slippery as ice. They walked two out of three transect lines. All scats and termite dust had been washed away, and it was hard to see claw marks on slick bark. They tramped back to camp, warmed themselves over dinner, and vowed to continue in the morning.

Water seeped through seams, dripping all night. They rose early, sleep-deprived, ate breakfast, then hiked into the dense jungle past where they had been the day before. Movement was so slow that at 9.45am they decided to cut the expedition short. In the style of a jungle telegraph, Chai radioed Remmy, another researcher who was stationed at the Bukit Atur fire tower; Remmy called Wai Pak at the field centre; and Wai Pak called Wong, who was servicing the car in Lahad Datu. He agreed to pick them up that evening. The message was relayed back.

The team continued north to the third transect but conditions worsened. As they slid down a steep riverbank, Gillian wondered how they would ever get back. They scrambled up the other side and completed their work, but there was no chance they would be back in time to meet Wong. Luckily, the men knew the area well. The Infrapro camp wasn't far away. If they got there, they could radio for a pickup. They followed the meandering Lumparai River westwards. At about 4pm, with only about 400m to go, the river stood between them and their destination; behind them, the alternate choice of a five-hour hike and slippery slopes through dense jungle.

Chai and Gillian waded into the water until it touched their armpits and seeped into the packs on their backs. "Do you want to cross?" Gillian asked. "Yes" came Chai's reply. Gillian went first. Halfway across, her pack filled with water, threatening to pull her under. Scared, she yelled to Ade for help. He dropped his pack on the bank and launched in, arriving at Gillian just as her feet anchored to the other side. "You know, Chai isn't the best swimmer," he confessed. As if on cue, Chai, behind them, called out. He was continuing across.

Things happened so quickly then. Chai was out of his depth, calling for help. Ade was kicking hard to reach him. Gillian knew Ade was a strong swimmer and she was relieved when he got there. Then Chai's head disappeared under the surface. Gillian jumped in, her heart pounding. When she reached Ade, Chai was gone. She took a deep breath, duck-dived, opened her eyes in the murky water, and felt around with her outstretched arms. Two metres below the surface, a current pulled her. She kicked against it, sucked in a lungful of air, then dived again. And again. Every time she came up for breath, she scanned the bank, hoping Chai would wave back. She was caught in a nightmare, wishing herself to wake up. After an hour, her strength was gone; the current threatened to carry her away too.

Gillian crawled up the bank and sat next to the distraught Ade. It was getting dark and Gillian was shivering. They locked eyes. "I need you to come with me. We can't do anything more. We need to cross this river, or we could die too," she said. Gillian put the radios and GPS in plastic bags. They left the backpacks where they were, and swam across one last time with plastic clenched between their chattering teeth.

One radio survived the ordeal, and they managed to raise Wong through an intermittent signal. He deciphered three words: Chai, Infapro, camp. As he drove his half-fixed vehicle in their direction with steering fluid leaking, Gillian and Ade followed their hand compass west until they hit a road. They called Wong again. This time the signal was marginally better. Gill tried to tell him Chai was dead, but her words were lost in crackle. Wong said he was on his way. Gillian and Ade turned north and continued for fifteen more minutes. "We walked past the camp, in too much shock to want to talk to anyone," Gillian wrote in her report.

Wong met them on the road at 7pm. His first question was "Where's Chai?" The answer upended him the same way the elephants had once rolled his truck. He cradled his head in his hands as realisation spread through his body. As adrenalin coursed, Wong pushed aside the emotion and took charge. He handed out dry shirts, then drove his shivering assistants back to the research centre to warm up and eat something. They swapped to a more road-worthy car, before driving to Lahad Datu police station to file a report. While Ade and Gillian were being interviewed, Wong did the hardest thing he had ever had to do. He called Chai's father.

Exactly a decade after Chai's death, Wong and I are working next to each other on his bench desk. He has been remote and pensive all day. Before I close my laptop for the night, he recounts the conversation. It's one he hopes he will never have to make again. Wong puts down his steaming mug, diverting his eyes. Outwardly, he stares into the depths of his fish tank; inwardly, into the depths of his soul. Time may have dulled the pain's immediacy, but Wong is still visibly shaken.

It was past 1.30am when Wong left the station and he was back there at seven the next morning, waiting for the police rescue team. About seventy people tried to find Chai that day. Just as Gillian had the day before, Wong dived in the middle of the stream. Others searched the banks. Nothing. As the cool moist air descended, fishing nets were stretched across the stream and dragged along the bottom. At dark, still nothing. On the second day, divers from the fire service descended into the river's deepest point. Wong watched their bubbles move back and forth. Still no success. Rain kept falling, and the river kept rising. At 2pm, it became dangerous so the rescue was abandoned.

On day three, the search team split into two. One worked downstream, one up. Wong's group was again thwarted by heavy rain and aborted mid-afternoon. It wasn't until Wong was driving back to the field centre that he heard Chai's body had been found. Bile churned in his stomach like the muddy river, rising to his throat. He swallowed hard, choking back tears to keep from falling apart. Reality hit. Chai wasn't coming back; his valuable life extinguished. Wong intercepted the car carrying Chai's body. With the help of the rescuers, he transferred the corpse to the back of his vehicle and took it to the hospital morgue.

Wong struggled to continue his research after Chai's death. His world seemed to implode, and he clawed to the surface for air. If not for two things later that year, he might not have emerged: the BEARTREK project and a cub called Cerah.

CHAPTER 10

Moving Mountains

"Come on Joe, we have bears to find!"

Chris Morgan's filming was eventually approved and, just before the film crew's planned arrival, the Wildlife Department entrusted Wong with another cub. As he drove to Sandakan airport to pick up Chris, Wong was excited to share his news. The cub's presence would give Chris an unparalleled opportunity to film a sun bear cub in its natural environment. Just as importantly, Wong had been given a second chance, and he vowed not to make the same mistakes again. The first baby steps of a soft release were underway—this time, the transition to the wild would be much slower, giving him time to fatten up the cub and her time to hone her food-finding skills. Cerah meant 'bright' and she promised a bright future for bear rehabilitation and the BEARTREK project.

For the next three weeks, while Wong flitted between his roles as tour guide and leading man, he was propelled into the surreal world of shotgun microphones and light meters. "I grew up watching wildlife films and it was very cool to be in one," he tells me. He jumped on and off his motorbike more times than he cares to remember. The two antennae on his handlebars wobbled like a longhorn beetle as he slung his leg over the seat and set off beside Chris, returning soon after for another take.

Filming BEARTREK with Chris Morgan. Courtesy Cede Prudente

Wong helped executive producer John Taylor lug the heavy equipment across the suspension bridge at the Bornean Rainforest Lodge. The humidity was oppressive as they laboured up the rainforest tower, catching their breath on the third crow's nest, seventy-five metres above the ground. Joe opened his camera case and started assembling. Wong had no idea what Joe was doing. It had been a long day. His smile and positivity were fading. Filming was so much more time-consuming than he had imagined, and he was getting frustrated. "Come on Joe, we have bears to find!" he said, only partly in jest. Eventually Joe tightened the last bolt, securing his camera to a large pole called a jib. He directed Chris and Wong into position for the shot—Wong in his lucky hat, holding his H aerial out, Chris pointing the direction. Joe swept the camera above their heads, showing the flimsy wooden bridge slats below. Once Joe was happy with the take, he beckoned Wong to the viewfinder. The shot was exquisite. "From that moment on," Chris tells me, "whatever the location, Wong would shout 'Jib it Joe!'"

Over time, they ticked off the visual wish-list of shots in Joe's head. Eventually, there was only one elusive shot remaining, and on the last day, it happened. The camera pointed in the right direction as a rhinoceros hornbill launched from its perch at eye-level, pinion feathers extended like fingers, its red appendage leading the way.

When Chris and Joe returned to the US to the editing studio, their funds were dangerously low. In this era before drones, the helicopter needed for aerial shots had devoured their last US$3,000, and the cost of production loomed into the future. BEARTREK wasn't a typical box office money-maker, so they approached the non-profit Public Broadcasting Service (PBS), begging for funding by showing a clip of their work. PBS was impressed, offering them an opportunity they couldn't refuse: making a miniseries called Bears of the Last Frontier, which aired in 2011. Life became a whirlwind for Chris after that. His star rose over the following years from filmmaker to host and narrator. He gathered awards which led to a guest appearance on the late-night David Letterman Show. BEARTREK was shuffled to the back burner, but never off simmer. It took on a life of its own, spawning both a 'bear ambassador program', and, to respond to the public's reduced attention span, a new short film production company called UPROAR.

In 2017, the film was finally ready for a limited screening for stakeholders. Wong flew to Seattle. He and Chris were nervous in equal measure as they took their adjacent plush seats in the front row. Chris had watched the finished film a few times with donors present, but he was much more anxious this time, hoping it met Wong's approval. As the credits began rolling on a dramatic Canadian sunrise, the headlights of Chris's motorbike dipped as he navigated a rough remote road. A lonely grizzly pawed the river. Wong was transfixed, transported to countries he had only dreamed of. Then came Borneo and his own story. Memories of filming flooded back as the disjointed takes came together into a cohesive and compelling tale.

Before Wong's eyes, Chris wove his motorbike through the jumble of honking traffic in Lahad Datu. Overhanging awnings on the multi-storeys above sheltered a colourful splash of drying laundry; steam rose from a Chinese dumpling stand. He saw his home through the eyes of an outsider and it gave him a new perspective. As Chris turned onto the unpaved logging road, dust rose around him dulling his shiny steel panniers. The creases in his duffel bags, strapped to the flat surfaces, caught sediment. He waved a greeting at an oil palm worker leaning on his scythe, then the GB sticker announcing his country of origin disappeared into the dust.

Then, as the footage neared Danum Valley, oil palms were replaced by more natural growth. The tyres of an endless queue of heavily laden logging trucks dwarfed those of Chris's touring bike. They were piled high with thirty-metre-long ancient hardwoods, ribbons of bark hanging like torn clothes off a rape victim. Wong felt emotion catch in his throat.

Finally, as Chris entered the heavily humid air of the reserve, human sounds were replaced by a symphony of natural calls, amplified as they bounced off slopes and gullies. Down a muddy track, he arrived at Wong's field site, coming to a stop by a haphazardly draped blue and white tarpaulin.

It can be confronting to see yourself on film, but Wong had been privy to some of the daily rushes. A younger version of himself rose from the wooden table strewn with books and equipment, tilting his head to avoid hanging hurricane lanterns and bananas. As he watched himself pour two plastic tumblers of instant coffee, he remembered concentrating on speaking clearly, making sure he didn't look straight into the lens while he and Chris lamented about the devastation of the rainforest. "It is impossible for humans to recreate the rainforest," Wong said to the camera. "When the trees are gone, they are gone."

As the theatre lights rose, Chris dared to glance over at Wong, hoping for a sign of approval. Tears were streaming down Wong's face. It was more validation than he could have asked for. "If the biologists were happy with this film, I was happy with this film," Chris tells me later, via technology on opposite sides of the world. Even with a screen between us, I sense a deep connection between Chris and Wong. Chris recounts tales of crawling through the mud with Wong, marvelling at crazy insects while the camera rested. He tells of a mutual understanding, both fathers grappling with work away from their families. Chris pauses, silence dragging as he unsuccessfully attempts to corral his emotions. "There is something special about Wong," he says eventually, through tears. "He's a great ambassador for conservation… we need more Wongs in the world."

The documentary's London premiere is a few short hours away. As he counts down the hours, Wong spends the day contemplating the ostentatious architecture of an imperial past, built partly on the bent back of his own nation. Before long, he will button his starched shirt and slide on a suit jacket—feeling out of place, yet completely where he needs to be. I wish I could be there, but I suffice with pouring a glass of wine in my Australian living room and opening the link to the film Chris has given me.

Within the first few minutes, I am captivated by the wide vistas of Alaska and the magnificence of grizzly bears. A story of hope and adventure unfolds, from the macro to the micro, with the crowning climatic conclusion the story of little Cerah. My heart melts as Chris extends his hand and Cerah's long pink tongue licks off the salty sweat. Her dog-like snout pushes against the bars like a toddler against glass, exposing healthy pink gums. Cerah reaches out and Chris grasps her paw as if he is a parent guiding her over a busy road. Watching on, Wong's youthful pride is palpable. It is obvious from the film that Cerah stole his heart like Little One before her. I watch Wong open the cage, clucking to grab Cerah's attention. She is free. Uncontrollable joy courses through her limbs, turning her in circles. She bounces off branches, covering herself with leaves. Cerah stands on her hind legs, her arms flailing like she's swatting a fly. She shimmies up a sapling, hangs upside down by one arm, then slides down. It's poetic, every blissful moment of the footage engorging my heart. I raise my glass in toast.

Gradually, after Chris and the film team left Borneo, Wong came to terms with Chai's loss, as he realised the importance of his work. All around the world, man's influence was impacting on wildlife and natural systems. In the last two years alone, the Chinese river dolphin and the Caribbean monk seal had been declared extinct. As Wong clawed back his resilience, the dream of a sun bear rescue centre re-emerged. This time, the three-legged stool of money, skill, and location was balanced—the team of Wong, Ian, Robert, Cynthia, and Nancy had the power to make change.

In 2008, as part of his role at the Sabah Forestry Department, Robert managed a large swathe of land adjacent to Sepilok which was also part of the Kabili-Sepilok Forest Reserve. On it, he had built an environmental education facility called the Rainforest Discovery Centre (RDC) which he calls the 'friendly interface' between the Forestry Department and the public. Robert and the director, now known as the Chief Conservator of Forests, were open to the idea of integrating a sun bear facility.

On our strategically timed Skype interview, the sun not yet up in Scotland but just setting in Australia, Ian Hall tells me ninety percent of any new design job is figuring out the brief and matching it to the site. He and Wong itched to explore. Robert met them at the RDC entrance, handed them a map, and pointed down the path. They meandered through discovery trails, stopping to rotate their compass before continuing towards the jewel in the crown—a 237m-long canopy walkway strung between two towers. Excitedly, they climbed the spiral staircase, turning circles like a liana vine, to a vantage point twenty-five metres above the ground. Possibilities were laid out like a cake cabinet before them, and questions ricocheted off the canopy: Could they create bear pens directly beneath? How would they fence the rainforest to ensure the animals didn't escape? What size buildings did they need? What sort of access was required? How did the slopes affect the design? Slowly the centre materialised in their minds like a mirage. The edges were fuzzy, but the framework was stable.

When they were certain they were picturing the same thing, Wong bounced the ideas off Cynthia and more brainstorming began. The same Sylvia who had worked with Wong in Danum Valley, had accepted a position with Cynthia at LEAP. She and her colleague Heather (who had once worked in law) crafted all the ideas into a proposal. It was presented to the Forestry Department, which managed the Forest Reserve, and Sabah Wildlife, keeper of the bears. Wong felt confident—he knew the Sabah Wildlife Director, Laurentius Ambu, was receiving complaints about bear welfare. He knew his plan offered a solution.

None of them expected the answer they got: if they based the Bornean Sun Bear Conservation Centre at the Rainforest Discovery Centre, Sabah Wildlife wasn't going to give them the bears. The reasons were never convincingly articulated, likely political. Sabah Wildlife had started its life as a department within Forestry and clawed its independence. Perhaps moving the bears back to Forestry land appeared a backward step. Rather than dismiss the idea entirely, however, the director was willing to reconsider the plan if the centre was built on Sabah Wildlife land next to the Orangutan Centre. Wong and Ian laced up their boots and began trudging through the forest again. They were unaware that the future of Sepilok's bears would be tied to the fate of the Sumatran Rhino.

Sumatran rhinos are one of the world's most ancient mammals: fossil records show they have roamed earth for over twenty million years. Just like bear bile and paws, however, rhino horn (a hardened mass of hair), is a sought-after ingredient in Chinese medicine. Sumatran rhinos were relatively common throughout Borneo into the early twentieth century, but rubber plantations, superseded by a lacework of logging roads, made it easier for hunters to find their prey. Even though Malaysia joined the Convention of International Trade of Endangered Species of Wild Fauna and Flora (CITES) in 1977, the government failed to create a human line of defence protecting the dwindling rhino population from poachers.

By 1984, expert Nico Van Strien estimated the entire wild population in Southeast Asia at between 481 and 873. An emergency meeting was called in Singapore—it was agreed something had to be done. Perhaps fighting poaching was too difficult, or financial support wasn't forthcoming, but the Asian Rhino Group, created by the World Conservation Union (directed partly by international specialists) decided to capture 'doomed' animals and attempt to breed them in captivity through a network of experienced international and national zoos. Shortly after the agreement, two of the US zoos pulled out due to high costs. Then a public outcry rose when some of the captives were shipped to established breeding programs in the remaining US zoos, and a change of government resulted in a wave of nationalistic bravado which, in turn, resulted in the creation of two captive breeding programs in Malaysia—one in West Malaysia and one in Sabah. It seems incredible now, but the same new government that refused to send animals to the US and UK, gifted a precious solitary female to the king of Thailand, removing her from the gene pool. She died a year later, strangled by the fence in her lonely enclosure.

In March 1987, the first rhino caught in Sabah died in the trap. Three more captured between 1984 and 1995 died from trapping injuries. Those animals who made it over the first hurdle were cared for by well-meaning but often ignorant keepers who fed them grain rather than the wide range of leaves and whole branches they were used to. Grain was a staple of the more common white rhino, a species not even in the same genus. It caused the Sumatran rhino's guts to twist, leading to a painful death. Then the calf Erong, who had been caught in the wild, was fed full-cream milk which he couldn't digest. He drew his last breath in front of his keepers.

The gender balance of the captive rhinos in West Malaysia was heavily skewed towards males, and in Sabah it was the opposite. The two genetic pools were considered different sub-species, so they didn't share studs. This assumption (which was later proved incorrect by DNA studies) seriously impacted the success of the program which was further affected by a choice not to use artificial insemination.

In the wild, numbers continued to fall. By 1992 (as Wong tracked muntjacs in Taiwan), there were an estimated maximum of seven rhinos living free in Tabin Wildlife Reserve and twenty-three in Danum Valley. Poaching continued unabated. On August 9th, 1994, the Jakarta Post reported a further twelve Sumatran rhino horns were confiscated in Taiwan, smuggled from Malaysia. In the space of a human lifetime, the iconic horned mammal had gone from prevalent to close to extinction in Borneo.

The last breeding-program rhino was caught in Sabah in 1995. By then, nearly half of the forty captured animals were dead, and the program hadn't produced a single offspring. Spirits temporarily rose when the pair at Sepilok, female Gelugob and male Tanjung, successfully mated. Gelugob miscarried three months later.

In 2003, the West Malaysian breeding program suffered another devastating blow. Over an eighteen-day period, five more rhinos died. Officially a fly-borne parasite was blamed, but some experts believed poor hygiene was more probable. Out of a total of forty-four captured rhinos, there were no successful captive births in Malaysia. A total of only two offspring were produced, both in the Cincinnati Zoo, sired by Ipuh whose stuffed carcass now stares accusingly through Perspex at the University of Cincinnati.

Fifteen years on, as I research the disaster from my sterile Australian office, with the benefit of hindsight I am inclined to think efforts would have been better spent on protection and anti-poaching enforcement. But then the image of tuskless African elephant carcasses piled high flashes across my social media newsfeed. It appears the success of a ranger program is equally as unpredictable. Wong has come to believe the worldwide wildlife war must be fought on many fronts. While captive breeding with the aim of release is a good insurance policy, it can only be successful if it is based on a well-researched understanding of the species and safe, healthy habitat is simultaneously secured.

As Wong strolled towards the Sepilok vet office one early morning in August 2006, ranger James ran out from the rhino paddock crying, screaming "Tanjung is dead!" Pandemonium broke out, staff buzzing like flies, Wong following on their heels. When he reached the enclosure, Tanjung was pinned by a large branch. The splintered protrusions where it had split from the tree above looked like a fist of daggers. Together they lifted the murder weapon, but nothing could be done. Tanjung wasn't breathing.

The atmosphere was sombre that afternoon as Dr San, who had caught the first flight from Kota Kinabalu, sliced through

Tanjung's hairy hide to answer hanging questions. Wong focused his camera, recording what could well be the death throes of a species. Still in her pen, he could hear Gelugob crying out for her friend as she paced restlessly. Perhaps she too knew her kind were doomed. Tanjung's spinal cord was completely severed, so at least his death was fast. The lonely Gelugob was moved to the zoo in Kota Kinabalu, the Sepilok rhino enclosure abandoned.

Two years later, in 2008, Wong and architect Ian stepped over missing planks along the abandoned ironwood walkway with an uneasy reverence for the enclosure's past inhabitants. They followed the perimeter fence, climbing rickety steps and slashing through overgrown encroachments. At the far reaches, where the second sun bear observation platform now stands, they sat on the dilapidated rhino feeding deck in silence. Their necks crooked to the sky as they imagined bears high in the massive trees. "I could picture it then," Ian tells me. "It was at that point we realised we could make it work."

The men returned through the dilapidated buildings, their drainage channels consumed by advancing vines. Orange mildew crept up concrete walls towards faded facia boards. The corners of the tin roof had been folded back like a sardine can by inquisitive orangutans. They tapped walls—the structure was sound, so it would save money to use, rather than tear down. Wong greeted the nine bears like old friends as he passed their cages. He inspected their cages with new eyes, wondering if the frame would support an office and visitor centre. Maybe the old rhino sleeping stalls could be converted into the bear house? Wong started seeing the advantages of the new site: its proximity to Sepilok Orangutan Rehabilitation Centre meant they could share veterinary staff. The possibility of attracting some of the current hundred thousand yearly visitors meant BSBCC might eventually be able to survive without donations.

Ian, Wong, and Wai Pak travelled in search of the perfect cage and enclosure—Ian to the Singapore Zoo, Wong to Gabriella's centre in Kalimantan, Wong and Wai Pak to Free the Bears in Cambodia. When they returned, they combined their learning into a checklist: the maximum number of bears per pen, access for feeding trays, distance between water sources for wash-down, drainage inside each cage, the most effective locking mechanisms, width of corridors for keeper safety. Such details were incorporated into the first draft of new concept plans. With Cynthia's help, Wong then broke the proposed build into three manageable stages and costed each step. "I had to come up with a business plan of how I was going to raise all the funds for construction and how I was going to maintain the centre after it opened to the public," Wong explains. Phase one included the bear house, training pens, food preparation area, and a one-hectare fenced enclosure. Phase two focused on repair and construction of the boardwalk and observation area including refurbishment and renovation of the old buildings to create staff offices and a visitor centre. Phase three expanded capacity with construction of a second bear house.

The team at LEAP sprang into action—sending the proposal across a network of US zoos and foundations asking for donations. The goal of RM1.3 million (about US$300,000) would enable them to build the first bear house and the first enclosure. They had no idea how much money they would raise, so they also put out feelers to organisations willing to help build. The first confirmed group was fifty scouts from Ian's home of Edinburgh, who donated willing hands and backs for three weeks. Next, a group from Raleigh International.

Slowly, the money trickled in—US$10,000 from here, US$20,000 from there. At that rate, however, Cynthia knew it would take years to be able to complete phase one. She sat beside Wong at the round glass table in her office scrolling through her

MOVING MOUNTAINS

laptop spreadsheet to show him the figures. She proposed a major fundraising event, the likes of which Sabah had never seen. It would take the better part of a year to organise, but in a past life, Cynthia had owned a nightclub and run successful events, both in Borneo and overseas. She knew how much power events had for raising both fast cash and awareness.

LEAP took on the role of Event Manager. They hired dreadlocked friend and musician Amir Yussof to arrange performers, organise the sound system, and find artists willing to donate pieces for an auction. Amir rang his contacts in Kuala Lumpur. As I talk to him online, (now on a different trajectory with a hobby farm in New Zealand), I can't imagine anyone saying no to his deeply resonant James Earl Jones-like voice crafted from "years of whisky and cigarettes."

All the wealthy companies and prominent politicians in Sabah were invited. Deposits needed to be paid and air tickets booked for performers, so LEAP Inc. board members extended a bridging loan. It was late 2008 and ripples from the global financial crisis were starting to reach Malaysian shores. With two weeks to go, Cynthia was nervous as bookings were only trickling in. Before Cynthia travelled to Danum for a meeting, knowing she would be out of phone range for the next three days, she drew a financial line in the sand. If ticket sales hadn't reached it when she got back, she would cancel the event. They would retreat to lick their wounds.

As Cynthia handed over her ticket at the airport counter for the return journey, her phone vibrated with messages downloading in rapid fire. She held her breath and scrolled through. Her shoulders slumped. With only ten days to go, not only would they not make money, but they would actually lose it. She stared unseeing at palm rows below the plane, retreating internally as her heart sank to her stomach, but by the time the tyres bounced on the tarmac, she had gathered every ounce of sinew. She wasn't a quitter. At the office, she shepherded her staff together. "Let's do this thing!" she said. Like parts of an atom, Sylvia, Heather, Winnie, and Jacquie revolved around her centre, bouncing off each other in action. "We just called everybody—the Director of Forestry; the Minister of Tourism, Culture, and Environment, to garner their help with table sales, and the calls started coming in," she tells me. "It was definitely the moment it became real."

The morning of November 14th, 2008 arrived. In a few short hours, guests would descend on the Shangri La Tanjung Aru Resort ballroom. The event production team slotted the final pieces together: Amir directed men on ladders adjusting a bank of coloured spotlights on the scaffold which framed the stage; swathes of green cloth were draped like a rainforest canopy; banquet staff smoothed black tablecloths and placed polished cutlery; florists strategically dropped fuchsia orchid blossoms around the VIP centrepiece (a bed of bird-of-paradise flowers extending skyward); LEAP staff in sun bear shirts flitted. Cynthia was omnipresent. Run sheet in hand, she straightened the Chief Minister's place card and barked orders into her walkie-talkie with her phone glued to the other ear.

And then it began: a parade of dinner jackets and bow ties was ushered by similarly dressed waiters, nametags and youth the only indication of rank. Opponents settled into a one-night truce, having jovial conversations over grasped hands. Palm plantation managers mingled with conservationists, right wing with left. Voices lowered to whispers and petered out as Amir stepped up to the microphone, flanked by two other well-known musicians. He strummed a new song, "Calling on You," which he had written for the event. "We are not so different, you and I," it began. By the time he reached the last phrase, the mood in the room had shifted. "Give me more time," he sang, "Help me survive."

Celebrity after celebrity graced the stage, from television personality Daphne Iking and actor-cum-comedian Jit Murad, to Miss World 1998's second runner-up Lina Teoh. Well-known musicians sang "Return to Pooh Corner," John Lennon's "Imagine," and a rewritten version of The Jungle Book's "Bare Necessities." Paintings from local artists, including Wong's sister Siew Lee, were auctioned. Plates progressed—eaten and cleared. It was Wong's turn to approach the podium, his wire-rimmed glasses glinting under the spotlight. He grasped a microphone and outlined the problem through the story of Cerah, imploring government, industry, society, and science to come together in a solution. "He didn't blame or shame anybody," Cynthia tells me. "It was just very real... very candid."

Then it was her turn to connect the dots. Looking much calmer than she had a few hours before, in a black suit and postbox-red lipstick, Cynthia expertly congealed the narrative with a real-time PowerPoint of the RM650,000 raised so far that evening larger than life behind her. As applause died, she faced the who's who of Sabah. A power imbalance reflected back like a great white shark baring its teeth. Without flinching, Cynthia looked directly at the head of the government and said, "I would like to ask the Chief Minister to match it." All eyes were glued to the stage as Musa Bin Haji Aman followed with his own speech. "I think you are all waiting to hear my answer to Cynthia," he concluded. "Well, Cynthia, on behalf of the government, I will match you one to one."

On the night of the Bear Necessities event, a five-year agreement was signed between LEAP (which handled accounting and administration), the Forestry Department, and Sabah Wildlife. A board which would meet every three months was established. Although Ian wasn't able to vote, he was usually at the meetings. "I guess I was there as an adviser," Ian tells me. "In the early days, so much was about the construction and planning." Issues were batted back and forth as they attempted to overcome raised challenges of secure cages, poor runoff, animal sewage treatment, visitor access, and inquisitive orangutans. "The Wildlife

Department was worried about orangutans getting in, not being able to escape, and having fights with bears," Iain explains. "Some of the early designs included an electric fence on the outside to keep the orangutans out!"

Their fears were well founded. As Wai Pak unlocked the door to his temporary office in the old quarantine building, shards of plaster covered his desk. Dust was suspended in a shaft of light coming from a gaping hole in the ceiling. He held his breath, checked the corners for stowaways, then took stock—the only thing gone was his cassette tapes. He walked back outside to investigate. A roof sheet was missing. The culprit was nowhere in sight, but from the strength required, he knew exactly who to blame. Not the female orangutan who pried open doors, sneaked to the fridge, and stole Wong's lunch then sat within view, eating it on the roof. This crime smacked of the more troublesome male. Before anyone became injured, Sabah Wildlife relocated him, most likely deep within the reserve.

Life in Sabah is a constant negotiation between nature and architecture, but with the culprit removed, Ian felt more confident in his designs. The plans went out to tender and he and Wong moved onto the next big challenge—dividing the old rainforest enclosure into smaller sections. Ian explains an electric fence needs to be straight; otherwise, when you tension the wire, it will try to pull the fence over. They had no idea how they were going to find a straight line through the forest for the internal barriers, and, since they didn't know of anyone else who had tried, they really didn't know how close they could go to the trees. Ian and Wong settled on their own criteria—at least two metres from any tree trunks.

They tied a machete holster on their belts and grabbed a roll of string, some red tape, a hammer, a compass, and an armful of wooden posts. Ian held one end of the string while Wong walked with the other like Theseus in the labyrinth. He got about ten metres, then, stumped by a tree, retreated. Wong stopped to look around, flicked a leech off his arm before it took hold, and launched out again in another direction. Jubilant, he called Ian forward to hammer a post and stick high-visibility red tape on top, before setting off again and glancing over his shoulder at the waving flag.

Eventually all parties were happy with the final design; contractors were chosen. There was one more step before ground could be broken: the forest needed to be cleansed from rhino failures, which meant forest spirits would have to be asked to welcome and protect the bears.

CHAPTER 11

Many Hands, Many Gods

*"...your staff is your hands and feet...
all the limbs help each other."*

On Friday July 17th, 2009, three elderly women stepped gingerly across the brown earth where the bear house would stand, mud squishing through their slide-on sandals as they approached six wooden platforms the size of coffee-table tops, splayed in a circle like petals. They took their places on one platform each, turning outward toward the gathering. An eclectic sea of faces looked back, Wong notable by his absence. Cynthia Ong and the Minister for Tourism, Culture and Environment were still flushed from their heartfelt welcomes. Cynthia's brother Robert stood by a group of Junior Rangers, distinguished sliver flecks yet to pepper his temples. Ian Hall's head poked above the crowd like a poppy in grass, with the logo of Little One on his chest. He was flustered—the digger had been smoothing the site only an hour before. The Scottish scout volunteers he had been instrumental in inviting stood in a row, the past week's work scrubbed from under their nails.

In a cultural contrast, the three women were dressed in black skirts and elbow-length jackets, with bright yellow brocade around the cuffs and the bodice accentuated by a row of gold spherical buttons. Simple black and white striped hoods framed their worn faces, lying flat down their backs like hair, the peaks standing tall. One held a large parang, or knife. The women were traditional Kadazan Dusun high priestesses called Bobohizans. The last of their kind—more endangered than sun bears—their job was to pay respects and appease the forest spirits, and to ask permission to build. Also in the circle stood the women's tall, well-groomed male apprentice. His hair was parted and greased down, and he looked no older than the scouts. He faced inward, eyes downcast, minding the struggling kindled fire between them. Cradled in his hands, a live cockerel twitched, its bright red comb wobbling.

Ian's gaze settled on the cockerel as his mind flitted through the past few days. It was Cynthia who had proposed the ceremony, but as a conscientious Buddhist, Wai Pak refused to help source the bird, so he had accepted the task. "We need an ayam jantan bertaji, don't forget the taji, taji is important," Sue from LEAP had instructed him. Usually a weapon in cockfighting, the cockerel's heel spur, or taji, was essential. Its power would be used to cleanse the earth in a sacrificial ceremony called a Mongimpi. I am conflicted when I first hear about the cleansing from Wong. Internally I am questioning the difference between a belief in the power of cockerel feet and the scientifically unsubstantiated practice of ingesting rhino horn for virility, yet I am respectful of Indigenous practice.

As Ian waited for the proceedings to begin, he felt honoured to witness such a dying ritual but lacked clarity around his culpability in the bird's imminent death. He knew the bird was bred to eat, and still would be. Its death was probably by knife in either instance. He remembered the unpleasant smell of mould, urine, and death as he approached the poultry farm. He had been accosted soon after by cramped squalor, live birds climbing dead ones, cages under a direct sun, feathers flying from bald patches. He had turned and fled, instead asking for a friend's recommendation and plucking the healthy beast before him from its free-range village life. He contemplated the importance of treating all nature with respect.

The preamble prayer began quietly in Kadazan, dragging him from his reverie. The priestess gestured to the cardinal points then he held his breath in anticipation of violence as the parang was placed against the cockerel's throat. In one smooth, almost gentle motion, its throat was slit. Blood stained the earth. Relief—the experience was far less traumatic than the poultry farm, for him and the cockerel. Just as he relaxed, the headless chicken came back to life. He scanned the crowd. Death was too close for some of the scouts. Not forewarned, their anguished faces turned away.

The Bobohizan pronounced the ceremony a success. The offering had been accepted and understood. A more familiar Western ground-breaking followed. The head of the Forestry Department, the Wildlife Department, the Tourism Minster, and Cynthia joined the women in the inner circle, with ribboned white shovels strategically placed in front of them. The husky tones of Amir Yussof launched into his song "Calling on You" for the second time, with a token canopy protecting his sound system from the rain. Malaysian Junior Rangers provided the crowd with fact sheets about sun bears, a younger generation accepting the baton of stewardship. The multicultural ceremony concluded as a stocky young scout pursed his lips around his chanter, inflated the lung under his armpit, and, together with his compatriots, played a haunting melody on the bagpipes. The tune resonated through the forest, acknowledging mistakes of a colonial past and offering hope for a more compassionate and collaborative future.

Over 14,000km away, Wong humbly accepted applause, stepping from behind the podium. He glanced at his watch, sparing a thought for the cleansing ceremony, a cultural world away. He was at the Columbus Zoo and Aquarium in Ohio, the last stop on an awareness and fundraising tour which he had combined with a family vacation. The zoo had contributed financially to his research, so he felt it important to present his findings and ask for their continued support. A week before he had been in New York sipping from crystal in Nancy Abraham's stately living room. Evie had been on his knee and Winnie beside him on the floral couch, both in lacy white dresses. A crowd of the city's elite—their wallets exposed—listened intently to his summation of sun bears. Ohio was the last stop. He was looking forward to getting back to Montana, shedding his chameleon skin, and pulling his focus back to his PhD. Managing his many worlds was draining with BSBCC and sun bears far more insistent than his keyboard. He constantly wondered how Wai Pak was coping.

With the forest's blessing, Wai Pak juggled bear welfare, contractors, VIPs, and volunteers. The fifty Scottish scouts farewelled the bears. With their kilts folded neatly at the bottom of their luggage in preparation for departure, they surveyed their handiwork with pride. A strong comradery had developed as they sweated in front of the huge standard fan to adjust to the climate, then dug a wiggly trench and formed the wall's wire mesh. Through two nights they had laboured under temporary florescent lights to the rumble of the cement mixer, passing buckets of sludge and slapping them on the frame to fashion an organic-looking wall with built-in planter alcoves. Wai Pak had watered the seedlings, and they wondered how different the wall would look if they ever came back. It was their legacy—they had grown along with the wall. They said goodbye to baby Suria who had swung across the roof of her cage, trying to catch a glimpse of the action, and Kuamut, who had barked in protest through her sleep-disturbed night.

The second group of volunteers, from Raleigh International, dug backbreaking trenches around the entire enclosure circumference, starting work on the next secret weapon. Ian followed earth piles like mole mounds to find them taking a break, gulping from their water bottles, sharing a joke, living an adventure. He smiled as he remembered his own first impressions of this unforgiving environment. The pile of metal spikes next to them had dwindled since the morning. They had made good progress. Every ten centimetres along the fence line, spikes disappeared into the earth to a depth of four feet. He wiggled one: it was secure. Further along the line, an arch of fiery splinters fell as the welder linked them with a horizontal bar. The structure was called an underground portcullis, and it was based on the design of a medieval castle gate. Ian hoped it would thwart any sun bear attempt to tunnel.

A new volunteer team from Camps International was on its way and relationships were being forged with World Challenge in the UK and Dragonfly Group in Hong Kong. The Bear Action Team (BATs) volunteers were as international as the UN, and they brought in a thousand pairs of willing hands before Arkitrek handed the program over to BSBCC to manage. In October, the first individual volunteer, Californian photographer Jocelyn Stokes, flew in from another centre in Korea. She struggled to focus her lens in the dark cages, avoiding flash which would scare the bears. In the afternoon she probed Wai Pak for quirky traits then sat at a desk crafting short bios for the website. "Every day our volunteers give us is a day we don't have to pay a contractor," Wong tells me gratefully.

Buildings grew slowly and steadily from the mud like the ironwood trees surrounding them. Every day, the construction crew faced, and overcame, the challenges of an inhospitable environment with a laissez faire approach. They were under the incredulous eye of Ian's assistant Billy Dunn, an architecture graduate from the UK with a textbook understanding of workplace health and safety. By the end of September 2009, concreters had poured the bear house floor and columns while singing Beatles tunes. There wasn't a radio or a steel-toed boot in sight. By the beginning of November, builders balanced up swaying scaffolding and teetered on roof beams nailing corrugated sheets, cigarettes glued to their bottom lips. Billy suspended the safety elements of his Western education as two workers jumped into the excavator bucket for a rollercoaster ride to earth with smiles illuminating their faces, their children onsite watching with glee. By the end of January 2010, despite rainy season delays, experienced welders (without eye protection), put the final touches to the sliding bars, pulleys, clamps, locks, and counterweights that would make operations safe for bears and keepers. After a week off for Chinese New Year in February, they started on construction of the fences. Soon the bears would be in their new home, and, funding willing, the contractors would begin on the visitor centre, gift shop, observation platform, and boardwalk.

That's all in the past now, and I'm about to see the new centre in person for the first time. Wong thinks I am coming tomorrow, but I have checked into my hotel and the magnetic pull of BSBCC has drawn me to the edge of the rainforest. I am nervous. I know the bear house is operational, and the broken-down buildings have been transformed, but I wonder if the design will please my Western aesthetic. As I saunter past the roadside vendor, the smell of curry puffs wafts in my direction. At the parking lot, a small crowd gathers around a tree, where a young macaque entertains with aerial antics. Behind them, a large black and white sign immortalises Little One, announcing the way.

As I step onto the boardwalk crossing the stream, I squint with the glint from shiny stainless-steel handrails. A wheelchair-friendly path meanders deeper into green. It integrates with the environment, a transition from the bustling car park behind. Then, just as a feel I have been swallowed by the jungle, the trees part to reveal a patio clearing. Saplings strive upward from the centre of concrete soft-edged tables. The trunk space cut-outs seem ambitious. The meandering scout wall supports a film of mildew softened by greenery. Meter-cubed cages, designed by Singaporean landscapers Salad Dressing, protect shrubs from orangutan interference, encouraging new growth to poke out of the gaps. An oxidised iron stencil of the BSBCC logo stands tall, complemented by ironwood stools made from the remnants of trees reluctantly sacrificed.

I step through the open door, incognito, and hand over the entrance fee to a round-faced smiling woman in a hijab. On the other side of the airy room, sliding doors open to the forest edge. A small shop spills from the corner, displaying well-chosen gifts. I hear a canned version of Wong's voice projecting from the screen in a small theatre to the right, where four tourists sit on benches, enthralled. I pass through the building and climb stairs to the familiar observation landing. High in the tree before me, a bear naps, her leg swinging below. From the parking lot, I have been guided on a journey, leaving the human world behind. Sleeping sensibilities have awakened as I become animal. I feel inconsequential, welcomed into the sun bear's world, a privileged witness. I drink in the rainforest and smile, my fears dispelled.

Three years later, as I walk the same path again, the saplings have grown to trees. Shade-projecting branches now extend over the tables, integrated. Tomorrow evening the outdoor area will be transformed into Wong's restaurant. His wok and gas burner will be pulled from the cupboard along with a mix-match of plates and mugs to feed about forty—staff and their families. In Australia, most office parties would be catered by professionals but, like an Italian Nona, Wong revels in the opportunity to show his appreciation by serving his staff. The celebration amalgamates Christmas, Chinese New Year, New Year's Day, and several smaller festivals and religious holidays into a cultural concoction.

Wong's nervousness is palpable as he mumbles his shopping list. His culinary reputation is on the line, and nothing short of gushing praise is acceptable. We start at a tiny temporary wet market on the side of the road which sprouts organically from the cracked pavement opposite the Muslim school most mornings. There are no fancy marquees here, just small-time farmers and fishermen selling the previous day's catch or the morning's harvest. Reef sharks share a makeshift plywood table with their iridescent blue parrotfish and red emperor prey, equal in death. Two large enamel bowls, propped on upturned crates, display pipi meat and prawns. The stallholder hoists a large grouper by its gills, so Wong can inspect the clarity of its eyes. Notes are exchanged, the fish is wrapped in plastic, and Wong slides it into the hessian bag over the crook of his arm. Wong's eyes dart over the stalls as we retreat, looking for evidence of illegal turtle eggs. He sees no difference between the health of the oceans and the rainforest, calling out unsustainable practices when he sees them.

The second market looks like a carbon copy of the first, but we aren't here for fish—we have come for pork belly. In deference to the national religion, it's illegal in Malaysia to openly display pig flesh, so, like a stoner buying weed, Wong has befriended his butcher. Things in Sabah are much more relaxed than in mainland West Malaysia, where breaches by Muslim believers can result in fines and jail time. Eating during Ramadan, cooking with sake, and owning a dog are all offences. Wong tells me things got out of hand in 2016 when the Halal certification board tried to ban the term 'hot dog'. They weren't successful.

Our third stop is a narrow food shop in a modern row. Red and gold festive paper decorations in the window are telltale signs of Chinese owners, and, as Wong discusses cuts of beef in Mandarin, I try to identify fragrances and decipher products. The shelves tell a story of a colonial past, a multicultural present, and a reluctance to dismiss tradition. To my surprise, along with a splattering of Malay, Arabic, and Mandarin, every label includes English titles. Heinz salad dressing and mint sauce placate British expatriates next to two-kilo tins of Mother's Choice margarine. A row of MasterFoods spice jars stands to attention next to haphazardly hanging plastic bags of Chinese spices with hand-written stickers, their corners curling. I wonder which animal produced the 'Frozen Halal Boneless Meat' or what makes the minced beef 'Indian' when it's produced in Kuala Lumpur. On the wall-hanging price list in English and Malay, omasum (which I learn is the third stomach of the cow) is not only a different product from tripe, but it costs twice as much. Interestingly, it's much more expensive than tenderloin.

We've one more grocery stop before the cooking begins. This time it's a large, insanely busy supermarket. I push the trolley while Wong fills it: a bag of garlic; a bag of onions; five litres of palm oil (from an entire aisle of the destructive amber liquid); a fruit box full of individually wrapped mandarins which are traditional for Chinese New Year; five bottles of soy sauce, oyster sauce, and fish sauce; and several kilos of chicken parts. While I guard the trolley in the loading zone, Wong goes to get the car and a brightly dressed toddler squeals past me in delight, chased by her father.

Away from the mayhem, the open display of gallons of palm oil is troubling me. I'm used to it being hidden behind clandestine labelling. I question Wong why he doesn't use an alternative. "In the past it was all I could afford," he says. "Now I know other cooking oils, like soya, take more land to produce the same volume. The reality is there are so many people in the world, if we grew another cooking oil, more forest would be gone. The Amazon would be converted into soya bean. The only choice we have right now is to support sustainable palm oil initiatives to minimise the environmental damage."

Wong feeds his fish while I start peeling garlic. To his amusement, I've only got a few cloves done when he returns. "Do it like this," he says, putting about thirty cloves in a stainless mixing bowl with another upturned on top. He shakes the two roughly, like a James Bond bartender, and, lo and behold, the garlic peels itself. I frantically chop while Wong stirs curry spices in a huge pot. The grainy fragrance tickles my nostrils, snagging on the back of my throat. I'm charged with stirring until the oil turns rust-orange. Then Wong tosses cubed beef to seal and slow cook. At 10.30pm I leave him at the stove with a couple more hours to go, his laptop on the counter streaming a Chinese soap to keep him awake.

The party is only hours away. With the bears fed and the bear house kitchen scrubbed and hosed, the animal keepers pitch in by rubbing spices into grouper steaks and wrapping them individually in foil. In the nearest pen, Bermuda's nose wrinkles and he's hoping an extra enrichment is coming his way. One of the staff members sits behind the reception desk peeling more garlic, and my credibility rises a notch when I show him the trick I learnt last night. Three new volunteers bend over the staff kitchen sink peeling prawns. Orangutan Wilma sits on her haunches on the roof, under the shade of a tree, watching Wong lay out his mise en place. By 5pm, sweat pouring from his brow, Wong holds court at the fry station. The staff gather around the drink coolers chomping on potato chips and telling jokes. The theatrics of Penang Char Keow Teow begin as Wong throws handfuls of ingredients in the wok and tosses. If things had been different and he hadn't gone to Taiwan, I can't help but think he would have been Malaysia's answer to Jamie Oliver.

Nearby, slight-boned maintenance man Ronny and gym-built Jeremy ingeniously try to speed up barbecue coals with a leaf blower. Before long, marinated lamb, chicken, corn on the cob, and the fish packets are sizzling. Wilma wants to come down from her vantage point and investigate, but Jerome keeps her at bay by pointing his uncharged slingshot in her direction—she's destructive at times. Bored, she decides to shred a tree branch and make a nest instead.

I shrink to the periphery voyeuristically, with my attention ducking in and out of pockets of conversation. I am reminded of Wong's description of his management style. "Kakitangan is the Malay word for staff," he said. "Kaki is foot, tangan is hand, so your staff is your hands and feet... all the limbs help each other. I am the brain of this body, but we need all the body parts to be functional." He struggles sometimes with friction between the animal keepers and visitor centre staff. They are halves of a whole, but the former focus only on welfare, the latter on creating a tourism experience. Social events like this one help smooth the edges.

The next afternoon, the office, which seemed palatial when it was built, is straining at the seams. There's an overwhelming smell of varnish from newly installed floor to ceiling cupboards. They encroach on the already tight aisles between the centre row of desks and the wall. I am squatting at Lin May's desk while she and Thye Lim are in Tabin, and I have fallen into pace with the workday of others around me.

The weekly staff meeting is about to begin. I close my laptop and swivel my chair to face Wong's alcove office. BSBCC's eligible bachelor, Jeremy, is laughing with Ina about something that happened at the party. The rest of BSBCC's twenty-six staff are propped against walls or perched on desks, intermingled with volunteers. I am struck by the melting pot around me, a spectrum of skin tones and face shapes. Wong has told me his staff come from three different regions and eleven ethnic groups. Faiths are equally as diverse: Muslims, Christians, Buddhists, Taoists, and atheists.

Wong opens the meeting in English by outlining the process and encouraging newcomers and visitors to ask questions. We 'non-regulars' introduce ourselves, also in English, then Wong swaps back and forth between three languages for maximum understanding. All his staff learnt English in school, but their grasp differs. Ronny and David are much more comfortable in Malay while education officer Gloria (who's been at BSBCC almost as long as David) is used to dealing with international groups. Her understanding is nuanced in either. Accountant Audrey answers in English, with the occasional Mandarin word thrown in for clarification. I am struck by the ease with which Wong navigates and negotiates this multilingual communication and translates for clarity. It's chaotic and dynamic, like table tennis with three balls in play.

The discussion begins with wildlife safety. Wong tells the volunteers to give extra berth to black-faced orangutans, who are more dangerous and always making trouble at lunch time. He laughs, then becomes serious. "If they approach you move away, if they run, you run. I was sent to hospital after being charged by an orangutan," he warns. Wong arranges the distribution of radios: "If you are alone on the second platform when a family of macaques show up, call for help. I am not always in front of the CCTV, but if I see them coming, I can warn you."

Then, twenty minutes into the meeting, an orangutan (not black-faced) appears at the sliding glass door, trying to open it. Gloria scrambles to slide the bolt and close other windows. Wong is momentarily upstaged, and appears frustrated. He's had a long day and wants to get home. As soon as the shuffling and chatter dies, he asks for input from the bear team and maintenance team. I zone out to the melodic sound of Malay punctuated by the occasional English word or bear name as Ronny and David report... Jelita... bio-composite... tree-planting... "Holy shit!" I snap back to attention as Wong translates. It appears Azzry is investigating a possible tunnel attempt, a vulnerable spot in security. I am struck by the need for constant vigilance: this is no ordinary workplace.

The Buddhist Temple, Sandakan.

The next morning, Wong drives me to the Buddhist temple in Sandakan. We turn uphill to the south of town. A row of concrete figures leads us through a massive three-arch gate where we park under vivid blue skies and walk onto the three-sided temple balcony. Red, gold, and pink Chinese lanterns lead the way to the entrance, in preparation for the holidays. As we round the veranda, expansive views of the harbour catch my breath. Beyond the city to the left, the Sulu Sea glistens. Ships heading for the narrow entrance ply the waters between here and the nearby Philippines. On the lawn below, an auspicious swastika hedge symbolises good fortune and eternal life, used for thousands of years before it was flipped and commandeered by Adolf Hitler.

Wong stops at an elaborately carved wooden pagoda-like sculpture. He spends a minute with hands to his temples in prayer, then removes his shoes and steps over the threshold onto mirrored tile. He comes to his knees in front of an elaborate gold effigy twice his height, and touches his forehead to the floor. It's a private moment. Instead, I walk away slightly flustered, focusing on a series of golden dragons wrapped around columns, their heads extending menacingly.

As we drive back to Wong's home, I tentatively question him about his faith. After his research assistant's death, Wong found solace in Chai's religion, prompted by Chai's parents' generosity of spirit and forgiveness. He now calls himself both a Taoist and a Buddhist. The two worldviews mingle with his own blend of belief in the spirits of the forest. The ancient Metta Sutta prose helped him make sense of his loss and understand his place in the world, and it became a code he tries to emulate. Prompted by his old school friend Tze Ling, he has recently started investigating the holistic power of age-old principles like positive thought, gratitude, and universal law. He says the concepts resonate intuitively, and I agree.

That evening, I open my laptop, searching for a translation of the Metta Sutta.

"Let them be able and upright, straightforward and gentle in speech, humble and not conceited, contented and easily satisfied, unburdened with duties and frugal in their ways, peaceful and calm and wise and skilful, not proud or demanding in nature," I read. I'm struck by the similarities between the translation and the 1927 Desiderata which hung on the back of the toilet door in my childhood home—my own kindness code. I contemplated its prose so often, the words are etched in my memory. "Go placidly amid the noise and haste and remember what peace there may be in silence. As far as possible, without surrender, be on good terms with all persons… Speak your truth quietly and clearly; and listen to others, even the dull and ignorant, they too have their story."

I read on: "So, with a boundless heart, one should cherish all living beings; radiating kindness over the entire world… freed from hatred and ill-will." The Desiderata interrupts my thoughts again, "You are a child of the universe, no less than the trees and the stars. You have a right to be here... The universe is unfolding as it should."

We are not so different, Wong and I.

CHAPTER 12

A New Home

"Things never go as you expect."

After years of planning, the time had come to move the twelve bears one step closer to freedom. Wong was both nervous and elated. He had flown from Montana especially for this, and in only ten days he would travel back to the United States to write up the research for his PhD. He hadn't seen his precious bears for almost two years. Speaking softly, moving slowly, and offering a hand for them to smell through the cage, he reconnected with his fur family. "Is this Suria?" he asked, turning to Wai Pak Ng. Some of the cubs, like Suria, were new and other faces had faded from his memory in his absence. Realisation of the promises he had made to Little One and Ann were so close he could taste them, but if the process didn't go as planned, he would miss watching the bears take their first steps on rainforest soil. The potential for disaster had made it hard to sleep on the plane, and the strain showed on his face. A frantic ten days lay ahead. It wasn't much time to move the bears from their cramped quarters to the new bear house, integrate them into social groups and release them into the new forest enclosure. Especially since, only a few days before, Wai Pak had been bitten by a bear. The welfare of his team was foremost in Wong's thoughts. Planning for as many contingencies as possible was all he could do.

Together, Wong and Wai Pak had assembled an international volunteer bear team of extraordinary expertise. As I thumb through their names in Wong's report, a quote from Indigenous Australian Lilla Watson springs to mind: "If you come here to help me, then you are wasting your time. But if you come because you understand that your liberation is bound with mine, then let us work together." She was talking about Indigenous reconciliation, but she could just as well have been speaking about the global environment.

Cambodian Free the Bears program manager Vuthy Choun arrived from Phom Penh, where he cared for a hundred rescued sun bears and moon bears. Vuthy was charged with helping set up the electric fence. Dutch-born Annemarie Weegenaar, bear and vet team director for Animals Asia in Vietnam, had first met Wong when she worked with Gabriella Fredriksson in Indonesian Borneo. She was an expert in bear integration and familiar with the challenges. American Maria Trenary maintained the health of sun bears at the Oakland Zoo, California and had travelled with Wong from the US. They had driven the last six hours from Kota Kinabalu gathering supplies while Maria acclimatised to the heat, the smells, and the abundance of dogs wandering around uncollared and ignored. Maria came to monitor the health of the bears and help with any medical emergencies. Two Australian filmmakers, Malaysia-born Dr Audrey Low and director Howard Jackson from Wildhoop Productions, were poised to capture every moment on film, hoping to create a short film titled Big Dream, Little Bears. This assembled dream team was supported by Wong's bear crew and regulars: Dr Cecelia Boklin, the head vet from Sepilok Orangutan Rehabilitation Centre, and ranger Elis Tambing who possessed legendary precision with an anaesthetic dart.

The days that followed were fraught with logistical acrobatics. If one step happened out of order, the end picture would be jumbled. With careful planning, each bear should end up in the right cage, next to bears with whom he or she would socialise. To do this they needed to be introduced into the same cage one at a time until social groups were formed. Individual bears would then be trained with the electric fence before friendship groups could be released into the forest enclosure. The odds were stacked against success, and, as Wong tells me with a wry smile, "things never go as you expect." None of the team thought they would manage to accomplish the complete picture, but Wong's passion and drive kept them riding a wave of optimism. "Everyone around him picked up that enthusiasm and just wanted to make it work," Annemarie remembers. It appears Wong has this effect on more than just me.

Even with the numerous welded locks and bolts, when Vuthy inspected the structure, he found the guillotine den doors were not secure. The bears could possibly escape. The construction crew were called for last-minute adjustments. The outside doors were about a metre off the ground and Vuthy wasn't confident that the bears would climb down, so they progressed onto crafting wooden ramps using dense, unyielding ironwood. Meanwhile, they were still racing to get electricity connected. If it wasn't coursing through the six-kilometre-long fence later in the week, the bears would remain under house arrest. An inspection of the fence perimeter identified another problem. "The terrain was quite uneven and some of the mesh was not getting low enough to the ground," Annemarie explains. Even with the portcullis, there was a risk that the bears could sneak under the wire and escape.

Progress was regularly halted by tropical rain which turned solid earth to mud in minutes and dislodged dangerous branches. After a particularly heavy deluge, Wong dragged the film crew through the rainforest to check the integrity of the fence for the tenth time. Together they walked the entire inside length removing branches and twigs that touched the wire. Thankfully, there was no damage, but so much adrenalin was coursing through Wong's body that he had to crack jokes to keep sane. He was well outside his comfort zone. He knew of no one who had ever attempted to create a natural rainforest enclosure. In comparison, enclosures at Free the Bears rescue centre in Cambodia, where Vuthy worked, were built around sparse trees; and Animals Asia Vietnam centres had started with degraded farmland and planted from scratch.

At a bonding breakfast on day two, conducted in the mutual language of English, Wong's dedication was infectious. He took the team to meet the bears. The three older males were housed in their own cells while some of the younger females had already been integrated. Unfortunately, the youngest female, yearling Suria, had proven too playful. She had annoyed the other females so much that she was back in solitary confinement, and, as Wong and Audrey delighted in watching her climb the bars, they noticed a wound on her stomach. It seemed she had been attacked during the attempt at integration, highlighting just how dangerous this process can be for the bears. Wong's heart skipped a beat. He would never forgive himself if Suria succumbed to another bear just as Little One had so many years before. They immediately put her on a fasting regime so she could be anesthetised and assessed.

On day three, the wound had expanded to reveal a hole into Suria's stomach cavity. Elis drew anaesthetic fluid into his dart like a syringe, ensuring the carbon dioxide canister was in place. He fluffed the bright red feather designed to keep it true, then pressurised the fluid just before he took aim. The bears knew Elis, and, as they smelt him coming, panic set in. Their pace quickened. Alarm barks cracked through the rainforest. Macaques stopped in their tracks, and bars rattled as Om climbed in an effort to escape. Suria frantically ran in circles as Elis approached her cage. Maybe she hoped he'd miss a moving target. Despite the chaos, Elis remained focused and accurately discharged his weapon through the bars before withdrawing out of olfactory range. As the dart found its mark, a sleeve covering the needle moved back and the pressurised chamber released, pushing a plunger forward into Suria's thick skin. I'm having difficulty picturing this so Maria clarifies for me: "It's a little like giving an injection with your hand, but the dart is giving it for you. You can dial the pressure up and down. If you are very close to the bear you can lower the pressure, so it doesn't hit them as hard, and if they are further away you have to hit them a little harder." Within seconds, Suria was swaying like an alcoholic, licking her wound, and trying desperately to remain awake. The other bears' heart-rates gradually returned to normal. They had escaped for the moment.

As soon as Suria was unconscious, the team sprang into action, opening the heavy steel bar door, lifting her twenty-five-kilo body into a heavy tarp sling, manning each corner for the walk to the shiny new bear house where they hoisted her onto the stainless-steel operating table. Dr Cecelia shaved Suria's fur to reveal that the wound had been made by another bear's claw and was starting to heal already. She cleaned the entry and exit holes and determined that a couple of stitches wouldn't go amiss. The skin was so tough, however, that her surgical needles wouldn't penetrate. She ended up improvising with a stronger hypodermic needle. Wong looked on, confidence draining from his face as his promise to Ann flashed across his mind. There was no denying the risks of integration.

Suria spread out like a shag rug on the sterilised concrete floor of her new, larger den to recover. As fate would have it, the smallest and youngest bear had leapfrogged the two older bears planned for relocation that day. Back on schedule, old man Om came next. Elis estimated his weight then loaded the appropriate volume of anaesthetic and fired. Om was not impressed, pulling out the dart and throwing it aside before succumbing to the medication.

He endured more injections as he lay on the operating table, and each one was noted in the medical records I pore over: Vitamin B to combat stress, a general antibiotic, and Ivermectin to kill worms and parasites. Wong tells me wild animals live happily in a symbiotic relationship with parasites, but when stress is thrown into the mix, a normally innocuous parasite can burden their system.

Annemarie focused on measuring every part of Om from his paws to his penis. Maria monitored vital signs and Dr Cecelia collected blood samples. Wong hovered ever-present, overseeing the process when, unexpectedly, Om started to stir twenty-six minutes into his exam. His head weaved from side to side like Stevie Wonder mid-chorus. "Heads up!" yelled Wong, and the team instantly moved back from the bench. At sixty kilos, Om was the biggest bear Wong had ever handled, but the dosage had probably been more suitable for a forty-kilo bear. It's an inexact science—dart placement and bear stimulation (including movement) play a part. Maria's wits sharpened. At Oakland Zoo she would have suggested a top-up but here the pace simply quickened. Om was moved into his new den to slowly wake up—the proverbial 'bear with a sore head'.

With scarcely time to chug a litre of water, Elis, Wai Pak, and Vuthy moved onto another old male bear, Ah Chung. Meanwhile, little Suria gained consciousness and threw up. Time was tight. The more Maria recounts the experience, the more detail is dragged from her memory: "We would monitor each bear on recovery until they had their head up, and then meet up with the next bear as they were coming into the bear house."

Moving the remaining bears over the next few days was hot and thirsty work. There was no electricity to run the fans, so they worked hard, fast, and early to avoid the thirty-five-degree midday heat which sapped their energy and overheated the bears. Maria giggles as she tells me, "Before I arrived, Wong told me 'you are going to sweat all day long!' and he was right." With oppressive humidity during daylight hours, bear nerves and people nerves were on edge from the constant hammering and welding. After the sun set, logistical discussions continued well into the evening, peppered with humour and 'in jokes' indicative of a deepening connection. Repetition spawned efficiency, and by the fifth day, the twelfth bear moved house in less than fifteen minutes. The first step was complete. Wong breathed a sigh of relief as Annemarie, feeling satisfied with the accomplishment, packed her bags and flew back to her day job of rescuing bears from bile farming in China.

Now that the electric fence was finally live, fence training came next. Jelita was one of the most inquisitive of bears, so it wasn't a surprise when she was the first of the female bear group to venture into the concrete-floored training pen. Electricity pulsed through the wire intermittently, and touching it was a game of Russian Roulette. She tentatively nudged the barrier with her nose once, then twice. The third time she was not so lucky. As the bear team watched quietly from a distance, she reeled from a high-voltage shock, then pirouetted, ran back inside the den, and flew up the bars to cuddle with her two female roommates in the metal bear hammock. She was as far away from the perceived threat as she could get. Jelita may not have considered this a success, but Wong certainly did.

As fence training continued over the next two days, integration also began. With twelve bears and six forest enclosures, creating bear friendship groups was essential if all bears were going to have significant outdoor time. Developing playmates was also important for psychological wellbeing. Integration has even greater importance in 2018, with two bear houses full to capacity and forty-four bears to juggle.

The older male bears were positioned in neighbouring dens for the first few days. They tolerated each other well, so on the seventh day, the door between them was lifted. The team stood by with buckets of water on hand to douse hot-headed bears if things got out of hand. Fire extinguishers and pepper spray were within reach, but there were strict instructions that they would only be used in life-threatening emergencies. The last resorts stayed in their holsters, as Om and Ah Chung cavorted together for two hours, rolling on the floor and swinging from a double tyre swing until they collapsed together in total satisfied exhaustion.

Wong didn't sleep much that night. Scenarios flooded his mind. Stopping their flow would have been akin to holding water in his hands. Nevertheless, when daylight crept across the sky, he was ready. Jelita had led the pack with fence training, and, as the outside trapdoor opened, her curious nature could not be contained. Fresh organic air seeped in, clashing with the metallic residue on her tongue. She stuck her muzzle outside to test the unfamiliar scent. Just out of reach, a bee seemed to beckon her. Lin May tells me that Jelita has remarkably beautiful eyes. This was the moment the sun's rays kissed them for the first time. Looking up from her safe haven, Jelita could see the forest canopy. Her instinct was to climb up away from danger, but she was fearful of the space between the ramp and the nearest tree. She looked sideways at the fence. Scaling the wire that 'bit' her before was simply not an option.

Watching intently, Wong was convinced Jelita's unique V-shaped chest mark would claim victory, but even with his encouraging words, the hours slid by. Talking to me from the comfort of her home in California, Maria is a world away from the bears, but she remembers the frustration as the memories come flooding back. "We all had that dream that they were going to see the sky and rush out into the forest, but they were very cautious," she says. Disappointment weighed heavily on Wong's shoulders as he made the executive decision to lock the bears in for the night and try again the next day.

To coax Jelita out in the morning, the new ramp from her door to the forest floor was covered with branches and peppered with treats. Wai Pak even tossed bananas over the fence every time her head protruded, but to no avail. In the wild she would be accompanied by her mother up until the age of about two, but after years of sensory deprivation, she was content to simply swing on her new tyre and splash in the overflowing sink in the corner of her larger pen. Not to be outdone by the other females, baby Suria, who was still in isolation, managed to squeeze her bottom into her sink to cool down, sitting expectantly like a human toddler at bath time.

The hour hand progressed relentlessly until the bear team was forced to disperse. First Vuthy flew back to Cambodia predicting, in his parting remark, that it could take up to ten years for all the bears to gather courage to venture outside. Then, after a poignant handover to Wai Pak, whom Wong called "my right hand, my left hand, and my soul", Wong too departed for America. They had accomplished part of the puzzle but there was still more to do.

Over the next month, Maria kept herself sane by gathering bear poo and doing faecal analyses. Without a centrifuge to spin the droppings, she delved into the recesses of her memory for old-school alternatives. She successfully used a sugar solution and pilfered microscopes from Dr Cecilia's laboratory to improvise. Meanwhile, persistent Wai Pak, aided by a new full-time bear-keeper, David Tair, tried to coax the bears out. Wai Pak gave up on Jelita and moved on to Om, who preferred to pull the strategically placed branches inside his den and roll in them, releasing the fragrant leaf oils onto his fur.

Wai Pak's frustration escalated as the day approached when the film crew, Audrey and Howard, would fly back to Australia. Impatience silenced intelligence the day before they left. Without consulting Wong, he decided to take a massive risk. Only a few weeks before, Wai Pak had warned the volunteer team to stay well away from baby Suria's bars for fear of injury, yet the tropical heat seemed to have affected his reasoning. He stepped inside the enclosure. David stood by the gate ready, his fingers poised on the latch if Wai Pak needed to run. Wai Pak attempted to coax the huge Om out of the door by offering him a big hard plastic Kong toy. In trying to reach it, Om extended half his body down the ramp, but thankfully, considering the deadly power behind those six-centimetre claws, he clung tight to the perceived security of concrete with his paws.

Wong could hear Wai Pak's stress when they spoke on the phone that night, and, knowing he really had little control from the other side of the world, he agreed to let Wai Pak try coaxing much smaller Suria outside the following day. Inaction can be debilitating, so Wai Pak was ecstatic that he could now do something. He had been part of Suria's rescue team—the first of many experiences he would have confiscating cubs from remote villagers who swore they had been abandoned by their mother. During the long road journey back to BSBCC, he and Suria had bonded. Even with this connection, Wai Pak had never been given the opportunity to 'play' with a baby bear before, so he was over the moon. His thick leather gloves grappled with the latch, and his heart pounded in his chest as he entered the enclosure and approached the waist-high open trapdoor to Suria's den. He dribbled honey droplets from a supermarket squeeze-bottle along the ramp.

Even a bear Suria's size has dangerous teeth and claws. Maria, watching from a safe distance, knew sun bears have a fierce disposition when they feel threatened. She breathed a sigh of relief as Suria, who was tired of isolation, enthusiastically jostled with her new human playmate in the doorway—her jaws wide open, her paws playfully slapping the air. Turning backward and lying on her stomach, Suria slid down the wall, but the second her paws hit ground she lost her nerve and scurried back up. A little more honey, strategically placed, and she gave it a second go. This time her fear was surpassed by the chance to play. Suria chased Wai Pak around the pen for twenty minutes before realising she was actually outside. Then she didn't want to go back in. An exhausted Wai Pak eventually picked her up. Once she was safely secure, he couldn't stop giggling as he called Wong. "I hugged a bear!" Adrenalin coursing, he kept saying it out loud as if to remind himself.

Within two days, Suria climbed high into the trees, and, slowly, other bears followed. The smallest bear was leading the way again.

Outside can be a very scary place. Courtesy BSBCC.

CHAPTER 13

Learning and Giving

"Do what you do best."

The last few months of 2010 were especially difficult as Wong waded through literature in a foreign language, trying to understand conflicting advice from his supervisors, and juggling decisions about the Centre from the other side of the world. His upcoming dissertation defences loomed—one open to the public, another closed-room session to the committee. It was the final hurdle. He was nervous. His friend and fellow student Tammy Mildenstein calmed him. "They don't let you present until they know you are ready," she said.

Wong ran his finger under his collar. Its stiffness cut into his neck. A sea of students and professors faced him, their eyes intent, their smiles encouraging. On a nod from Chris Servheen, he led the room through his research questions, methods, results, and analysis. He had found a synchronicity between rainforest fruiting and pig reproduction. When aromatic white tree petals carpeted the forest floor from a mass flowering event, it seemed to trigger mass mating. The pig's gestation period, slightly longer than fruit production, meant an abundance of food when their young were born. It enabled females to pass on adequate nutrition and survive the depleting nursing period.

Wong finished his presentation and asked for questions. He was comfortable that he answered them well. Before he knew it, the public dispersed, many congratulating him as they exited the door. His committee remained. Their comments batted back and forth like a tennis match, not always in agreement. Wong took notes and asked questions. He had a month to tidy up loose ends and submit. As they rose to leave, each mentor shook Wong's hand. "Congratulations, Doctor Wong," they said.

Wong felt proud as he watched the thawing hills disappear below the aircraft wing. The end of his PhD journey was in sight and he was looking forward to the next adventure. He wondered if noisy bear Ah Lun had grown. If Juliani, with folds of fur framing his face, would still recognise him. He and Chia-Chien were excited about the prospect of settling down in their own home, but until they could, she had taken the girls back to Taiwan and temporarily enrolled them in the same school where her mother taught, giving Wong time to search for somewhere to live and somewhere for Winnie to study.

With so much going on, Wong struggled to make the final thesis changes; his heart was divided. The month flew by, and he was granted two more weeks. Those last two weeks were like the final days of a pregnancy, except the gestation had taken nine years, not nine months. All he wanted was for the baby to be born. He knew he could have been more thorough, but other commitments took precedence. The well-being of the bears was pressing. Finally submitting his thesis came as a relief.

With one less thing on his plate, the BSBCC dream took shape. The Malaysian Ministry of Tourism agreed to fund phase two (the observation platform and access boardwalk); and the visitor centre, office, and giftshop were underway, thanks to the charity arm of palm oil company Sime Darby. Wong was featured in a book called Wildlife Heroes which was read by a feisty no-nonsense forestry worker called Gloria Ganang. Inspired, she gave up the possibility of her dream job at World Wide Fund for Nature (WWF) to become his education officer. Meanwhile, in Taiwan, Winnie struggled to settle because her Mandarin was poor. By the time Wong found a house with a good school nearby, she was starting to fit in. "If we went to Sandakan, Winnie would have to learn in three different languages," Chia-Chien tells me during an interview. With her mother's counsel, she was reluctant to uproot her daughter again. "They decided it was better for the kids to stay in Taiwan and not move them anymore," Wong adds when I ask how he felt about the decision. He's holding back out of respect, but I get the feeling he had little say.

Almost everyone I interview for this book mentions how Wong's dedication to sun bears impacts his personal life, how he struggles being away from his family. The difficulty of maintaining a cross-ocean marriage is as unfathomable to me as the ocean between them—the life he and Chia-Chien led was not what either one expected. There were times when cracks threatened the foundation, but in 2017 welds appear to have added strength. Chia-Chien used to feel he chose bears over her, but not anymore. "Only he studied the sun bears; he's the only person for them; I had to let him go," she tells me. "Do you see yourself moving to Sabah one day?" I ask. "Yes, after Evie goes to university." It's long-term planning I can only admire.

In May 2011, as he adjusted to extended periods alone, Wong suffered another blow. The letter from his PhD committee to the program director hit him like a falling tree. "It is with regret that we have concluded that Wong has not met the requirements for a satisfactory dissertation in Wildlife Biology at the University of Montana," he read. The rest was a blur... "clear he didn't understand his analyses" ... "no strong link between well-developed questions" ... "discussion not supported by data" ... "lacking rigour." In a typical 'academic sandwich' where feedback tries to end on a high note, the knife sunk deeper with platitudes: "We recognise that Wong has done a significant amount of work to collect a complex data set under very difficult field conditions over several years and we greatly admire him for this amazing effort." He was "welcome to reapply for the program." The knife twisted.

Anger and puzzlement rose within him in equal measure. Wong thought he had addressed the committee's concerns. He's still unsure what actually happened. Trying to grasp how things went so wrong, I question his supervisor, Chris Servheen, who's still in America. He wasn't in agreement with the letter: "It was a complicated system of reviews, committees, and deadlines that had to be met. He took longer than he was supposed to take. Some of it had to do with rewriting his analysis, some of it had to do with rewriting his thesis, and it was complicated for him to get it done in the time period. The rest of the committee were really rigorous with this time issue and he made choices to put BSBCC ahead of his study."

Wong was the last PhD student Chris ever supervised and he is immensely proud of what Wong has achieved. "There are plenty of people with PhDs that do nothing but publish papers—they never really accomplish anything on the ground," he says. "I think not getting his PhD was a small matter in terms of the conservation of sun bears. His world-renowned effort to do what he is doing is far more important... I'm proud to know him."

When I met Wong in Borneo, one humid day in December 2012, I knew nothing of his recent academic struggle. I was visiting Borneo with a decade-long bucket-list goal to see orangutans, and as I hunkered on the viewing platform at Sepilok Orangutan Rehabilitation Sanctuary, my repellent hood pulled low and my glasses fogging, the experience fell short of expectation. Later, the hotel concierge, hoping to improve my wildlife experience, scribbled Wong's phone number on the corner of my notebook. I prepared my best journalistic voice and picked up the phone.

They say people look like their pets, and on that first meeting Wong looked like I imagined a sun bear. His amenable round face was framed by short cropped black hair which could easily be mistaken for fur. He had grown just as tall as he needed to be—any more would have been a waste. I leaned towards the extended arm and broad hands gripped mine. Wong was well groomed with a disarming smile, intelligence evident in every sinew of his stocky frame. I followed his yellow rubber boots through the overgrown jungle and musty-smelling abandoned buildings while he painted a verbal picture of his future.

As Wong walked me back to the BSBCC entrance, my mind spinning with the bears I had just seen, I asked what I could do to help. "Do what you do best," came the powerful reply. What was my best, I wondered? I ticked possibilities off my fingers during my flight back to Australia: I taught public relations at the University of the Sunshine Coast; I was a freelance writer and magazine editor; I had published a guidebook about travelling with children. Which of these were most useful?

I started by introducing Wong to Dr Sheila Peake, International Relations Project Manager at the University of the Sunshine Coast. Sheila flew to Borneo to meet Wong, conduct a risk assessment, and discuss potential research and education projects. They hit it off immediately. Unlike some academics and conservationists with species- or discipline-driven tunnel vision, Sheila says Wong's holistic approach to Borneo's environment was refreshing. Her help came at an opportune time: 2013 was a difficult year for the Centre. Wong squeezed the life from every ringgit, but the board suggested he cut staff, and his blood pressure rose every time payday approached.

Two science students started the ball rolling with a month's placement at BSBCC while Sheila explored other possibilities. The bear community is almost incestuous. Before long, USC was working with Matt Hunt, CEO of Free the Bears, Cambodia; Wong was working with researcher Hank Harlow from the University of Wyoming; and Hank started a research project with Free the Bears under a Fulbright scholarship.

Sheila roped in Senior Lecturer in Art and Design at USC, Kevin Todd, who was no stranger to Malaysia, having lived in Kuala Lumpur in 1995 and designed the airport floor I have crossed numerous times. Kevin was already involved in a program giving third-year students the opportunity to create new displays at Lataba Elephant Hall in Kruger National Park, South Africa. He listened, intrigued, as she suggested extending the project geographically to include Borneo. Before he knew it, Kevin was back in the tropics, discussing sign placement and crafting a semblance of story along the aerial walkway, with Gloria at his side. Unlike Lataba, these signs were outside in a harsh climate at the whim of wildlife. Orangutan opposing thumbs had been known to worry screws into submission. He promised to investigate materials capable of outsmarting primates.

Gloria emailed Kevin the final interpretive information in three languages. Meanwhile he skimmed the cream of students, emailing individual invitations to participate. Successful candidates eagerly squashed into his office to brainstorm design concepts: What sizes were the signs? How could they reflect the location's organic nature? Did they want colours to contrast with the rainforest or blend in? How would they differentiate each language? Which fonts, and what size? With a general understanding, and ideas itching to translate to paper, Kevin (acting as their art director) sent the students away to create fifteen concept designs. He met with them each subsequent week during the semester.

Kevin arrived in Borneo with full-size samples rolled tightly into a tube protruding from his armpit. He gently unfurled them on the long table in the staff room, grabbing anything heavy to hold down the corners, Gloria and Wong excitedly looking on. Over the following days, staff members gave their input, and a buzz of conversations bounced off the office walls as they took ownership. With the favourite concepts chosen, Kevin rolled the papers again. This time they had notes scribbled in the margins. Now the real work on the first twenty-five signs would begin. While the students worked, Kevin researched materials, eventually settling on light, transportable, modular aluminium sections with inks printed straight onto metal and a scratch-resistant coating.

While Kevin and his team manipulated the first concepts in 2013, I developed a different student opportunity: the creation of a sun bear adoption program, to be launched at fundraising events in both Australia and Malaysia. With a blessing from the Head of School, and federal funding for the students, I stood in front of every public relations class, the imploring face of sun bear Natalie beckoning behind me. An unprecedented twenty students vied for four positions. Like a reality TV producer, I sifted through their written applications, massaging skills until they complemented. In early September, the team was formed: high-achieving Saira worked in the marketing department at Australia Zoo and volunteered with animal conservation; conscientious Courtney was very organised with keen leadership skills, but had never been out of the country; Hungary-born mum Krissy brought a worldliness and self-motivated maturity; Nerilyn was an avid traveller with a Filipino family, event-management experience, and a keen sense of humour.

Our first meeting took place in November. Tasks were allocated, details honed. Over the next six weeks Gloria emailed information about bear needs and costs. The students created exclusive and non-exclusive bear adoption options called 'share bear' and 'my bear', and five bear gifts with equally engaging names. Modelling on campaigns like Oxfam, visitors could buy honey, hammocks, enrichment, food, and medicine. Local companies printed flyers and banners at no charge; Wildhoop Productions gave us permission to screen their movie Big Dream, Little Bears; and Saira's connections led to Australia

Zoo donating their wildlife hospital as the venue. We were interviewed on ABC radio and bookings rolled in. On January 30th, 2014, seventy eager people flooded into the small theatre. They gasped at the right moments, and were moist-eyed as the credits rolled, dipping hands into pockets and parting with notes. A week later, still buoyed with adrenalin, we flew to Borneo for a repeat performance.

The PR team: Courtney Angel, Saira Manns, Sarah Pye, Nerilyn Vetter, Krissy Morris.

It was 4pm on February 13th. The last stage of the project was about to begin. The students were ready, their bright green 'Save Sun Bears' T-shirts matching my own. They tacked posters on the glass windows advertising bear gifts, handed out flyers in the parking lot, and filled the reservation spreadsheet. Nerilyn and Krissy squeezed chairs into the theatrette, Courtney placed brochures on each one, and Saira tested the sound system. Torches were handed out to three staff to guide guests from the parking lot and rope strung across the observation staircase to discourage exploration.

Wong wanted to feed us all before the crowd appeared. He lit up the iron gas burner, glancing at a selection of stainless-steel bowls splayed before his wok containing peeled prawns, rice noodles, and bean sprouts. A two-storey egg tray was also within reach. Young orangutan Michelle was poised on the roof eves, a sentry ready to welcome guests. Sweet soy and garlic steam wafted down the path as the first young couple arrived. Wong was still not in his uniform but, instead of being flustered, he handed them a plate and chopsticks, instantly making new friends. Michelle was uncomfortable with so many humans. She climbed down and slunk away, her knuckles dragging. Mobile phones and wide eyes followed her exit. When she was out of sight, the humans shuffled inside, taking seats in the theatrette and spilling out of the openings. Of the forty-one who booked, thirty-three were there. Looking around, I couldn't imagine how we would have accommodated the rest.

Courtney grabbed attention by describing how the project capped off her own public relations degree. She invited the team forward. A huge fake cheque for AU$1,200 under Nerilyn's arm had been lovingly glued on cardboard that morning. I felt proud as I asked Wong to join us. I shook his hand and presented our donation, overcome with emotion, then moved to the back of the room as Wong commandeered it. I was struck by both his professionalism and magnetism as he enveloped the room in his dreams. Every eye followed his gesticulating arms, his energy rippling through the crowd. Thye Lim turned the lights down and the movie began.

Enthralled visitors from places as far flung as Scandinavia watched Om being lifted into his den·for the first time, and gasped at the climax when Wai Pak coaxed courageous little Suria into the forest. As Dr Audrey Low spoke her last piece to camera, the room erupted in applause. Then it was student Saira's turn—a call to action. Her enthusiasm was tangible as she used slides to explain the bear gifts and adoption options. Chairs scraped as the audience rose and inundated the shop in a flurry of generosity. In fifteen minutes, we made an extra seven hundred ringgit.

The following morning, adrenalin still flowing, we wandered together to the observation platform to say goodbye to the bears, a mix of emotions raw on our skin. A sub-adult in the nearest pen scaled the trunk closest to us, stopping at eye level. Time suspended as she held our gaze. When she broke the spell—a second, a minute, a lifetime later—I glanced around. The tears on four Australian faces mirrored my own.

Sheila and Kevin put Wong's name forward for the university's highest accolade—an honorary doctorate. Their nomination was scrutinised by a committee which included the chancellor and vice-chancellor, and was eventually successful. I ask Vice-Chancellor Greg Hill how Wong met the criteria. He tells me it was an easy decision: doing significant good is one part; being a leader in the field is the other. "It must have been pretty disheartening and miserable in the early days," Greg says, his own wildlife-research background and figurehead role ensuring he understands more than most. "Setting up the Conservation Centre was one thing, but going through all the hurdles and getting the funds to make it happen, getting the right staff and facilities for animals... he must have to pinch himself occasionally."

When Wong heard of his successful nomination, he was astounded. Long resigned to the choice he made to put bears ahead of his PhD, he still smarted with the knowledge of how much work he had done without recognition. Finally, it seemed, his commitment would be acknowledged. On days like this, Wong felt like the leader of a rising resistance of environmental warriors.

On September 29th, 2016, he stood to attention, in line between two other robed figures. He straightened his floppy cap, and glanced down at the kangaroos bounding across the necktie he'd chosen in deference to his hosts. He wondered if Chia-Chien was equally as nervous in the audience. It was good to have her here since her plan to join him in Australia was almost thwarted by a typhoon expected to hit Taiwan the day she departed. Wong was ushered forward as the academic parade made its way to the stage. He straightened his posture self-consciously and stepped up to take his seat, flanked by professors. He scanned the crowd, and smiled when he found his wife.

The vice-chancellor approached the podium, looking quite different from the man in a white shirt and braces Wong had met at the Centre's official opening in 2014. Wong listened as Greg sung his praises, saying he embodied the criteria for the university's highest honour. Applause erupted as he rose from his seat and passed the gowned row of academics. He extended his arm to accept a white folder, the gold logo of the University of the Sunshine Coast glinting under spotlights. Wong told of his work then thanked the university. "As a non-profit conservation organisation, we have very limited funding, and without the help from USC, we would not have been able to achieve what we have today," he said. "I hope the partnership between us can continue to benefit both institutions."

The next day, Wong and Greg signed an agreement to continue the relationship. The two organisations would grow together. Students would increase their international experience, academics would share their knowledge, and bears would benefit. "It's a good fit," Greg tells me, "whether it is writing about Wong, working with the bears, designing signage, conservation projects, or tourism." The grain of connection I tossed in Sheila's direction so long before had taken on a life of its own, the roots spreading, powered by her tenacity.

As the Centre grew, collaborations between BSBCC and other universities developed. One of the recipients was West Malaysian Biology and Psychology student Charina Pria. In her second week as intern in the bear house, Charina grasped a stainless-steel food tray in each hand. This was her favourite part of the day. She tested herself on bear names as she walked down the middle of the corridor: Simone's face was identifiable by a dab of orange, Loki's by a small bald patch, Wan Wan's by her cute pink nose. Their behaviours were different too, something she hadn't considered before she arrived. Wan Wan might look cute, but she had a wicked temper, her bravado betrayed by her fear of the outdoors. Charina smiled at her favourite bear, Sigalung, who was already sticking his tongue out in anticipation as she approached. She had helped integrate him with a male that morning, recording his behaviour on the form every minute. His reaction had been far more animated than with the female bears, prompting her to wonder if he might be gay. Charina whispered sweetly as she slid the tray in Sigalung's direction. Balancing another three trays up her arm like a waitress, she walked sideways, keeping her face to Bermuda. She knew she shouldn't assume his meaning, yet he seemed offended if she turned her back.

Wong understood that research generated knowledge while education passed it on, the two inextricably linked. Personally, he may not have published many academic papers, but he saw the importance of developing BSBCC's education department to act as a conduit, disseminating new knowledge to local communities where it could be applied. It grew to encompass three arms: daily interpretation for visitors, guiding visiting groups, and school outreach in collaboration with government departments and NGOs. "If we can incorporate the knowledge on local flora and fauna into the school curriculum, it would save lots of effort," Wong tells me shortly after meeting with the newly formed Sabah Environmental Education Network. "The Ministry of

Education representative says they don't have enough qualified teachers to teach wildlife conservation, so the next step may be teacher training." It's a long-term goal, but Wong is no stranger to long-term thinking. "Maybe in five or six years we can have a system in place."

Gloria's education team expanded to five, but even so, there were times she felt stretched. She listened carefully as the newest recruit multi-tasked at the second observation platform, focusing the telescope on Tan Tan resting high in a tree while chatting to visitors. She was enthusiastic, and she listened intently to the content; it appeared her new employee had learnt well in the bear house. She made a mental note to offer praise when the shift changed, then glanced at her watch. It was nearly time for rotation; the retail staff would take over for two hours on the front line. Usually, Gloria relished her time out on the platform, but this time her mind was elsewhere. It was the middle of the school term—their busiest time. A group of secondary school students was expected onsite in the morning, and the logistics of their visit were still unclear.

As I sit in BSBCC's office flipping through annual reports, I am astounded at how quickly the education program grew in Gloria's capable hands. Nineteen visits to schools in 2015 increased to fifty-four in three years, educating over 13,500 children in 2017 alone. There is so much demand, they haven't visited the same school twice. Onsite group visits grew almost thirty percent over the same three years, impacting over five thousand people. In 2017, a new education arm appeared in the reports: community talks. With it, Gloria and her team could start to address those people directly involved in animal harm or help. I put the reports back on the shelf and help load boxes into the back of Wong's car, then slide into the back seat with Jeremy and Ina in front. We have a long drive into the state's interior ahead. Tomorrow we educate.

I'm awake before Ina's alarm, stretching my travel-weary bones, stirred by a chorus of trainee roosters in the riverside town of Sukau, their voices cracking like pubescent boys. The sky to the east is tinged with purple as the homestay around me comes to life. As we drive away, mist rises off the overgrown soccer field and a woman in a java sarong stops hanging her washing to wave farewell. I am perched high in the middle of the back seat, so I can see the convoy of four-wheel-drive vehicles in front of us. Our destination is the remote Malbumi Group oil palm plantation, our aim to inform the workers about wildlife. This collaborative effort was organised by an NGO called Hutan (which means forest). The Sabah Wildlife Department and the Forestry Department lead the way; the Sabah Police follow in an ancient blue Land Rover with character-building bench seats. The team from the Fire Department is running late, so they will meet us there.

Jeremy is at the wheel and, for now, he's rolled up the sleeves of his khaki uniform showing tattoos extending up his muscular arms. Wong worries about the message this gives children, so he'll cover them again before he starts his presentation. Beside him, soft-spoken Ina's navy, bejewelled hijab looks like the night sky. It's folded and pinned under her chin. She broke her arm badly in an accident in 2016, so she's glad to have Jeremy there to drive and lift the heavy boxes.

We pull over at the river and watch pigtail macaques scurry along the bank while a blue and white tug pushes a flat-bed barge through the muddy flow in our direction. Jeremy backs down the ramp using side mirrors, without hesitation. Before long, we disembark the ferry and drive slowly. The road is flanked by endless palms, and punctuated with piles of bright red fruit awaiting collection. An Indonesian migrant worker with a long sickle-shaped blade reaches into the fronds to cut another bunch. In contrast to the rainforest, the ground is dry, causing clouds of dust to obscure our view and cast a sepia hue. Blue flashing lights on the back of the police vehicle cut through the thick air. For an hour it feels like we are approaching the stomach of the beast. The palms, like fast food, provide necessary energy, yet negatively impact the body as a whole. We are the probiotic, hoping to restore balance.

Eventually we approach a boom gate. A toothless guard, with her hair severely pulled back, raises her arm in a slow-motion greeting. Our narrow vision widens as we enter a clearing peppered with a gathering of solid brick two-tone-blue buildings. We unload our displays at a covered outdoor meeting room where wooden church pews face a whitewashed wall which doubles as a projection screen. A crowd of workers is already gathering. They are excited about a day away from the hard work in the field, and the atmosphere is festive. They jump to their feet for the national anthem, singing strongly to compensate for a scratchy recording, cupping hands before them in prayer.

Ina sits beside me all morning, translating as needed. In turn, the presenters talk about wildlife, environmental conservation, law, and safety. Many of the workers are migrants. They know little about the law, protected animals, or environmental damage, but they are the very people who risk injury from wildlife, who stumble over poachers' shell casings and snares, who decide whether to dump unused fertiliser in the river. Like most Westerners, I have been sold a story of environmental heroes battling evil plantation companies. Yet all morning, the workers are enthralled, and they ask detailed questions about how to change their behaviour. "I have broken the law in the past," one man admits. The regional police chief, Tukiman, responds: "That's the past," he says. "If you break the law from now on, you have no excuse."

At lunchtime the workers turn Ina's bleached sun bear skull in their hands; they watch the video of climbing sun bears in awe, stuff endangered bird charts into back pockets, squint down the sights of confiscated homemade weapons, and climb into the seat of the fire truck. Primary school children swarm in, classes done for the day. Ina tells tales of Debbie, the fork-tongued sun bear, to scrubbed, wide-eyed faces. Her questions meet enthusiastically raised hands.

The charismatic plantation manager seeks me out to recount tales of seeing sun bears eating palm fruit during his daily border checks and fleeting glimpses of the elusive clouded leopard. He says the plantation owner Edward Ang supports a reforestation program next to the plantation. He has planted over 2,000 native forest trees and purchased machinery to help Sabah Wildlife Department maintain habitats. This makes the manager very proud. In any other setting, I would have taken this animated, disarming man for a conservationist. It's a day of changing perceptions.

CHAPTER 14

Bongkud, Koko and Gutuk

*Individual bears take shape like landmarks
in the mist as I draw closer.*

I find myself contemplating climate change, apathy, fear, risk, and politics. Do we avoid climate-change discussion out of denial, or out of fear of causing further harm? It took Australia nine years to ratify the Kyoto Protocol; the political football is often tossed around with employment statistics. Was this deliberately misleading the masses, or political head-in-the-sand behaviour? Will history's hindsight conclude ignorance or wilful neglect as we grieve a world that once was?

On July 13th, 2015, the year before his honorary doctorate, Wong came face to face with the direct consequences of climate change. The visitor centre had been open to the public for about eighteen months. The office staff were preparing to go home, the reception team balancing the takings; and, with the crowds gone, Ronny was in the rainforest building new stairs from the observation platform to the fuse box.

The sky was heavy with clouds and the humid air was completely still. The organic smell of humus wafted from the forest floor, heavy on the senses, as the sky darkened. Heat was trapped under the platform, and even Ronny, acclimatised to the tropics, was sweating heavily as he worked. Sensing imminent rain, the bears started to play. Bongkud scampered up a tree next to the observation platform, higher and higher. She swayed back and forth, practising her wild bear skills.

Out of the corner of his eye, Ronny could see her climb. Such an independent bear, she was becoming self-sufficient—often building sleeping nests high in the trees and finding her own food by shredding termite-infested logs on the forest floor. It wouldn't be long before she could be returned to the wild habitat where she belonged. What a different bear she was from that day in 2012 when she arrived at the Centre with signs of severe malnourishment, sores on her head from rubbing her small cage in an effort to escape.

Damai, a fastidiously clean bear, wandered around the buttress roots at the base of the huge dipterocarp tree which dominated the rainforest pen as she decided which trunk to attempt. She could smell the rain coming, and wanted to get away from the impending mud and join in the fun above before irritating mosquitoes squashed between the pads of her paws. Ronny felt a sense of unease and called up: "Bongkud, Bongkud, go back to the bear house, go back!" But like a bulletproof teenager, she was oblivious to any danger—testing her boundaries.

Suddenly a wind came out of nowhere, creating a cacophony as it slalomed through the forest, branches colliding in its wake. A powerful lightning bolt a short distance away shook the ground where Ronny sheltered, causing him to catch his breath in surprise. He didn't have time to take action before a second bolt struck. This time it was much closer, and deafening. In a split second, he took in the scene: Damai and four other bears were running for the bear house. Then, instantly, everything around Ronny was whitewashed in bright light as the metal that supported the platform structure lit up like a fireball. His vision was gone. "It was just like I saw white paper," he remembers.

In the quarantine area fifty metres away all the metal bars glowed as electricity coursed through them. The bears' ears pricked up in fear at the intense impact as the huge hundred-year-old dipterocarp tree suffered a direct hit. The deafening crack could be heard from the office, but an adult orangutan taking shelter in the eaves restricted the staff from investigating.

It took Ronny's vision a few moments to return and, slowly, as the blood rushed to his optic nerves, the whitewash turned red. All the hairs on his arm were on end. He reached for the stainless-steel post next to him, but recoiled from the heat. The outside skin of the big tree was shredded, exposing its inner skeleton. Flakes of bark rained down. The mandatory rubber boots, which probably saved his life, were as warm as if they had been left in the midday sun. Time suspended and Ronny was so dazed he totally forgot about the bears. It felt like fifteen minutes before reality hit. He reached for the walkie-talkie on his belt and radioed the staff. The acrid smell of burning hair accosted his nostrils; he assumed it was his own.

As we sit at the BSBCC picnic table and he recounts the trauma of that May day, my heart aches for Ronny, whose eyes are moist with emotion. He is lucky to be alive, but cross-species survivor guilt plays with his mind. Bears are like people at BSBCC, and the trauma lingers as strong as if Bongkud were a blood relative. Perhaps even more so when you consider how few sun bears remain.

Rahim was the first person to make it to the platform. Taking in the situation, he approached the dazed Ronny while noticing Bongkud lying motionless in the enclosure beyond. Until Rahim mentioned the bear, Ronny had completely forgotten she was there. Her body lay where it had crashed from thirty metres above. The path of the lightning bolt was scorched into her fur from her neck to her abdomen where she had grasped the tree for support. The burning smell was intense as the bear team approached her lifeless body. Snapping into action like an emergency department triage team, bear-keeper Azzry organised a group to carry Bongkud's crisp body to the operating table. There was nothing that could be done to save her.

Wong was in Kota Kinabalu airport, waiting for a flight back to Sandakan. On the other side of the world, the journal Science had just published results of a study by the University of California, Berkeley, connecting lightning strikes to global warming. In the contiguous United States, it predicted a 12 percent increase in lightning per degree of global temperature change. Although he wasn't aware of the study, Wong had noticed the increasing unpredictability of Sabah's weather and he too suspected climate change. Just before boarding, he received a text saying there had been a lightning strike in the enclosure. It was followed shortly after by a rapid burst of updates: the power had tripped… a bear had been struck… Bongkud was dead. Wong's helpless heart sank as he willed the plane back to Sandakan. I imagine him checking the time every five minutes during the flight. He jumped straight in his car at the airport and drove past his house, directly to Sepilok. Any remaining hope dissolved as he looked upon Bongkud's charred body. Her fur was torched from her belly up her right arm and down to her groin; his nose twitched with the smell. Over the next couple of days, results of the necropsy revealed the only thing he could still hope for: she had died quickly from the lightning strike, not from the four-storey fall.

Pragmatic Wong sent her body to a taxidermist. Her skin is now displayed in Kota Kinabalu and her skeleton is used in BSBCC's education program. "She's still educating people," Wong tells me wistfully. The trees died more slowly. Over the next few days leaves shrivelled and flaked off like dry skin until the platform was carpeted with them. The smaller tree, to which Bongkud had clung, took two months to give up its ghost.

Bongkud. Courtesy Jocelyn Stokes

The forestry department surveyed the pen and identified those damaged trees which needed to be felled, then the centre closed for a couple of days to remove the fence and cut them down. All the bears were locked away, except Natalie who refused to come down from her nest. "Every time we fell a tree, something bad happens," Wong tells me. "It feels like the forest knows something is happening and it punishes us." It was 5pm when a visitor approached Wong saying there was a bear outside the fence. He followed quickly, only to see Natalie disappearing into the undergrowth. And so Natalie's thirty-seven-day escape adventure began.

Wong and his team had rescued a total of fifty-five bears over a nine-year period all at various stages of malnutrition. Sadly, Bongkud was not the first casualty. When one poor cub arrived, she had such bad osteoarthritis, caused by an improper diet, that her pelvic bone fractured when she tried to stand up, making euthanasia the only option. Little Suria, the brave cub who had led the way out of the bear house, was found dead in her pen one morning without any perceivable reason. Wong sent samples to the laboratory to unravel the mystery, but they went missing in the system. Officials and technicians pointed fingers, but no one lost their job and nothing was learnt. One of the other unlucky bears was Koko whose oil painting portrait hangs on the wall of the Centre as a memorial.

It was February 20th, 2012 when young Koko arrived after a seven-hour drive from Lok Kawi Zoo. Like Natalie and many of the bears at BSBCC, she had been captured by hunters the year before, her mother shot for body parts. Her owner, a man named Robert, had bought her from the poachers for three hundred and fifty ringgit (about US$80 or A$110). As she grew to about twenty kilos, realisation hit: this was not a cuddly pet, but a feisty, and potentially dangerous, animal. He sought advice from a friend working with the Sabah Wildlife Department who convinced him to surrender Koko to the zoo on the western side of Sabah.

Even now, when Wong's phone rings in the evening, his heart skips a beat like a parent waiting for a teenager to come home. When he received the call about Koko, the single bear house was stretched to capacity. Things haven't changed much since. There are now two bear houses, but they are still overflowing. Accepting another bear would put a strain on BSBCC, but there wasn't anywhere else for rescued bears to go, so Wong found a way to accept Koko. After she spent a month in quarantine, the team anxiously introduced her to two other yearlings, Mary and Debbie, to form a social group and free up space.

Just as they had when bears were moved into the new bear house, the first step of integration was moving the bears to adjacent dens. Strategically this was challenging because Koko's den was on the other side of the corridor. With a temporary plywood tunnel erected, they successfully lured Koko using a spot of honey until the bears were close enough to touch noses between the bars. The bear team lashed a branch inside her den, and after a year isolated in a cage barely big enough to turn around, Koko climbed along the branch, licking honey drops along its length, teasing bark strips with her claws.

Debbie and Koko made friends almost instantly as Koko stood on her hind legs, dancing in excitement close to the shared bars, but Mary was less accommodating. It was a slow process and several weeks passed before all three bears could share the same den. When Koko was finally introduced into the same cage, Debbie cavorted, climbed, and chased with her as they bared their teeth and jostled, then rolled, as one, across the den floor. Mary, the more serious and aloof of the three, remained less enthusiastic. Wanting Mary's attention, Koko teased her with taps on the back and annoying nips until Mary responded and barked to show her who was boss. Totally exhausted from a day of play, at night Koko and Debbie huddled together in the metal nest attached to the wall, keeping each other warm with Koko suckling her new best friend's ear for comfort.

Koko's rudimentary social group grew over the following year, as did the number of bears in residence. Eighteen months after her arrival, BSBCC was well over capacity with fifty-three bears and only three outdoor pens. The strain meant a logistical juggle ensued every time the bears were due for time in the rainforest. Managing time-share for the forest enclosure was a constant headache, the need to mingle social groups acute. Bears like adult male Bermuda didn't help matters. He wouldn't have a bar of integration, preferring to be alone. This put extra pressure on outdoor time. Wong decided to integrate the two young matriarchal groups, freeing up another pen for Bermuda. Even though two of the females were on heat, and therefore potentially more aggressive, Mary's group of six bears (which by then included Koko and Bongkud) was integrated with Natalie's group on September 9th, 2013.

Eventually, the newly combined gang of teenagers was let loose in the forest enclosure, and they proved to be favourites among visitors. Koko's relationship with Debbie soured when they competed for a favourite log, so she and Bongkud buddied up, wrestling and rolling together. Koko's favourite pastime was climbing to the very top of trees to reach termite nests high in the dead branches where her peers feared to go. Lin May held her breath as Koko tore bark in search of her prey and the branches cracked under her weight. Koko's traumatic past appeared long gone as she learnt, once again, to be a wild sun bear. Unfortunately, the good times didn't last. Koko's demise started with an oblong, thorny fruit.

Malaysian farmers, just like farmers all around the world, have used their knowledge and skill to improve the yield of strategic or lucrative crops. Sun bears love huge, spiky-skinned, pungent durian (duri means 'thorn' in Malay), which is endemic to the Bornean rainforest (you may remember it helped capture the escaped Natalie). Cultivated versions are, however, much larger, with larger seeds. Those larger seeds, as it turns out, can be fatal. "It's just something we didn't know," Wong tells me sadly.

August 17th, 2014 began with the bear feeding. Volunteers scooped cooled porridge from the huge stainless cooking pot, and divided it accurately into feeding trays using the weight chart on the wall. Snapping into action, a team of three delivered the food as quickly as possible to avoid stress to bears as they watched each other eating. Crouching down in front of a cage, with eyes focused on the bear within, Thy Lim lifted the trap door, slid the tray in, quickly putting the trap door back down with a clang reminiscent of old prison movies. In pens where there were two bears, the second helping was tipped onto a banana leaf worthy of any five-star tropical resort, and slid under the bars.

While the bears ate, the feeding team cut up over ten kilos of fruit in chunks before returning to collect the feeding trays. Many of the bears paced as they waited for the doors to the rainforest to open. The cleaning crew also waited, gathering their tools. It was then that Thy Lim noticed Koko had thrown up her breakfast, and she was drinking excessively. He made a note on her chart. For the next few days, Thy Lim and Wong were attentive. "She would eat the porridge and after two minutes it all came up, and it was like this for several days," Wong tells me. There was no sign of improvement and no indication what was causing her distress. An x-ray of her dietary system was needed, but at that time, such facilities didn't exist at Sepilok.

Taking a child for an x-ray can be an inconvenience, but taking a sun bear for an x-ray is an adventure with a whole different level of complexity. The nearest x-ray machine was in a medical clinic at Mile 8, a town twenty kilometres from Sepilok. Wong alerted the clinic while Koko was sedated for transport. His eyes dart sideways to access a mental image, and he smiles as he recounts the startled look on the other patients' faces as a sun bear was carried through the front door on a canvas stretcher. Frustratingly, after all that effort, nothing showed up on the x-ray, but Wong knew there was something wrong.

Koko was further sedated, and the team put her back in the transportation cage and drove her eight hours to Kota Kinabalu to a renowned wildlife vet who agreed to operate. Her distended stomach revealed its secret, a cultivated durian seed acting as a plug and restricting the digested contents of Koko's stomach from continuing down the small intestine.

Relieved, Wong thought they had averted disaster, and promptly removed all durian fruit from the walk-in refrigerator. The team nursed Koko back from the operation only to find she was still unable to keep food down. Without adequate sustenance, two days later Koko passed away. The subsequent necropsy found a second seed stuck in her oesophagus. Wong was devastated. He had vowed to take care of bears, not harm them. He had done the best he could, but Koko still died in his care.

I slide Koko's file back into the space on the BSBCC office shelf and grab another, voyeuristically flipping through bear medical records to get a sense of the mundane work behind maintaining forty-two bears. Rather than sending me to sleep, individual bears take shape like landmarks in the mist as I draw closer. Their histories provide glimpses into their traumas and celebrations, their friendships and foes. They tell a different story too, of a well-oiled process and organisational structure. Medical records of the older bears before Wong took over their care are sketchy at best, and from what I have been told, their care was equally as lackadaisical. Then, from 2009, records are complete and thorough.

Each bear undergoes an annual examination to record body weight, age, pad length and width, claw length, head circumference, chest girth, shank length, nipple colour, fat level, and evidence of any injury. These records paint a medical history much like our own: drugs given, reasons, amounts, blood counts (including electrolytes, renal function, liver function, and white cell count). As a non-medical professional, I cannot distinguish the Latin terms until I come across a test conducted on David's favourite bear, Om, on September 8th, 2011. It is a melioidosis serology test with negative results. I jump on Google to discover this is an infectious disease which lives in the soil, but it is the pathology note that grabs my attention. "Please note that the melioidosis IFAT testing is currently done only on human serum," it says. "It has never been tested for use or validated on animal serum. Please interpret results based on clinical symptoms." This footnote, more than anything else I see, awakens me to how little science is known about sun bears, and how important and ground-breaking Wong's research is.

I am starting to see double from reading endless records. It is 5pm. Ernie is shutting down her laptop, Audrey is gathering her lunch box, Jeremy is plugging in his walkie-talkie and turning off his brain for the night. Wong and I are last to leave, and we wander around the centre checking that all the doors are sufficiently locked to protect from marauding orangutans. As we turn off the lights on the rainforest aquarium, Wong appears annoyed that the office staff forgot this last step, but it is a half-hearted whinge, an indication of his extraordinary level of commitment to his fish than their lack of concern; not a real bone of contention.

We exit through the cloakroom where Ronny would have grabbed the footwear that saved his life. On the vertical end of the shelf, twenty-six dog-eared cards are slotted into a rack next to an old-fashioned punch-card machine. Wong grabs his timecard, and, as the machine takes a bite, he laughs that he's not done the required hours and is 'in the red' again. As he sticks the redundant card back in its sleeve, I ask why he punches in at all. He looks at me without understanding for a split second then shrugs. "Everyone does it," he says. "I want to make sure I am the same as the other staff." But of course, this could not be further from the truth.

As we double-lock the door, Wong casually tells me we have to make a stop at the bear house; Gutuk needs an operation. He doesn't seem particularly perturbed, and I remember this is a relatively common occurrence for him. "Do you want me to stay in the car?" I ask, but he shakes off my concern. I wonder if he sees my wide eyes as we walk up the steps and dip our shoe soles into disinfectant trays.

My heart races. At no time in my wildest dreams have I imagined being present for a bear operation, and I am beside myself with the enormity of the situation. Sun bears are a threatened species, and even though Gutuk is one of the oldest bears in the centre, blind, and in no way considered for release, his life, like Bongkud's and Koko's before him, represents a significant percentage of the species. Known as 'the bear who travelled far', Gutuk was one of the original bears at Sepilok when Wong conducted his survey. In 2009, before the bear house was built and when the old cages were at capacity, Wai Pak was asked to take a pregnant bear, Manis, from Lok Kawi Zoo. Believing she could be cared for better in the birthing den with CCTV coverage, he agreed and swapped old man Gutuk in her place. Just over a year later, Gutuk returned.

In front of us, the stainless-steel bench, cluttered with water bottles and mobile phones only an hour ago, is sparkling clean. Azzry and Andy are inside Gutuk's cage, lifting him by the scruff of the neck as you would a kitten. The loose skin folds in their four-handed grasp. They place his limp body on a sling and weigh him before transferring him, belly down, onto the cold metal surface. The tip of his twenty-five-centimetre-long tongue lolls from his mouth. I stare into glassy unseeing eyes, pushing away comparisons with a game-hunter's trophy rug. Gutuk's paw is bleeding. He is no stranger to bleeding. In fact, he has a very strange condition where he seeps blood through his skin, giving his fur a strange reddish hue. If his fur is brushed with a towel, it leaves a pink stain and an iron smell.

Dr Laura (called in just as she was heading home for the day) is moving in to look at the wound, while the rest of the team start routine measurements so they can push back the date of his next annual check-up. This is the first time I have witnessed Dr Laura at work. She might be only four years out of veterinary school, but the team's respect for her was earned when sun bear Panda lost a fight. It took Dr Laura three hours to reconstruct Panda's face. There's no sign of the injury now, partly attributable to the extraordinary healing power of sun bears, but mostly due to her expertise.

Dr Laura moves quickly and carefully with few words, her team meshing like clockwork. Gutuk's canines dominate as Andy opens his jaw, exposing healthy pink gums. My heart races as I move closer to look—a primeval instinct of dicing with death. Two sun bears in nearby cages pace back and forth as if in sympathy, and I can't help but wonder if it would be better to have the operating table out of sight.

I step back to observe. The discussion is in Malay. Wong translates. It appears Gutuk's index claw has grown too long and embedded in his palm. As I watch, Dr Laura pulls it out, treating the wound. Sun bear claws are unique in that the finger bones extend inside the vascularised claw, giving a strength which enables the arboreal antics I have gleefully witnessed. In order to trim his claws and avoid a repeat performance, a smartphone torch is utilised behind the claw as a low-tech x-ray. The light passes easily through the nail, but not the bone. Industrial-size clippers (similar to those Wong used at the goat farm) nibble away at the crescent-shaped claw. Simple and effective.

This injury is evidence of Gutuk's past psychological and physical trauma. Most bears' claws would file down on trees as they dig for termites and honey, but Gutuk's haven't done this because, other than briefly stepping outside in December 2015, he is too afraid to leave the safety of his cage. He might be the most travelled bear in the centre, but it's not been under his own steam. Gutuk is too old to learn new tricks or connect with the instincts of his youth. After years in small, restrictive cages with only concrete underfoot, rain, soil, and leaf litter are a distant memory. "From the day they are captured and kept as pets, most bears never climb the trees and dig the ground again," Wong tells me. To Gutuk, the forest is an alien planet of unknown creatures and sounds, and the fear is heightened by his poor eyesight. He is one of the saddest examples of bear mistreatment Wong has encountered, but Gutuk is not alone. Sometimes, as Wai Pak experienced when he coaxed baby Suria outside, it takes able-bodied rescued bears weeks or months to gather enough courage to venture from their barred security.

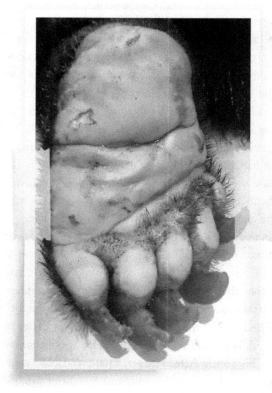

Gutuk's paw. Photographer Sarah Pye

As the team trim nails, I wander around the table, taking in every detail. Gutuk's age is showing. He is starting to lose the thick velvety fur of younger bears. His knees are tucked up under his belly in a yoga 'child's pose' which exposes the bottoms of his feet. This is a view I haven't seen before, the footprint is remarkably human. Gutuk's injury has seeped blood with every painful step, staining his sole with red streaks. The surrounding fur is matted from incessant licks. My maternal instinct is to spit on my fingers, wipe it clean, squeeze the puffy pads like cheeks, and kiss them better. I resist, instead sufficing with leaning into his motionless ear and whispering on behalf of my species, 'I'm sorry'.

Wong is keen to ease the reins on his staff, giving them enough responsibility to test their mettle and expand their skills. He rations out encouragement, and we retreat to the car before they complete the procedure. As we drive away, past Dr Laura's house, part of my heart remains on the operating table.

Leaning over the rail of the observation platform the next morning, I can feel Bongkud and Koko's energy. If they could counsel me from beyond the grave, would they accept the risk of death, singing the praises of their ability to climb to the highest treetops, to dig for hidden termite treasure, or swing from vines in the rain? The stump of the huge dipterocarp tree stands before me in testament. Another bear, Sunbero, languishes on its tabletop, light refracting through the folded wrinkles around his face. My thoughts are drawn to Gutuk shrinking in the shadows of his den, and I think I have my answer.

Contemplating freedom. Sarah Pye

CHAPTER 15

Too Close for Comfort

A chain saw coughs into life and destruction.
Before my ears, the forest falls to its knees.

However debilitating Gutuk's fear, it was justified. As Free the Bears CEO Matt Hunt tells me, "The wild is no bloody paradise."

As Wong sat on a chipped plastic chair, on the edge of the same path where he walked young Natalie, a lizard ran down the log behind him, its tail airborne. His well-worn lucky hat was fast on his head, his heavy cargo pants (repeatedly darned to keep them alive) stuffed into black boots. The walkie-talkie in his back-pocket buzzed into action. He switched it off before starting to speak into the documentary lens. "Human impact is great. Our species destroys nature and I feel a responsibility to protect it by telling nature's story so others know how special it is," he said.

Wong explained how sun bears are essential to the health of the rainforest. They are forest planters, eating fruit and dispersing seeds through their habitat, which keeps the ecosystem healthy. They are forest doctors, feeding on termites that threaten to fell trees if they are not kept in check. They are forest farmers, tilling the soil with their strong claws as they dig for food and enhance the nutrient cycle. And they are forest engineers, shaping homes for rainforest creatures by decimating stingless bee nests and leaving attractive cavities behind. He had done this so many times, the words rolled from his tongue, but his endless enthusiasm hadn't waned. He knew there was more to sun bears than their visual attractiveness, but he needed others to understand that the rainforest would be sick without them.

The cameraman scrolled through his phone for the last question. "What threatens sun bears?" he asked. Wong's smile faded. He slumped slightly as he explained they were in a constant fight for survival against poachers who wiped out populations faster than they could breed; their claws and canines were used as trophies, or ceremonial decoration; they were hunted for meat; their gall bladders taken for medicine; and cubs were sold into the pet trade. Survivors lived in shrunken forests, over thirty percent of their habitat gone to humans who had raped the land for resources and planted monoculture crops. Wong didn't touch on overpopulation—he had painted a bleak enough picture—but it wasn't far from his thoughts.

It's a thought which has been playing on my mind too. Are humans a weed species, I wonder, so adaptive we no longer know where our own native habitat is, so successful we threaten our own survival along with the survival of all other living things? Are we really the most intelligent life form? Knowing my interest, someone has sent me a video compilation of bears around the world doing 'humorous' things—swimming in a backyard pool, eating offered honey from a jar extended through a window, walking their cubs across a busy road, dismantling a bird feeder to get the seeds. These snippets are instantly endearing, but they serve to illustrate an alarming trend: bears (and all wildlife) are increasingly forced to interact with humans.

In November 2016, just as 195 countries prepared to sign the Paris Agreement and commit to emissions reductions, residents in a small remote village called Abai contacted Sabah Wildlife Department. A bear had been hanging around the periphery for a while, circling closer as he became bolder and hungrier. Villagers had been tolerant, but the bear had just broken into a house in broad daylight and stolen rice. They were worried for their safety. Testosterone-fuelled men inched within a few metres to take photos, then chased the bear away with arms flailing and voices raised. Sabah Wildlife sent the photos to Wong. It was hard to tell much from the angle, but Wong thought he could see a collar mark around the male bear's neck. Coupled with the unnatural daytime behaviour, and lack of fear around people, Wong thought it was probably a pet bear which had been released when it grew too big. "If the bear was semi-habituated, we needed to trap it and bring it to the centre," he tells me on a Skype call just as the intermittent Internet disconnects.

Wong hand-picked a bear team to join Dr Laura from the Wildlife Rescue Unit, travelling to the village by boat. It didn't take long to find their quarry skulking around the edges of civilisation. By 7pm, the 46-kilo beast slumped on a bed of leaves in the relocation cage, before the boat and car journey were reversed the next day. As dusk fell on August 24th, bolts slid home on the BSBCC quarantine cage. The plan was to observe the bear (now called Abai, after the town) and release him back into the wild in a couple of weeks.

Young bear-keeper Azzry hadn't been part of the rescue mission, but with the enthusiasm of youth, he and co-worker Lester checked on the bear at around 8pm. Abai had shaken off the anaesthetic and seemed quite relaxed as he climbed the bars. They offered fruit, which was refused, but Abai lapped every morsel of rice porridge with his long tongue.

Azzry was first at the quarantine area the next day. In the long-shadowed morning, he couldn't immediately see the bear. He pushed strands of hair from his eyes, stepping closer to pen number ten, a strange foreboding rising from his gut. It was replaced moments later by cold fear. An entire section of the bear cage had been ripped off, the metal snapped in two. Azzry turned full circle scanning his surroundings, sensitive to any movement or any flash of black; but nothing. He fumbled in his pocket for his phone and dialled Wong.

While Wong and the Sabah Wildlife rangers planned the re-capture, Azzry, Lester, and Dr Laura found fresh claw marks up a tree. Just as they had when Natalie escaped, teams fanned out through the forest reserve, and, to reduce human risk, both the Sepilok Orangutan Rehabilitation Centre and BSBCC were closed for the day. A relief team of vets arrived from Kota Kinabalu, and the search continued. They found tracks leading outside the area, but the ghost-like bear had disappeared.

Recriminations flew like shrapnel, the Director of Sabah Wildlife pointing the finger directly at Wong. The orangutan centre was permitted to reopen the following day with a 'shoot to kill' order in place if the bear returned and approached humans, but BSBCC remained closed until he provided explanation and apology.

Wong laboured over his written reply, stress furrowing his brow. Had he known it was a wild bear, he tells me a few days later, he would never have agreed to take it. As evidence, he shares images of barrel-traps folded open like food cans. "Wild bears will break anything and everything. As long as there is a place for them to put their mouth, they will chew; as long as there is a place for them to put their claws, they will peel edges; they will bite until they chip off their teeth; if it is a cement wall, they will keep scratching until they break through, " he says. "There was no way our facilities could hold an adult wild-caught bear. If he didn't escape that day, he would have the next."

Fast forward to September 2018, and reports of clashes between bears and humans had escalated. One bear bit a retired teacher as he defended his teenage son, and Wong installed camera traps to try and capture it. Then, in a case of déjà vu, another bear invaded a kitchen in Abai village. Sabah Wildlife trapped it, pressuring Wong to relocate it. With the previous bear on his mind, Wong was reluctant, but this one had injured himself trying to escape the cage. An open wound on his left leg needed treatment. With a new name, Ace was kept in the translocation cage for a couple of days until his aggression subsided, then moved to the strengthened quarantine area.

Two weeks later, Dr Nabila conducted a full body check. His wound was healing, but she beckoned Wong over to look at his paws. He had never seen anything like it. The pads were black and hairy, rather than the usual naked pink. Wong wondered if this was a genetic adaptation to the wet, muddy habitat. The skin was cracked and rough, perhaps caused by overly dry conditions since his capture. Wong fitted a collar around Ace's neck. There was much this bear could teach him.

Over the next few weeks, as the collar was tested, Ace tried to escape, breaking off two of his canine teeth in the attempt. One Sunday, Dr Chong, the dentist, performed root canal surgery. Two days later, November 5th, the last medical check before release took place. Wong breathed a sigh of relief—this bear would go back to the wild on his terms.

In the cool morning, as Wong and six other men manoeuvred the heavy cage down concrete stairs to a waiting boat at Sandakan dock, Ace's pink nostrils widened in the salt air. Clouds rolled in off the sea, rising as they hit land, releasing their load. As twin outboards pushed them upstream, the river narrowed. Finally, they reached the chosen reserve. It was only seven kilometres from the place where Ace was captured, with a fast-flowing stream between them and the village. Finding a gap along the bank was difficult, but after a few passes, they nosed in, and inched the cage from the moving deck to solid land. Wong glanced up at tall palms and ficus heavy with fruit. Beneath his feet he could see snails, a bear delicacy. It was a habitat far different from Danum or Tabin, but he was thankful there was plenty to keep Ace alive. He checked the collar around the bear's neck one last time, willing it to stay on and gather answers. As the door slid open, Ace climbed out and stopped. His eyes scanned the team, as if thanking them for their help. A few moments later, he was out of sight.

Wong is away at a conference. While I wait for his return, I am cocooned in a mosquito net on the top bunk of a small room at Paganakan Di Resort, which is used as housing for BSBCC volunteers. A set of double French windows opens onto a vast expanse of rainforest like the doors to C.S. Lewis's wardrobe. Through it, the eastern sky is tinged with orange, and rising moisture carries fungi pores into the canopy where they trigger a light rain which cools the roof and washes leaves. Out of sight, lianas circle ironwood buttresses, using their trunks as a ladder to reach sunlight. The vines spread at the top, stealing rays from below. At ground level, a dipterocarp tree being attacked by predatory insects excretes a chemical repellent, alerting family members by sending slow electrical pulses down what Professor Suzanne Simard calls the 'wood wide web' of roots. Somewhere out there, Abai roams, one citizen in a multicultural world.

The gecko who's been pooing on my mosquito net all night emits rapid-fire calls. Outside, a short-tailed, red-headed honeyeater darts between broad leaves, followed by its mate. In a palm, a squirrel chews any remaining goodness out of the blossom husks before running down the spine of a frond and leaping to a new tree. In my head, I hear a Cirque du Soleil audience gasp. Undistinguishable birds sing to the brand-new day, jubilant that they made it through the dark. What are they saying, I wonder? Is it one big news radio system batting back and forth? Does Abai hear the same as I? How far has he made it in the past few months?

The sound rises to a crescendo as the sun appears. I am reminded of a quote by American writer John Muir, founder of the Sierra Club: "When we try to pick out anything by itself, we find it hitched to everything else in the universe." In the distance, the melodic vocal gymnastics of an alto human voice calling believers to prayer echoes across nature's temple, in keeping with the forest ritual. As it subsides, another sound fills the space, jarring—a chain saw coughing into life and destruction. Before my ears, the forest falls to its knees.

The age-old battle between development and conservation flared in 2008 when a government plan was created to jump-start Sabah's economy by opening up a development corridor which included a bridge to connect the town of Sukau to Sandakan. It would improve access to oil palm plantations, enabling quicker access to medical care. It would also severely impact the tourism industry on the Kinabatangan River, open access to illegal poachers, and ring the death knell for wildlife. An environmental assessment was planned, but the forest was partly cleared for machinery storage well before its completion.

Sabah's state government was working toward expanding protected rainforest coverage to thirty percent of Sabah and protecting one million hectares of sea off the northern shore, creating the largest marine park in Malaysia. Wong saw the proposed bridge as a direct contradiction to this plan. He wasn't alone. In a tug-o'-war which plays throughout the world, the conservation community rallied. Communities were ideologically severed—some favouring progress over protection, others attempting to save natural assets.

At five hundred and sixty kilometres, Kinabatangan is the second-longest river in Malaysia, and the longest in Sabah. It's less than two hours' drive from Sepilok. Besides diverse flora, it's home to Muppet-like proboscis monkeys, screeching macaques, fleeting orangutans, gliding saltwater crocodiles, herding pigmy elephants, prehistoric armadillo-like pangolins, camouflaged clouded leopards, booming gibbons, and an elusively small number of sun bears. Feathered residents include darting iridescent blue kingfishers with pointed beaks longer than their heads, white-bellied sea eagles surveying their kingdom from strategically commandeered naked branches, purple herons with necks like a plumber's S-bend, and the iconic pied hornbill with a beak appendage like the sight on a rifle.

In the West, much of our knowledge about the creatures along the river comes from documentaries narrated by Sir David Attenborough. On his first visit in the 1950s, Attenborough was charged with the job of producing a series called Zoo Quest in which he travelled around the world with London Zoo curator Jack Lester. Like Victorian gentlemen, they captured animals for the zoo's collection, filming their habitats. Fate had it that Lester became ill from an undiagnosed tropical disease after presenting one instalment, and, since the program was already scheduled, Attenborough slid in front of the camera, never looking back. Most recently, Attenborough visited BSBCC in 2014, standing in the same spot on the observation platform where I had been two weeks before.

Kinabatangan River. Sarah Pye.

Few visitors leave Sabah without visiting the river he traversed. My daughter Amber and I are no exception. As dawn comes to the misty river, we are shepherded into a wooden longboat which carves a swathe through reflections of pink-tinged skies. Dense trees lean towards us, vines dripping like decorations. Glimpses of encroaching palm plantations through rainforest gaps give the impression of a Hollywood film set. The pristine paradise façade I see through the narrow view of my camera lens is in contrast to the reality of the white-bellied sea eagle flying overhead, its black feather tips spread. Beyond the jumbled green wildlife corridor, rich in food and nesting sites, the eagle sees uniform tufted trunks standing like soldiers at a border crossing, or graves in a war cemetery. The government may have legislated a hundred-and-fifty-metre-wide no-mans-land, but the river doesn't respect absolutes. It claws back the corners, meandering closer to the boundary and squeezing endangered species into an ever-shrinking fringe.

In 2017, it appeared the bridge would go ahead, meaning the environment would have been sacrificed. Then the plight of the remaining one and a half thousand pigmy elephants at Kinabatangan prompted Sir David Attenborough to reverse his normally unpolitical stance. "If this construction is allowed to go ahead, I am left in no doubt that the bridge will have significant negative effects on the region's wildlife, the Kinabatangan's thriving tourism industry, and on the image of Sabah as a whole," Attenborough wrote in a letter to Sabah's Chief Minister Musa Aman. It was the penny that tipped the scales. On April 19th, nine years after the fight began, Sabah Forest Department chief Conservator Sam Mannan announced they were scrapping the planned bridge. Wong and the rest of the hardworking conservation community celebrated briefly, then went back to work.

Wong was grateful for the weight of Attenborough's voice, yet he hoped by the next globally significant challenge in Sabah, the protests of the local conservation community would be loud enough. Intuitively, he knew Sabah needed a local figurehead, rather than a colonial one. "This is my country. I grew up here," Wong tells me. "I must protect my own country, and my own wildlife. It's not a responsibility I was given, but one I choose to take," he says as his shoulders slump slightly. "If I fail, I will have to deal with it every day. I can't just pack up and go home."

Wong's words unintentionally cut deep as I realise I fall in the category of people who can just 'go home'. Why, I wonder, am I not more vocal about habitat destruction in my own backyard? In the not-too-distant future, when I tell my grandchildren I used to see kangaroos every day on my university grounds, will I shrug off the change as progress, or will I accept my inaction as part of their demise?

Loss of habitat is only one of the ways development threatens wildlife in Borneo. "The pressures of hunting and poaching are increasing because habitat loss has caused bears to be confined in smaller areas, closer to humans," Wong explains. "There are more roads through the remaining wild pockets which makes it easier for hunters and poachers to access the forest."

When you approach Sabah from above, it looks like a calming, untouched Eden. As you get closer, light plantation green separates from forest dark, the harsh lines between like a child's colouring project. Fronds of oil palms become distinguishable from ancient knobbly and inter-connected canopies. Of the deceivingly untouched areas, a study led by Jane Bryan found only twenty-five percent of Sabah's forests were intact in 2009. Another thirty-one percent was classified on a continuum of degradation, with old and current logging roads leaving their hearts vulnerable. Even in areas where logging has ceased, these are the conduits poachers ply.

In Malaysia, it is illegal to enter protected forests without approval, illegal to carry a gun into the forest without a permit, illegal to hunt at night, and illegal to be found with an endangered species. Yet armed poachers are still rampant, outnumbering unarmed rangers. Sabah Wildlife Department prefers a soft educational approach to punitive enforcement, informing villagers of the law rather than slapping them in jail. Rangers often risk their lives to apprehend, only to see the offenders released a few months later. In 2016, for instance, Wong tells me only eleven poachers were charged in Sabah as opposed to around a hundred and fifty in West Malaysia. None of the prosecutions were successful in the courts, with offenders sometimes released on a technicality when the animal body parts in their bags were not properly identified. He is visibly angry as he explains every single rescued bear at BSBCC represents at least one wildlife crime. I shudder as he shows me camera trap photos of a bear who has chewed its own limb off to escape a snare, and a baby elephant with its hoof hanging, the red gaping wound most likely a death sentence. He doesn't think the situation will improve until consequences are more extreme. "It's about time killing protected wildlife was taken as seriously as killing humans," he says.

Sometimes, poachers only take one sun bear organ— the heart-sized gall bladder, prized for a chemical called ursodeoxycholic acid (UDCA), and leave the rest of the carcass to rot. Sun bears produce more of this acid than other mammals. Unlike the totally unsubstantiated medicinal benefits of rhino horn, UDCA improves healing in sun bears, and, to their detriment, it is also effective in the treatment of human fevers, haemorrhoids, and sprains. This led to its use for thousands of years in traditional Asian medicine. Now, however, synthetic alternatives to UDCA have been proven more effective. They are cheaper, and readily available in pharmacies worldwide with a prescription. Paradoxically, wild-caught bile is still favoured. In 2015, wildlife trade monitoring network TRAFFIC surveyed three hundred and sixty-five traditional Chinese medicine shops across Malaysia. Almost half of them had bear products for sale including whole gall bladders, bile pills, and bile powder. A whopping two hundred and ninety-three intact gallbladders were sighted in that snapshot survey. This statistic alone translates to almost three hundred dead bears.

It is possible to harvest bear bile without killing the bear, but this practice is paramount to torture. Thankfully, there is no state sanctioned bile industry in Malaysia, but in China, many bears face a thirty-year sentence contorted against rusty bars as they outgrow a small cage. Their gallbladders are milked up to twice a day with a catheter dripping the brownish-yellow liquid into a plastic bag in the same way maple trees in North America are tapped for syrup.

Sometimes, poachers use more than just the gallbladder. Like a discarded junkyard car, they methodically harvest paws for soup, and teeth as trophies. Parts are sold on the black market or brazenly displayed on a plastic tarp at the local market alongside live pangolins, monkeys, and civet cats. The cacophony of screeching is overwhelming, the stress palpable, and the risk of disease transmission between animals and humans high. On one occasion, reports reached Wong of a live cub being sold next to the carved remains of her own mother. More often, cubs are sold as pets or taken home to placate children.

Ina is on the platform today and, as I take a rest from reading depressing statistics, she draws my attention to Wawa and Dodop, sauntering in single file along a fallen log. Wawa was the first cub rescued in 2016, arriving at BSBCC in March. She was found by a Forest Management team alone, weak and dehydrated, her piercing blue eyes searching for her mother. She used every remaining ounce of her strength to bark warnings to the threatening human captors, but eventually surrendered in the corner of the quarantine cage, exhaustedly accepting her fate. Before Wawa was moved to the bear house, another young cub, Dodop, arrived with a very different story.

After separation from her own mother, Dodop was kept as a pet in a village near Ranau, confined to a small cage inside a house. Her captors thought they treated her 'like one of the family'— she had enough food, and she was loved. As she grew into her skin folds, Dodop became boisterous, instinctively testing her reach, the strength of her teeth, and the adeptness of her tongue. In desperation, her owner preferenced his family's safety over her needs by ripping out all four of her canine milk teeth from her jaw. Eventually, she was surrendered to Sabah Wildlife like a discarded Christmas puppy, the mental and physical damage done. Unlike Wawa who craved the wild, Dodop fussed and screamed for her human family, separated from the exploitive life she knew.

Eventually, in June, Wawa and Dodop were introduced. Wawa aggressively barked in a voice deeper than her size, shocking Dodop into response. Eventually, she approached and sniffed her new companion, before wrestling her to the floor. It wasn't long before they were inseparable. Wawa and Dodop offered each other the companionship they were missing. Wawa was outgoing and confident, Dodop happy to follow. As I watch them climb down from the log backwards, their faces turn towards me, Wawa's perfect black nose contrasts with the pink patches on Dodop's, reminding me families come in different packages.

Many scientists now believe we have entered the sixth period of mass extinction. The last was when the dinosaurs disappeared. In 2015, following the breeding debacle, the Sumatran Rhino was added to the statistic as the species took its last free lung of Malaysian air, and was declared extinct in the wild. There were only three remaining animals in captivity, and neither female was able to bear young. Eighteen months later, twenty-five-year-old Puntung developed a weeping abscess on her jaw and stopped eating. When she didn't respond to round-the-clock care and medication, an international emergency team of dental experts flew in. They sterilised their instruments, carved at the tissue, announced the procedure a success, and retreated—she hadn't died on their watch.

Unfortunately, tests revealed aggressive skin cancer. As a calf, Puntung had survived losing part of a limb in a poacher's snare, but the amputee wasn't going to triumph this time. Over the next two months, the aggressive growth distorted her face like elephantiasis. Just after dawn, on June 4th, 2017, Puntung was euthanised. Her uterus was sent to a waiting team, but no viable eggs were recovered. In February 2018, the last remaining female rhino, Iman, refused her favourite fruits. Partly clotted blood oozed from her vagina, a uterine tumour the cause.

On May 28th, 2019, only eight months after the Brazilian blue parrot is officially announced extinct in the wild, I am shocked when Iman's infertile mate Tam draws his last palliative breath. As I stare at my newsfeed, I feel as alone as Iman. Will sun bears be next? A line from BEARTREK springs to mind: "The orangutan is listed as critically endangered," Wong told Chris in 2007. "Sun bear numbers are much, much lower than the orangutan… If the orangutan is listed as critically endangered, I don't know how should I classify sun bears because they are so rare?"

His turn of phrase makes it seem classification was Wong's responsibility, and of course it wasn't, yet the weight on his shoulders was shocking. A dozen years after his question hung unanswered, long sleepless nights are taking their toll and disappointment sometimes shows in the lines around his eyes. His weight and his blood pressure are higher than they should be, his hand occasionally shakes, and he's worried his memory is fading.

Wong is on a race to save a species before he himself is lost.

CHAPTER 16

The Future for Sun Bears

*"If you keep destroying forest and confiscating
bears, you need to either build more facilities for
them, or get rid of them in some other way."*

t's September 2017. I am at the first-ever Sun Bear Symposium
in Kuala Lumpur. A Malaysian man stands to address the
room. Wrinkles around his playful eyes the colour of nutmeg
accentuate a serene smile as he says something like "I'm Balu—I
can't assume to speak for bears but..." I don't hear the rest. I'm
stuck on his name. A bear expert called Balu? Is it possible his
parents named him after the bear in Jungle Book, or is Balu a
common name? My train of thought has wandered so far, I've lost
the gist of the conversation. I snap myself back. "We need to look
from the point of view of the bear," the expert continues. "Sun
bears should have equal protection as humans." Such ideas may
not go very far in government chambers, but in this cohort, the
emotive language elicits a nod of approval from many.

The conference room is set with twelve tables of eight, which
host a hotchpotch of at least a dozen nationalities. Some have
come from as far away as Holland and Germany, Australia and
New Zealand. Others haven't travelled such a distance, but
since they originated in the less affluent countries of Vietnam,
Laos, Cambodia, and Indonesia, it's a significant investment for
them. Given the diversity, I am lucky that proceedings are being
conducted in English.

I glance around the room at the web of lives dedicated to saving sun bears. Gabriella Fredrickson sits behind me. The youthful exuberance that was in her eyes thirty years ago, when she, Wong, and Namura pioneered sun bear research, has been replaced with the weight of wisdom. Matt Hunt in his Free the Bears shirt, chairs this session; Lesley Small has flown from Taronga Zoo in Sydney; Wai Pak has left his research in the field to be here; Thye Lim and Lin May sit together like conjoined twins with golden sun bear markings blazoned across their black uniforms; Vuthy shares stories of electric fences with his old friend Anne Marie; Sheila is talking to Gloria about the next batch of animal ecology students; and Gloria is looking nervous about chairing the upcoming session on education. Peppered around the room are zookeepers, genetic experts, rangers, and rescuers. They all have one goal in mind—to do what they can to save this species.

A strange thought flits across my mind and I try to hold onto it before it dissolves. When I was a child, my family gathered round our newly acquired colour television for a program called This Is Your Life. The presenter, Eamonn Andrews, appeared from behind a curtain at some auspicious event holding a microphone, surprised a celebrity, then proceeded to invite them into the television studio. The celebrity's friends, holders of secrets, would share anecdotes and paint a picture of their life. I have a whimsical feeling I might spring from my chair, microphone in hand, and shove it under Wong's chin exclaiming, "Wong Siew Te, this is your life!" I imagine the subsequent sound bites: "I only got into bear research because of him", "Things were so different back then", "He gave me my first job", "You wanted to retire by fifty, how's that working out for you?" Surrounded by so many people whose lives have been impacted by this man, I realise why I've heard whispers referring to Gabriella as Mama Bear, and Wong as Papa Bear.

Matt Hunt starts by setting the scene. The International Union for the Conservation of Nature (IUCN) creates a comprehensive inventory of flora and fauna to evaluate extinction risks and create the IUCN Red List of Threatened Species. Of the world's eight bear species, six are threatened, and sun bears have been listed vulnerable since 2008. Polar bears, as the poster children for climate change, have their own celebrity profile, but the IUCN Bear Specialist Group (BSG), with a hundred and eighty members, focuses its efforts on the other five. They have joined with Free the Bears and TRAFFIC Southeast Asia to host the symposium, charged with creating a blueprint on which individual countries in the region can base their own national bear policies. Sun bears are the first cab off the rank.

I feel encouraged until Dave Garshelis, now BSG's Chairman, asks people to stand if they are working in the field, researching sun bears. Only ten people rise from their seats. Reality sets in, compounded by Dave's commentary—so far there have only been thirty-three research publications which focus solely on sun bears, as opposed to hundreds for other tropical species like orangutans. Among other things, this lack of scientific investigation means humans are still not sure how bear populations are changing, what habitats they need, or how climate change will impact survival.

Over the next two days, I am surprised to learn that much of what we know comes from bears in captivity. In-situ and ex-situ facilities collaborate much more than I had anticipated. In addition to the dog-eared justification that captive animals are awareness ambassadors, the limited captive breeding programs (designed to maintain bear numbers in captivity) have led to deeper understanding. For instance, experts now know sun bear gestation is about 96-110 days; geneticists have mapped where bears in rescue centres originated; studies of bear activity have led to advances in care; and metabolic and physiological monitoring has improved understanding of the range of temperatures sun bears can endure. As I scribble frantic notes, I realise I now know so much more than I did even a week ago. It appears a holistic response is needed, which incorporates all manner of sun bear interactions, from field work to conservation-focused zoos.

Wong's presentation is next. He starts with a history lesson of the ten-year journey at BSBCC since he gave birth to his four pillars of Animal Welfare, Education, Research and Rehabilitation. He feels content with what he and his team have achieved, but there is still a long way to go.

A young Tan Tan arrives at BSBCC. Courtesy BSBCC.

When it comes to the first pillar, Animal Welfare, Wong's individual charges live in luxury in comparison to other captive bears, and for that he is glad. For the second pillar, Gloria and her team have made significant inroads into Malaysian environmental education. Yet, even with BSBCC's outreach efforts, there is still a substantial lack of awareness about sun bears. In comparison, high-profile species like orangutans have stolen hearts, and their human champions have hijacked limited conservation funds. Wong says because these engaging primates share the same forests, efforts to save their habitat have, fortunately, had a positive flow-on effect. Over the past ten years, social media has also helped considerably. I snap to attention, taking a photo of him in full swing, as requested, forwarding it on before I forget, and knowing it will be on Facebook within the hour.

It's time for lunch and I slot into the buffet queue behind Matt Hunt. His mind is still on social media, which he tells me is a two-edged sword. Because sun bears are "the most insanely cute animals on the planet", he says the heart-melting cub images he shares online to raise awareness and funds, have sometimes been pilfered and used inappropriately to sell cubs. On the other hand, only last month, his Facebook newsfeed clogged with shared images of emaciated sun bears at the Bandung Zoo in Indonesia. A viral campaign to shut the zoo down had already resulted in over 850,000 petition signatures to president Widodo and world-wide media coverage (as this book went to press, the number had risen to 1.5 million). Awareness is often boosted by celebrity tourists at Free the Bears and BSBCC. In addition to David Attenborough, Wong has taken Sigourney Weaver (Gorillas in the Mist, Alien, Ghostbusters), Emma Thompson (Harry Potter, Nanny McPhee, Love Actually), and British ex-prime minister Tony Blair on tours of the bear house.

Wong's own celebrity status is growing. I can hear someone in the line behind me congratulate him on becoming a Wira Negaraku or 'My Country Hero'. "It's great for sun bear awareness," I hear them say. Wong agrees. He's not particularly comfortable at gala banquets in a suit and tie, but when the Malaysian Prime Minister shakes his hand, traction and awareness are generated. On August 31st every year, Malaysians celebrate Merdeka, or Malaysian Independence Day. The government awards people who have made an impact with an award akin to an Australia

Day medal. In 2014 and 2016, Wong was nominated in the environmental category, but he's yet to take home the ultimate coveted prize. He hopes to win one day so he can use the position to propel his conservation message.

My mind flashes back to the last day of June 2017. Wong excitedly fidgeted with his glasses during our regular Skype call. He'd been nominated as the global news giant CNN's Hero. There were only 24 other finalists. This was the big time—no wonder he couldn't sit still. He had spent the day taking direction from a film crew, and was still on a high. "The two-minute clip will be online soon," he said. Producer Kathleen Toner had interviewed him for a feature to go along with the film. Extra footage would be used if he made the top ten, in which case he would be flown to New York for a gala awards ceremony. Two weeks later, my own adrenalin kicked in as I searched for the results. Had he made it? If so, would he still find time to talk to me? The top ten popped up and I frantically scrolled. Not there.

At the symposium, Wong is back in his seat, leaning proudly forward as Thye Lim describes his own study of sun bear populations in Tabin Wildlife Reserve. Hair samples are one of the easiest ways to collect bear DNA so, together with a team of research assistants, Thye Lim has identified trees with regular sun bear scratching, then wrapped duct tape around the trunks with the sticky side out to collect samples without impacting individual animals. Strategically placed camera traps show that this process seems to be working, but the study is still in its early days. These initiatives inform Wong's third pillar: research. Hopefully, results will help Wong and Thye Lim determine how many bears are in the protected area, map their individual ranges, determine if they are related, and understand whether the population is genetically robust enough to survive. To the left of Wong, Gabriella nods her head in agreement. She knows how important it is to gather data. More sun bear researchers are needed. It's been difficult to attract them so far.

Wong's last pillar, rehabilitation, is the most controversial. In my warm and fuzzy naivete, I hadn't considered all the issues. As the first day of the symposium draws towards a conclusion, the risks faced by released bears, and the impacts to their wild neighbours, concern me. I individually corner Dave and Gabriella to form a more complete picture. "Do you support Wong's rehabilitation goal?" I ask. Neither has a straight answer.

Gabriella appreciates more than most the immense pressure Wong is under. More forest refugees arrive on a regular basis, and the bear house at BSBCC is at capacity. The forced high-density conditions threaten to choke the forest enclosure as bears degrade the forest. "If you keep destroying forest and confiscating bears, you need to either build more facilities for them, or get rid of them in some other way," she says with a wry smile. "Free the Bears has sent bears to foreign zoos, and Sabah Wildlife Department sent fifteen or so to the USA, but captive facilities are finite. They are expensive to run, and sun bears have long lives."

Gabriella says releasing more individuals into reduced forests, with limited food resources, can put both the released and the wild bears at risk. Socially, the wild resident bears don't accept newcomers, sometimes killing the competition or chasing them to the edge of the forest where they are in danger from humans. "The crux is that there is no point adding stress to the wild population of sun bears by adding rehabilitant bears in an ever-shrinking habitat that is, in most cases, not well protected… there is no conservation value in that," she says. Since poaching is still prevalent, protecting existing habitat is crucial, and until habitat is safe, governments need to build more enclosures for the orphans created by their trade policies.

Asked the same question, Dave initially quotes the IUCN Guidelines for the Placement of Confiscated Animals, which state that animals should be released only if there's a benefit to conservation. Issues such as spread of disease, behaviour abnormalities, or animal/human conflicts need to be considered, he says. Probed further, he thinks Wong may have kept past releases under the scientific radar until he could perfect the process. He thinks this is in response to the controversial release of two pandas in China in 2003. Both pandas died—one killed by another male panda in a territorial battle. The experimental attempt significantly impacted funding. The next five releases were kept quiet, but all five were successful. "It was a really dumb reaction by people because it was an experiment," Dave says. "What I am hoping is that on the path along the way, Wong is collecting the data that will inform why a release was successful, why wasn't it successful, or do we even know if it was successful."

Dave and Gabriella have differing opinions on bear release, but they both feel strongly that rehabilitation can be a tool for engagement. "People love a named animal going back to the wild," Dave tells me. "You can't generate that kind of emotion by doing science surveys." Gabriella agrees: "As long as Wong uses the release of captive bears to raise the topic of conservation and raise the protection of reserves, then perhaps the positives outweigh the negatives."

It's been a long day. Over a bowl of noodles with Wong, Thye Lim, and Lin May, I probe further on ways to reduce the risk of release. Their five-year dream is to shut down one of the bear houses at BSBCC after returning the majority of bears to the wild. It is an ambitious dream which begins with teaching cubs important skills from the moment they arrive.

Lin May coordinates the care of new arrivals like baby Noah, who I met from a distance. Each morning, she showers with non-perfumed soap and pulls back her shiny long hair, then dresses in black cargo pants and black sun bear T-shirt, attempting to look as little like a human as possible. It is intensive work, since the youngsters require four-hourly feedings. Slowly they learn to trust her enough that forest walking begins. If they are to survive in the wild, it is important to maintain or develop instinctual stranger danger, so Thye Lim hides behind trees, and when Lin May and a cub pass by, he jumps out, teaching them to be wary of their biggest enemy.

Walking bears in Sepilok was straightforward when Wai Pak and Wong taught Natalie how to climb trees, but with tourism numbers increasing and the profile of the centre gaining momentum, Lin May says she often finds herself trying to protect spooked cubs, who could easily be loved to death by encroaching tourists keen to get a photo. Thye Lim says moving cubs to a remote location would make training easier, alleviating the bears' anxiety. Young bears could grow up in the forest, transitioning to the wild quicker than ever before.

That goal identified, Thye Lim and Lin May recently clambered through the undergrowth at Tabin trying to think like sun bears until they found a potentially 'just right' location. It needed to be close to Sabah Wildlife's research facility, but not too close; safe from human traffic, near a river providing both drinking water and a physical barrier between released bears and threats, and not subject to flooding. Plans moved from napkins to blueprints. When everyone was content, they completed an occupation permit application to the Forestry Department and they now wait. If they get the tick of approval, the new centre will have space for up to ten bears, and, over time, the staff will expand to match. They hope to release four more bears in 2018—the first two at Tabin, the second two at another protected area. Yes, they assure me, data will be meticulously gathered to perfect the process.

"But what about poaching?" I ask Wong as he puts down his chopsticks. "The bears aren't safe in the wild." With BSBCC's first four pillars acting as triage, Wong says he's very aware of gaping holes, so he has added another four into BSBCC's charter.

The first three, Anti-poaching, Ecotourism, and Community Conservation work hand-in-hand.

The first pillar, Anti-poaching, requires more boots on the ground in the rainforest, boat patrols, road patrols, observation posts, camera traps, and a better system of prosecution. To propel this new pillar forward, Wong has found an ally in the United States government, which is keen to stem the illegal wildlife trade. They sent judges, public prosecutors, US Fish and Wildlife Service representatives, and US police officers to share their expertise at a conference in early 2017 (the third in a series) called Justice for Silent Victims III: Combatting Obstacles in Wildlife Crime Prosecution. Wong attended the workshops along with most of the region's wildlife officers, prestigious judges, investigators, and prosecutors. Together they learnt how to gather effective proof and apply the Wildlife Conservation Act with more success. If this first step leads to ongoing training, and Wildlife Officers are armed for their own protection (giving them more confidence to apprehend), Wong thinks the scales could be tipped in the sun bears' favour.

Wong draws breath and moves onto the second new pillar, Ecotourism. He prefers to call it Conservation Ecotourism, combining education, research, and the blossoming tourism industry together. I want to know more, but it's been a long day. Tiredness chips away at my optimism, and I wonder how Wong keeps positive. We pay the bill, then retreat to our respective hotels.

Ecotourism isn't new for Sabah. In the 1990s, Borneo's jungle drew nature lovers and adventurers from around the world. Trophy-hunter guns were replaced with cameras, and tourism's value to the GDP caused the government to take notice. Then, on April 23rd , 2000, as I sat in Australia planning my first trip to Borneo (subsequently cancelled), six armed Filipino Jihadist militants stormed the dining hall on the Malaysian island dive resort of Sipadan. They herded twenty-one frightened people onto waiting boats, forcing them at gunpoint to swim to a waiting mothership and transporting them to Jolo Island in the Philippines, about three hundred kilometres away. Ransoms were demanded, shots were fired, evangelists who offered themselves as mediators ending up as captives, and a journalist and television crew added to the tally. After undisclosed ransoms were paid, Libyan leader Muammar Gaddafi mediated, and the Philippines armed forces attacked. The stand-off ended on September 16th, 2000.

Sabah's tourism industry crossed its virtual fingers, hoping the world would forget. Instead, abductions continued. In early 2013, with a total of about fifty people snatched, the government formed the Eastern Sabah Security Command (ESSCOM) to patrol the 1,400 kilometres of Sabah's East Coast. Controlling the intricate web of islands was akin to a schoolyard game where children outwit and elude one central captor. Even with a sea curfew imposed at night, kidnappings continued. Worldwide condemnation and travel warnings reduced international tourism arrivals to a trickle.

Then, on May 14th, 2015, two days before Wong's birthday, another six militants tied their boat to the pylons beneath a Sandakan seafood restaurant under a cloak of darkness and climbed the ladder. As frightened diners watched, they grabbed the restaurant owner at gunpoint. She resisted and was knocked to the floor. Almost as an afterthought, they dragged a tourist along for extra collateral, revved their outboard engine, and headed back to the Philippines leaving stunned patrons cowering in their wake. Three months passed with demands and negotiations. Locals stopped going out for dinner in fear. Eventually, the restaurant owner was released, but the tourist was beheaded. As his family mourned, local waterfront restaurants shut their doors, leaving derelict buildings strutting into the bay, a memorial to the industry and the man.

Finally, abductions slowed, and brave tourists trickled back. Tourism now towers over the historic economic stronghold of the timber industry, becoming the second-largest export industry in Sabah after palm oil. In 2017, even with continuing travel advisories impacting the ability to secure travel insurance, the state earned RM7.8 billion from tourism compared with only RM1.85 billion from timber exports.

The impacts of tourism have the potential to harm the very attraction visitors seek. This is why Wong believes ecotourism is the answer. He is collaborating with Borneo Eco Tours and Sukau Rainforest Lodge owner Albert Teo to champion a tourism industry which works with nature. The two agree that you can't expect villagers to give up their agricultural or hunting livelihoods without a viable replacement. That's where Conservation Ecotourism comes in. Wong explains a percentage of Albert's profits are syphoned off to a non-profit arm called Borneo Ecotourism Solutions and Technologies (or BEST for short). Albert runs community projects hiring the children of farmers, fishermen, and hunters, giving them a wider range of livelihood choices. He's making a difference one family at a time. Wong is committed to help. He is also expanding BSBCC's volunteer options into a more developed program, giving travellers meaningful and immersive experiences, relieving pressure on his staffing requirements, and spreading an ecological message like ripples in a pond.

Even though the Sabah government is dragging its feet on a revised ecotourism master plan, a year behind schedule, Wong is encouraged that almost half of Sabah's landmass (3.54 million hectares) has been gazetted as permanent forest reserve. State parks, wildlife sanctuaries, and wildlife conservation areas add another 0.27 million hectares of protected forests. If ecotourism increases the economic and social value of wilderness areas, Wong thinks politicians will have the incentive to protect even more.

Wai Pak saunters into our conversation telling me about the third new pillar, Community Conservation, and relating it to his own research. Reports travelled the grapevine of sun bear sightings in a commercial acacia forest on Bengkoka Peninsula, right on the northeast tip of Borneo. Wai Pak, who is now working with Malaysia Nature Society, went to investigate. Sure enough, it seems bears might be living in nearby mangrove areas and wandering into plantations. Wai Pak is conducting a PhD project, through Sunway University, studying these bears in the midst of human habitation. With bears on their doorstep, the villagers are important stakeholders in their survival. He and Wong are putting a program in place in the community to support cottage industries and give locals an outlet to sell sun bear handicrafts at BSBCC's visitor centre. They are breeding a community of conservationists by default. "Hopefully, as communities realise a bear is worth more alive than dead, poaching will decrease," Wong adds.

"That's three new pillars, so what's the fourth?" I ask.

The last pillar of captive breeding comes with some very big ifs. If poaching can be brought under control, resulting in fewer bears needing shelter; if the government keeps its promise to protect more natural areas; and if more bears can be safely released to free up space, then, and only then, Wong will introduce captive breeding to help repopulate protected habitats. It is blue-sky thinking in the extreme, but this is a man who is used to dreaming big.

The responsibility of saving a species is heavy on the shoulders of this son of a tailor, who grew up in a small town outside Penang. He has come so far since he naïvely thought a wooden trap would hold a sun bear, since he grieved the loss of his field assistant, since he optimistically thought he could create a rescue centre while writing his PhD. Like his hero Jane Goodall, Wong now spends most of his time travelling—educating, advocating, and awareness-building.

Back in the conference room, Matt Hunt asks for volunteers to whittle two days of discussions into a draft vision statement for the species. My hand shoots in the air. Over coffee and lunch breaks, our team of four experiment, adjusting the ingredients into a morsel we hope will stick to the experts' palates and linger on their taste buds like honey. It's the last day, and I walk towards the podium as the nominated mouthpiece. It dawns on me that the people behind ninety pairs of eyes drilling into my soul could possibly turn our collective dream into reality. The five sentences on the shaking sheet of paper before me will be further massaged by experts but still their immensity hits home. After a nervous cough, I begin:

The sun bear thrives in viable populations throughout its entire historical range, fulfilling its ecological role within intact forests. Humans have learnt to live harmoniously with sun bears throughout the region due to political and cultural recognition of their intrinsic value. There is no longer a need for sun bear rescue centres. Those bears not fit for release are maintained under globally applied, high ex-situ standards and contribute to advocacy and education. The species has become a best-practice example of regional collaborative conservation and research.

CHAPTER 17

Debbie and Damai

"You are back where you belong, Debbie, I kept my promise."

It's March 4th, 2018, three days before the release of two bears and my plane has just touched down in Sandakan. Their journey to this point has been a longer one.

On January 6th, 2012, while many Christians celebrated the arrival of three wise men at a baby's manger in Bethlehem, Sabah Wildlife Department travelled to Lok Kawi Wildlife Park just outside of Sabah's capital of Kota Kinabalu to rescue a different kind of infant. The tiny six-month-old bear's history was sketchy. Wong was simply told she had been purchased from a Chinese pet trader and surrendered.

After her seven-hour-long journey, Debbie arrived at BSBCC just after dark. She was understandably stressed and angry, barking loudly as her cage was carried to her new den. Wong felt it was likely she hadn't been in captivity long. Her spirit was still intact. He was sure she missed her mother, and he longed to offer her his finger to suck. He knew it would calm her, but he didn't want to risk losing a digit. Debbie was too stressed to eat, but she was dehydrated from her long journey, noisily licking the electrolyte water Wong pushed towards her in a metal tray. As she drank, Wong examined her distinctive chest patch, a bright golden cocktail glass peppered with black dots. He talked softly to her, promising to take care of her and give her every chance of returning to the forest.

Two days after Debbie's arrival, Wong flew to Kota Kinabalu for the Sabah Wildlife Conservation Colloquium. Every break, he found a quiet corner, and called Wai Pak to check on Debbie's progress. She still wasn't eating, perhaps due to her injured forked tongue, but she was sleeping well and defecating, which indicated internal health. She wasn't comfortable with humans, pacing when the volunteers cleaned her cage, barking loudly to scare them away. Wai Pak told him she had sad eyes, and from experience, they both knew this meant their first impressions had been right: she hadn't long been separated from her mother.

When he returned, Wong set to making Debbie feel more comfortable by using honey as a tried and tested ice-breaker. First, he put a smear on the end of a pole so he could reach her where she cowered in her basket. After a few repeats, Debbie ventured onto the ground, following the sweet smell to the spout of the bottle Wong held between the bars. Slowly she let down her guard. Eventually, as he gained her trust, Debbie licked honey from Wong's flattened hand before relaxing enough to explore her cage in earnest.

A month later, Elis darted Debbie, and Doctor Nigel administered a complete health check. Debbie had put on weight well, reaching thirteen kilos. Her claws were strong, and blood tests showed she was free from disease. Half an hour after sedation, she was recovering back in her pen. With the all-clear, integration with Mary and Fulung could begin attempting to form a sun bear cub gang. On the last day of February, Mary and Debbie were moved into next-door dens so they could become familiar. Debbie wasn't happy, huffing and barking defensively, while Mary retreated to suckle her feet. Mary was moved back one cage, making more space between then. The next day, Debbie was more relaxed, watching Mary intently with curiosity rather than fear. Wai Pak then eliminated the den between them. Debbie approached, tentatively and gently touching and scratching her new playmate through the bars while Mary continued to suck her feet. A few days later, the same process took place on the other side with Fulung. This time it was easier. Fulung was a confident bear who made friends easily.

With the three bears playing happily in adjacent dens, on March 10th, 2012, it was time to remove the bars. Wai Pak scattered banana and pumpkin pieces across the concrete floor as a distraction, then opened the gates. The bears tolerated each other well while they were eating. When every morsel was gone, Fulung rose to his feet, towering above little Debbie, showing his dominance. Bravely, Debbie stood as tall as she was able, and bared her teeth in a 'don't mess with me' stance. She only reached Fulung's shoulders. Startled, Fulung shrugged, letting Debbie bite the loose skin around his neck, then pinned her to the ground with his comparative size, their friendship cemented. When Fulung lost interest after about ten minutes, Mary took over, jostling with the exhausted youngster until they both ran out of steam. Wong and Wai Pak were relieved. It had been a successful day: Debbie was no longer alone. Finally, she had someone to play with, cuddle, and annoy.

Later that year, on the evening of November 5th, 2012, a man called Blue Lum saw something that looked like a puppy in his carport. Dogs are everywhere in Sabah, so he didn't pay much attention, instead settling down to watch television. The 'dog' kept barking so Lum's son went out to investigate again, only to come face-to-face with a tiny four-month-old sun bear cub. Lum called the Civil Defence Department, and, before too long, officers captured the compliant cub.

When she arrived at BSBCC, the cub weighed less than five kilos. Wai Pak lifted her from a fragrant bed of pandanus leaves and she snuggled into his shoulder. Her tiny face was dwarfed by an oversized nose, complemented by puppy eyes and a downturned smile. It appeared her thin, broken-horseshoe chest marking had bought her luck; the cub was safe. She was named Damai after the town where she was found. It means 'peace' in Malay.

After three weeks in quarantine, it came time to introduce Damai to the bear house. Her unfamiliar smell startled the other bears. They barked, frightening her. Through strong metal bars, she could see them climbing and pacing, but the odour of fresh cut leaves calmed her. Damai used the bars to climb up to the fixed wall-basket and investigate. As anxiety gave way to joy, she swung on the suspended log which commanded centre stage.

Even though she wasn't any bigger than a small domestic dog, Wong and Lin May started bear training almost immediately. Amenable Damai followed them down the mosaic-paved path like a sooty shadow, settling down in the dense forest for a few hours each day, using her keen sense of smell to locate termites, ripping through decaying stumps, securing her prey with her darting tongue.

Walking Damai in the forest. Courtesy BSBCC.

As confidence grew, Damai scaled her first tree stump, perching on the top, clinging tightly with her oversized claws. Wong and Lin May recorded her adventures on the BSBCC blog like proud parents. Nearly 5,200km away, I followed along like an overseas grandmother.

Damai was a clever bear, and as she honed her skill, she preferred trunks wrapped with vines that acted as hand- and footholds. While on the ground, she was constantly alert, often standing on her hind legs intently staring into the distance, listening to the crack of branches, or deciphering the alarm calls of gibbons. Occasionally she felt threatened when she came across an infant orangutan or macaque. She stood bravely and huffed a warning. If that didn't work, her vocals escalated to a bark and she retreated up the nearest tree. As time went on, she became less anxious, eventually feeling safe enough to straddle a branch like a panther and take naps above Lin May's head.

While Damai was forest training, three more bears were integrated into the sun bear cub gang: Ah Bui, Koko, and Bongkud. By August 2013, when they were considered sub-adults, the team of six was ready to graduate to the forest pen. Bongkud excitedly climbed high in the liana vine, unaware her penchant for climbing would lead to her eventual death. Debbie followed behind while Ah Bui sunned herself on a fallen tree log. With a succession of thuds, Fulung heard David tossing whole coconuts from the other side of the fence. He grabbed one under his arm, like a rugby player bracing for a tackle, and retreated to the base of the huge tree. Pleased with himself, he repeatedly sunk his black claws into its tough outer layer, ripping it back to expose the fibrous core, then deftly piercing the softest eye. Pivoting on his back, he balanced the sphere on the balls of his hind feet so he could suck and lick coconut water. Smelling sweet liquid, Debbie ambled over to investigate. She wanted some, and complained in a high-pitched voice. Before long, she realised he wasn't going to share. She sauntered off and found her own. It took her longer than Fulung to get to the prize, but her perseverance was finally rewarded.

By the time she was eleven months old, Damai had put on almost twenty kilos. Her forest-walking days were numbered. Her strength was now potentially dangerous to humans, so she too joined the cub gang. Just as they had done with Debbie's integration, the sliding doors between dens were opened one at a time. At first Damai brushed off Mary and Debbie as they came close to sniff her fur. It was persistent Fulung who eventually convinced her to play; he simply wouldn't be ignored. They wrestled together, softly biting and clawing as they rolled across the concrete floor. Debbie and Mary climbed up into the basket, perched like balcony seating at the opera, and watched the entertainment below. Tired, Damai retreated to the sink in the corner of the den, amusing herself by splashing water while the others ignored her.

Damai was still one step away from the forest enclosure. Before she was exposed to the high-voltage forest fence, she needed to master the training pen where the voltage could be adjusted. Wong and the team placed fruit pieces and dribbled honey very close to the wire, then opened the door to Damai's den. As her tongue extended to reach the honey, her back touched the wire, and her flight instinct kicked in. Within seconds, she was back in her den. It took a week, and four more zaps, before Wong felt confident enough to extend the seven bears' integration area to include the training pen. A week after that, Damai stood framed in her pen's open door, her paws folded over its sill, staring out at the forest.

Koko tried especially hard to introduce her playmate to the outdoors, and before long they were chasing up trees together. Unlike some of the more traumatised bears, Damai delighted in her surroundings, curiously bending branches and rolling in leaves. Through it all, her bottom lip hung at the corners to reveal her pink gums—a Doberman smile without the slobber.

At 10am on July 30th, 2013, somewhere around her first birthday, Damai grew sleepy. She wandered to her favourite tree and started to climb. Lin May watched her from the observation platform expecting her to find a comfortable branch for a nap as she had so many times before. Instead, Damai bent the supple branches in her mouth, breaking and assembling them until she had fashioned her first nest. It might not have been as beautiful as an orangutan's, but once it was lined with a few leaves, she played in the treetop until her eyes grew heavy, snuggling in for the rest of the day. Lin May wondered how she had learnt this essential survival skill. Had a distant memory of her mother been triggered, or was it instinct? Either way, it was another important milestone which indicated Damai would one day be ready for release.

Four years and nine months later, that time has come. I'm following Wong like a puppy, trying not to get under the feet of Will and Chris, the two cameramen, as they conduct piece-to-camera interviews in the bear house. Chris is determined he isn't going to get lost in the forest with Thye Lim like he did last time. Wong suggests camera angles; he's more adept than he was during the filming of BEARTREK and facts roll off his tongue in usable soundbites. He is talking about the release process, and as I listen, I can feel the excitement welling in my throat.

I survey the bears, wondering what they are thinking. Simone stands to attention, watching with interest, her paws flat against the bars as if in surrender. She's oblivious to roof damage above her head caused by a widow-maker limb. Montom barks loudly in protest at the sight of the unfamiliar tripod. Bermuda's tongue protrudes out of the side of his mouth in defiant anger. Damai comforts herself, sitting on the ground sucking her back paw and emitting plunger-like sounds, her heavy collar slipping around her neck. Debbie anxiously paces. She hasn't been in the bear house since her collar was fitted three weeks ago and she no longer feels comfortable confined.

Tomorrow is release day, and there's a no-nonsense atmosphere in the bear house as the team prepares to dart Debbie and Damai then transfer them to relocation cages for the long journey to Tabin Wildlife Reserve—and freedom.

In the corner, the petite frame of Dr Nabila in black boots, a black shirt, and black hijab makes me think of a movie ninja warrior, her youthful features causing me to unwittingly contemplate the march of time on my own. She checks her oversize watch then picks up the dart gun, loading anaesthetic from her tackle box. I wrap the loops of a face mask around my ears, and push my fingers into blue surgical gloves. Thye Lim climbs next to Damai's cage with a squeeze bottle of honey in his hand, attempting to distract her while Dr Nabila aims, but she smells danger and, instead, climbs frantically and anxiously. The dart goes in. Damai reaches behind her back to pull it out. Barking in protest, she climbs down the bars and starts pacing. Wong checks his watch. Time moves like molasses but Damai isn't slowing with it. Eventually her limbs grow heavy and she sinks to the concrete, but she's uncomfortable, rotating her collar with both paws. Either she has been under-dosed, or the dart didn't hit its mark. Dr Nabila decides to boost her Zoletil using a syringe. Thye Lim grabs a blue-handled broom from the rack for protection. The two go in. Another wait. Damai sneezes as her head grows heavy. She shakes her head to try and stay awake, and her heavy tongue protrudes from her mouth. Wong is pacing, the uncomfortable expression on his face matching Damai's. Dr Nabila asks Elis for advice. They administer another top-up with Wong holding a towel over Damai's eyes. With her final ounce of energy, she licks her lips, then she's gone. Swiftly, she is lifted onto a canvas tarpaulin and the corners come together to be hooked on a scale. At forty-one kilos, she's the perfect size for an adult female.

With Damai on the operating table, the team breaks into a well-rehearsed dance intensified by the presence of the film crew: measuring tapes stretch, ink pads appear, footprints press on white paper, gums and pupils are inspected, KY jelly and thermometer are pushed up the anus, and all the while shutters click. As Wong unscrews Damai's radio collar and cuts a new one to size, he speaks to the camera. Damai's radio collar has been misbehaving. She's already wearing her second and he only has one left. Wong hopes this one is more reliable. All finished, Damai is carried outside in the sling where the translocation cage awaits. Thye Lim pulls her through onto the soft carpet of withered leaves and the bolt slides into place. One down, one to go.

Debbie is pacing rapidly, but the dart goes in true. The process is much less intense. Since her collar is working perfectly, it only takes a few minutes. I hover at the periphery. Debbie's temperature is high, and Thye Lim pushes wrapped frozen ice blocks under her chest while he roughly plucks a few hair samples, sliding them into an envelope. Before too long, she is flat on her stomach in the translocation cage, with the bottom of her usually pink back paws black like a gorilla's. Thye Lim and Azzry prepare for a long night on watch.

Wong raps on my door at 2am. I'm up and dressed in an instant. We congregate at the bear house. Debbie pierces the forest with her barking as she and Damai are lifted into the back of two Toyotas in a convoy of five. Damai's pacing shakes the car and Debbie snorts while she circles, pushing the dry leaves aside in protest. Lin May and Wong calm them both down with a bottle of electrolyte water. A sheet of plywood is lashed to the top and back of the cages so the bears can't vandalise the car. At 3am, car doors clunk in unison. We are off.

The darkness adds to the sensation of adventure as we travel southeast to Lahad Datu. This rural fishing town borders a large bay in the South China Sea, at the end of the Philippines' Sulu Islands. Sea gypsies ply the waters in the archipelago, often settling in Malaysia unnoticed. The town has a reputation for lawlessness. "Trouble always breaks out prior to elections here," Wong tells me. Knowing an election is looming, I feel slightly uneasy. We pull over at a 24 Jam restaurant for breakfast and check how the bears are faring. Damai has managed to bend two bars apart, and her claw marks are almost through the plywood. It's a quick breakfast.

As the rising sun colours the horizon, we turn left down the fifty-kilometre unpaved road to Tabin Wildlife Reserve. The right fork leads to Danum Valley Conservation Area, where Wong's research was conducted. A dust cloud rises as we slow to navigate gouges left by palm oil and logging trucks. The endlessly ordered rows of trees clock by; the ground between them is carpeted with a legume vine to reduce weeds. Wildlife sightings increase as we approach the edge of the reserve. Two bearded pigs run across the road before us, and pigtail macaques announce our arrival. As we near the locked gate, a Wallace's hawk-eagle, named after the British botanist, stands like a sentry on the electric fence post designed to keep elephants off the road.

At the concrete pad just outside Tabin Wildlife Resort, marked with a huge yellow H, a crowd of hotel staff gather around the bears' cages. The sky is clear, the intense heat overwhelming. We strain to differentiate between the sounds of motorbikes and helicopters. Suddenly, like the theme tune from Jaws, a repeating thud draws closer. The six-seater helicopter appears over the treetops, and lands before us.

Author Sarah Pye as part of the release team..

Thye Lim's list of travelling companions is determined by weight and task. The set-up team goes first with the box of emergency provisions, just in case the weather turns. I climb into the front seat on the second transport wave. As we levitate, I look through the glass window beneath my feet to see the ground crew hooking a cable into the cargo net swaddling Damai's cage. Wong sits behind me with Will the cameraman, and his commentary to camera is inaudible through my headset. Below me, a sea of palms is slowly replaced by uneven green, a chalky river cutting a swathe. The occasional tall dipterocarp pierces the canopy. David Haskell referred to a similar sight in the Amazon jungle as "sky islands in a sea of rainforest" and it seems particularly apt. Based on the size of Tabin, Wong estimates it has a carrying capacity of one hundred and twenty bears. He has no idea how many wild bears there are, but, somewhere down there, Natalie roams.

Next to me, the pilot, a heavyset man, concentrates with every sinew, as Damai's cage swings below. We inch along at thirty-five nautical miles an hour as he attempts to keep the horizon on his instruments flat. I can't help thinking if we crash, we'll never be found. After fifteen minutes, a grey blemish appears in the distance, like acne. This bald spot is the mud volcano where Natalie found freedom. It is the only possible landing in Tabin Wildlife Reserve, conveniently located right in the centre, as far from human habitation as it is possible to be. Gracefully, we near the ground, then place our load on the crusted mud and come to rest beside it, forcefully blowing mud dust up Damai's twitching nose.

Thye Lim and Andy rush to her cage across cratered elephant footprints. Wong grabs the last corner and they lift in unison, taking her to the safety and coolness of the forest cover and tipping the cage on its side so the door can easily slide. Will and Lin May dance around them like mosquitoes, their lenses exposed. I watch as a Gopro camera is attached to the cage, and another is strategically placed in the direction Damai is expected to run. Will sets up his heavy professional camera beyond that, and Thye Lim ties a white nylon rope around the guillotine door. Wong leans against the far side of a tree with the other end in his hand.

CAPTION: Damai is nearly free. Courtesy BSBCC.

270

It's 10.45am. The moment has come. My heart pounds in my chest so strongly I am sure the others can hear it. From a respectable distance, I see Wong give one strong tug. The bars fall away and Damai strolls out, looking far calmer than I feel. She rises to her feet, sniffing the air. A note of honey on the outside of her cage stops her in her tracks. She doubles back to savour every morsel. She can smell bananas too, so she walks toward the five-kilo sack slumped against a tree. On the way, the alien tripod grabs her attention and she investigates, smudging the Gopro lens with honey breath. Lin May chuckles beside me. Damai recognises that voice. A distant memory climbing trees together flashes across her subconscious. She turns and walks towards us. "Damai, Damai!" Thye Lim distracts her, running deep into the forest away from his fiancée. "Go, go!" he yells to Lin May as we scramble away. Damai follows him around the green forest border of the mud flat. Thye Lim turns hard right towards the open sky, his boots sinking into mud. Damai stops, pivots. Within seconds, she's gone.

I can feel tears welling, noticing the same in Lin May's eyes. I want to stop and give her a hug but there's no time. To the west, a soft, insistent thud announces Debbie's imminent arrival. The performance is repeated, the only unpredictable element being Debbie's reaction. Thye Lim doesn't think she'll hang around like Damai, and he is right. As soon as the gate is open, she's off like a racehorse in the opposite direction from the strategically placed tripod.

I had imagined jubilant celebration but there are two dangerous bears on the loose and work to be done, so we cradle our individual emotions. Andy and Thye Lim attach camera traps to trees at hip height. Lin May scatters the bananas as a parting gift. Azzry keeps track of the bears' direction with the H-shaped aerial in one hand and VHF in the other. Rain droplets bounce in the elephant puddles—the weather is turning and we need to leave. As I zip my rain-jacket, I imagine Debbie and Damai climbing skyward. Wong's words before he pulled the rope are stuck in my memory. He crouched by Debbie's cage, fingering the scar she gave him as a cub. "You are back where you belong, Debbie, I kept my promise."

Debbie in her natural habitat. Courtesy Jocelyn Stokes.

Epilogue

"I don't have any other choice but to keep going."

"How are Debbie and Damai?" I ask Wong on a Skype call in late July 2018. I hear masked grief in his voice. Both their signals have stopped. His reasoning teeters between pessimism and optimism while he talks me through the possibilities. Perhaps both collars stopped working—but that would be quite a coincidence. Maybe they lost enough weight while they learnt to fend for themselves then they (like Natalie) dropped their collars—but then he would still receive a stationary signal.

He's trying to stay positive, but admits he thinks they are both dead. If Debbie and Damai reached the same stage of starvation as the bears during the famine, instinct would have led them to curl up in a womb-like cavity, and the collar would be unable to transmit. Wong can't be sure exactly what happened until he sends in a search party. The helplessness and uncertainty he felt during the famine has returned. I sit quietly while this news sinks in. He is in the middle of preparations for three more releases which will be filmed by Dame Judi Dench for her Wild Borneo Adventure documentary. He's no longer sure whether to go ahead.

A wave of complicit survivor guilt washes over me. Was the release a mistake because the ending might not be a happy one?

What part did I play in that? Am I complicit for consuming too many resources which impact climate change—the real culprit? Am I at fault simply by being human? In a split second, my admiration of Wong's unrelenting commitment deepens. So too my understanding of apathy and inaction around climate change. I fight the fear of doing the wrong thing, knowing inaction is decision by default.

A month after our conversation, Wong gives his parting advice to Thye Lim, who is leading a search party through the same type of dense jungle that nearly killed him on the rescue mission for Natalie's collar. He is better prepared and more respectful of the forest this time, taking enough supplies for contingencies. When he finds Debbie's collar, Thye Lim raises it to his nostrils. It's a 'clean drop'—there's no lingering smell of death. He searches for signs of bones. Nothing. Even though she lost enough weight to shed the collar, it appears Debbie might still be alive, her fate dangling like a modifier. He longs to continue the search for Damai's collar, but she's disappeared into a part of the forest so dense Wong won't condone a search. The loss of Chai is still raw.

The news that Debbie might still be alive prompts Wong to go ahead with plans to release more bears. Then a disaster of a different kind strikes. At 5pm on August 13th, 2018, Wong steps out of a Sandakan shop into a wall of oppressive humidity which instantly drenches him in sweat. Not far away, in Sepilok, the same ominous blanket of moisture foreshadows a wind unlike any other. In a few short minutes, it gallops through the forest like a harras of horses, twisting the green canopy in its wake. As the trunk of one giant splinters, it doubles over and collapses, crushing the second observation platform into a twisted wreckage of tin, steel, and ironwood. Within minutes, three other trees succumb, dragging saplings down, flattening the electric fence.

As quickly as it came, the wind tsunami is gone, leaving a deafening silence in its wake. When Wong's phone rings, he is already halfway back. He's thankful that the centre is closed for the day and there is no human injury, but he's worried there are still four bears unaccounted for. When he pulls up at the bear house, Dr Nabila is loading her dart gun. With a sense of foreboding, Tan Tan, Fulung, and Ah Lun run towards the bear house unaided. Wawa, nicknamed 'the Explorer', remains in the damaged pen. She is uninjured, but indecision has frozen her to the spot. Dr Nabila carefully steps over fallen shards, raises her arm, and aims. As the dart hits home, it jolts Wawa's subconscious into flight mode. She can feel her legs growing heavy, but she wills them on, tripping over her front paws as she runs towards her pen, slumping onto the cold concrete floor, unconsciousness taking hold.

When I talk to Wong the next day, he is exhausted both mentally and physically. The Centre is closed while he assesses possible damage to the remaining observation platform. Filzah, from Arkitrek is tweaking the platform design and the contractor is preparing a quote. Since the land and structures are owned by Sabah Wildlife Department, he doesn't have independent insurance, but he knows if he asks for repair funds, the red tape might drag on for months. It looks like the funds he has raised for bear releases will have to be diverted. "Are you feeling depressed about it?" I ask. He admits he is, but answers "I don't have any other choice but to keep going." Hope floats.

It's October 9th, 2018. The media have exploded over the Intergovernmental Panel on Climate Change (IPCC) report, released yesterday. "Final call to save the world from climate catastrophe," says the BBC. "The clock is ticking…" says the Washington Post. "Next decade critical," says the Sydney Morning Herald. I put sensationalism aside, instead devouring an outline of the report's findings as it compares impacts in a world one and a half degrees hotter, versus two degrees hotter. The picture is bleak in either instance. We have missed the chance to avoid climate change; mitigation is the only redeemable option. Scientists are begging policy-makers to step off their coal-fired trajectory—to claw back land and plant forests, the lungs of our planet. I imagine a row of eminent scientists teetering on the edge of a cliff saying, "If you don't listen, I'll jump."

The report urges personal responsibility around what we eat, how we use energy, and our level of consumerism. It paints a dystopic future where reefs are dead and islands sunken; where ocean temperatures have decimated fish stocks and grains strive to grow in acidic soils; where humans struggle to breathe, and oxygen-making trees are unable to keep up. Did we really think we were so far above nature? That we were immune to her contagious wheezing? Do we really think we can eat money or breathe power?

Now it's March 19th, 2020, and humans' erroneous belief of dominance over nature has been exposed for the illusion it always was. Nature is fighting back. If only we had heeded the warning seventeen years ago when the previous coronavirus jumped from a wildlife species (possibly civet cat or bat) to humans. By the time it was contained, severe acute respiratory syndrome (SARS), as it was named, spread through thirty countries and killed 800 people. Although the scientific community cannot be categorically certain, it appears SARS originated in a Chinese wet market where caged wildlife from different habitats, different regions, and even different countries were sold for food or collection. In response to that virus, conservationists and medical researchers called for an end to the wildlife trade, and specifically Chinese wet markets. But still the practice continues. Sun bears find themselves caged next to muntjacs, pangolins next to bats, and macaques within scratching distance of macaws. Prisoners of the wildlife war, they unwittingly carry diseases capable of mass devastation. This time, the novel, or new, coronavirus (SARS-CoV-2) is spreading quickly, killing thousands and bringing economies to their knees. BSBCC is in lock-down, struggling to find the funds to feed the bears without the expected contribution of tourist dollars. And my Australian home has become my castle with the drawbridge lifted.

My thoughts flash back to a conversation in 2016, as I sat in the passenger seat beside Wong. "If we have to evacuate Sepilok for any reason, I will simply open the cages and let the bears fend for themselves," he said back then. I remember feeling shocked with Wong's disaster-plan pragmatism, as an apocalyptic image formed in my imagination. Back then, he was referring to climate change. The crisis we now find ourselves in has a different name, yet the question still remains: how does he keep going, knowing the odds are in favour of failure?

Finally I understand. Wong fights for survival of us all. Like sun bears, we are in danger; both victims and perpetrators. As author Wayne Lynch says, "We should fight for these things as if our life depends on it, because it does."

The BSBCC team, 2020

If you are inspired to help sun bears, here are a few ideas:

- Lend this book to your friends or add it to the reading list in your book club
- Like and share BSBCC's social media sites on Facebook and Instagram
- Adopt a sun bear and follow their progress
- Choose ecotourism or a volunteer experience for your next holiday
- Reuse, recycle, and reduce your own consumption at home
- Choose sustainable products and banks that support sustainable projects
- Vote for pro-environmental policies
- Support or volunteer with conservation groups in your own area – the entire environment needs help, not just sun bears!

🌐 www.bsbcc.org.my

f www.facebook.com/sunbear.bsbcc

SARAH PYE is available for speaking engagements,
keynote addresses, and workshops. For more
information, visit www.sarahrpye.com.
You are invited to join the sun bear conversation and community
at the Saving Sun Bears Facebook group. See you there!
This book is printed on demand (POD) which
reduces waste and saves our trees.

COMING SOON!

Chapter books for children aged 8-12:

Wildlife Wong and the Sun Bear

Wildlife Wong and the Pygmy Elephant

Wildlife Wong and the Orangutan